CW00497690

Oxleas:

History, Conservation and Connection in a suburban Woodland

Tom Wareham

Copyright © 2020 Tom Wareham

Tom Wareham asserts his moral right to be identified as the author of this work under the Copyright, Designs and Patents Act 1988.

Original and modified cover art by Luz Adriana Villa and CoverDesignStudio.com

ISBN:

DEDICATION

To friends of Oxleas Woodlands –
and friends of woodlands everywhere

CONTENTS

'The wood...never fades, it never cheats. It has mystery but not falsity. It is staunch and even majestic but never overpowering. It is a place of quiet and conflict, of absolute peace and tigerish bloodiness, of passion and death. It is a contrast of power and delicacy, space and littleness. Yet all the time, throughout the year, it has its own special atmosphere. You have only to walk a yard under the trees in order to become under its spell, to sense the change, the sometimes startling, sometimes soothing difference in the spirit of the air, There is some precious quality brought about by the close gathering of trees into a wood that defies analysis...It is the wood of little and great trees, of flowers and water, of squirrel and fox, bird and badger, of light and shadowiness, that has the everlasting vibration of life in it, that special rare atmosphere, at once soothing and refreshing and somehow elevating...'

H E Bates. *Through the Woods.* 1936.

ACKNOWLEDGMENTS

My thanks for their help to staff at The British Library, The National Archive, the London Metropolitan Archive, Historic England Archive, the National Portrait Gallery. I am particularly indebted to staff at the Greenwich Heritage Centre for their help and patient forbearance. My very special thanks to the Estate of Francis Dodd for permission to use the artist's portrait of Charles Grinling.

Special thanks also to Chris for her suggestions and checking the manuscript. Thanks also to Bee Twidale and Laurie Baker for help with source material. And special thanks to Maggie Jones for checking and commenting on the chapter on the Campaign to Save Oxleas Woods.

Oxleas – an introduction.

If you are interested in history and love Nature, and woodlands in particular, this book is definitely for you. But I hope you will find more in it than is suggested by 'history', 'Nature' and 'woodlands'. When I set out to write this book, my aim was to somehow promote a love of the stretch of ancient woodland that has survived for millennia on the southern side of Shooters Hill in south-east London. Those already familiar with the area will know that the woodlands really consist of a number of different woods – each with its own name. Collectively they are often referred to as the 'Shooters Hill Woodlands' but for the sake of brevity I have given them the name of 'Oxleas Woodlands', after the largest and most well-known of the woods.

Oxleas is my attempt to tell the story of the woodland and the people who lived in it in the past. But in writing this book, I also came to realise that knowing the woodland's past also required an understanding of its present; and understanding the woods as they are now also requires a personal engagement with them. In some ways, this book conforms to the current genre of 'New Nature Writing' – but in other ways it differs. It is, in a sense, a blend of both 'new' and 'old' nature writing.

In the 19th and early-20th centuries many nature writers produced their work in the form of a travelogue or journey record. There is a long tradition of this going back beyond, for example, William Lambarde's famous *Perambulation of Kent'* in the late-16th century. As a genre it developed its own form, allowing the authors to combine natural history with a form of guide to the local sites, buildings, monuments etc. It is a form which gave rise to the travel guides with which we are so familiar today.

If we go back to the nature-writers and poets of the late-18th century and early-19th century, we find deliberate and defining attempts to explore our psychological relationship to Nature and the landscape. In *Remarks on Forest Scenery and other Woodland Views,* (1791) William Gilpin, (one of the foremost 18th century writers on natural scenery and the picturesque), set out not just to describe woodland scenery but, at the same time, to attach his emotional response to it. Wordsworth (among others) followed the same vein in much of his poetry, allowing his psychological connection to the landscape to channel more mystic or philosophical thoughts.

There is, of course, a huge difference between the nature-appreciating literature of the Romantic period and the guide books of today. Because what was lost over the course of time was the subtler element of engagement with the object that was being described. The modern guidebook has become detached from its author. It may tell you what to go and see, but it doesn't tell you how the author him or herself felt about it when they them self saw it. That sense of personal connection seems to have virtually disappeared from nature writing after the First World War – and perhaps it is hardly surprising given what had just occurred.

What changed, of course, was the sense of connection to nature and the landscape. The late 19th century saw the final wave of urbanisation of the population, the intensification of agriculture and the rise of the 'mechanical'. It was only in the late 20th century that the pendulum began to swing back as the cost that had been paid for these great changes became obvious. The devastation of the natural landscape, intensification of agriculture, pollution, species extinction, uncontrolled urban development and road building, and climate change – can all be attributed, if only in part, to our disconnection with Nature. And as the public response to these issues has begun to change, so has an element of literature in the form of 'New Nature Writing'.

'New Nature Writing' very much sets out to establish the connection that its authors have with nature. In some ways this book does that too. It is structured as a form of guide to each of the woods and meadows that constitute the woodlands on Shooters Hill. So, the reader can use it either literally as a companion to walking in the woods, or as a means of visiting them in their imagination.

Had I intended to write a straightforward history of the woods; the book would have been structured chronologically. It would have been simpler, certainly, but the result would have been an objectification of the woodland. Instead of seeing it as a living entity, something which needs to be valued and conserved, it would have been reduced to a form of monument to the past. Its flora and fauna reduced to an incidental presence against a more important backdrop. In fact, the reverse is true. The history of the woodland contributes to what exists now, because what we see there today is part of a historical process. The trees and shrubs that make up the woods are not static. They are part of a living process of change; and the buildings that once stood in the woods have also left their imprint on both the landscape and the woods that cover it. The echo of their former occupants adds another layer to what we experience when we wander through the trees today. Virtually all of the former residents interacted with the woodland in some way. Some more than others. And in turn the woodland interacted with them. As we will see, many of those who came to live in the woods also came to value them in some way, whether seeing it as an economic resource, or as a place of inspiration and personal restoration.

One of the earliest of these was the artisan poet Robert Bloomfield (1766-1823) who influenced and inspired both John Clare and William Wordsworth. Born in Suffolk, Bloomfield worked on the land until 1781 when he was sent to London to work as a shoemaker. He knew the Woolwich area well and married the daughter of a shipwright at the Woolwich Dockyard. Most significantly he knew Shooters Hill and, like many who came after him, found it a place where he could find both tranquility and psychological restoration. In his poem *Shooters Hill* he addresses himself to the allegorical persona of 'Health' who he seeks in the woodland on the top of the hill:

I seek thee where, with all his might,

The joyous bird his rapture tells,

Amidst the half-excluded light,

That gilds the fox-glove's pendant bells;

Where, cheerly up this bold hill's side

The deep'ning groves triumphant climb;

In groves Delight and Peace abide,

And Wisdom markes the lapse of time.

To hide me from the public eye,

To keep the throne of Reason clear,

Amidst fresh air to breathe or die,

I took my staff and wander'd here,

Suppressing every sigh that heaves,

And coveting no wealth but thee,

I nestle in the honied leaves,

And hug my stolen liberty.

...

This far-seen monumental tower [1]

Records th' achievements of the brave,

And Angria's subjugated power,

Who plunder'd on the eastern wave.

---

[1] Severndroog Castle.

I would not that such turrets rise

To point out where my bones are laid;

Save that some wandering bard might prize

The comforts of its broad cool shade.

Bloomfield clearly recognised and appreciated the healing power of nature and of woodland in particular. Like Bloomfield, many of us today value the woodland for its visual beauty and the sense of restoration that it brings as we wander through it. This book touches upon that aspect of the woodlands, but it also addresses the threats that they face too. Oxleas is the besieged survivor of something much greater. It was once part of a much more extensive woodland and rural landscape, populated by flora and fauna that have now been driven out because of us and the demands of modern urban society. As a result it is also a symbol for Nature in the broader sense, literally threatened by the demands we place upon it.

Like woodland everywhere, if the Oxleas woodlands - together with their remaining flora and fauna - are to survive, we need to reconnect with them, to learn to value them – and then to protect them from all the threats they face including, most importantly, ourselves.

Chapter 1- A green blob on the landscape

I came up to London from the West Country in the late 1970s, intending to stay for just a few years while I studied for a degree. But, like so many other London residents I know, I never escaped again. Like some of my ancestors, I became entrapped. As much as I loathed the overcrowding, the endless streets and buildings, the noise and pollution – and the incessant haste and bustle of everything – various things combined to keep me here. Some of these were very good things, others more questionable. However, the point is that I was lucky in that I landed in the comparatively leafy London borough of Greenwich. The unlucky bit was that for the first fifteen years my wife and I lived in one the most polluted and grubby parts of the borough: one of those bits where the tourists never go. Although we were fortunate then to have a few sparrows in our tiny back garden, they struggled to make themselves heard above the roar of traffic heading for the nearby Blackwall Tunnel; and at night our sleep was regularly interrupted by the clank of gas cylinders from a commercial supply depot behind the house.

We survived all this because we were lucky enough to be able escape to the country whenever we could. Eventually we were able to make something of a move and found a house only a few miles away, on the southern slopes of Shooters Hill. After the dark confinement of our small Victorian terraced house, the house we found, was light and airy and cheerful. In truth the house is just an ordinary 1930s semi – but what made it so immediately attractive is that it had panoramic views across south-east London towards the North Downs of Kent. From our back windows it was possible to see that London ended somewhere. In fact when the sun shines it is possible to see the fields and hedgerows on the Downs around Biggin Hill. And everywhere, there are trees. As you gaze across the miles of urbscape, trees erupt everywhere like frozen green explosions, blurring the hardness of the city lines and, during the summer, adding subtle green smudges to the grey and brown.

Now I know that, to many people, this little claim might seem risible. But the fact is that the vast majority of Londoners can't see a tree from their house, let alone the surrounding country-side itself. Best of all, though, from the small book-stuffed room at the front of the house where I work, I can see the trees of Ox-leas Woodlands only a few hundred feet away. The woodlands of Shooters Hill are our neighbors.

I would hazard a guess that most of the six million people who live in greater London give little thought to its topography. I didn't, myself, until comparatively recently. I knew that if you work in, or even visit, the centre of town, you are aware that when heading north from the Thames, there are sometimes low hills to climb. Trafalgar Square, and the road known as The Strand, for example, sit on higher ground. In the City itself, the ground rises steeply from the river up towards Cornhill. The Bank of England sits about 100' higher than the Thames. In fact it sits on a ridge of higher ground which extends from Holland Park to Whitechapel in the east. Even in the good old East End the ground rises from the Thames to the gravel terrace of the infamous Radcliffe Highway, above Wapping and Limehouse. This proximity of high ground to the shallow edge of the navigable Thames was almost certainly what inclined the Romans to establish a settlement where the City now sits. At the time, Londinium sat at an intersection where the lowest crossing point met the furthest extent of navigation for ocean going ships.

South of the river, though, the picture was and still is a little different. The area here is low lying from Battersea to Greenwich. Until the 18th century, the area was marshy and unhealthy. Although London expanded south of the river by the 16th century, it grew faster and further on the north side. Development on the south bank of the Thames beyond Southwark, when it finally came in the 18th century, had more to do with the needs of the shipping industry and the associated maritime trades. South London expanded eastwards hugging the Thames.

But to understand the context more clearly, we need to take a longer view, that is, in the sense of a longer distance view. If we were floating somewhere above the south-east of England at very high altitude, we would see that London itself sits between the fork of two great lines of hills. The fork – more a funnel –opens out towards the North Sea terminating in the north-east near Ipswich, and to the south-west at Dover. The two tines of this fork come together at the North Wessex Downs, near Marlborough. It is from near here, at Goring, that the Thames itself breaks through the narrow end of the funnel, winding its way in an easterly direction.

North of London, the lines of hills extends in a south-westerly direction from around Bury St Edmunds via Luton and the Chilterns, to the junction at Marlborough. From this point another line of hills runs south-east to Alton in Hampshire, where they divide to embrace the Kentish, Surrey and Sussex Weald. The line of hills which runs along the southern basin of the Weald and which we know better as the South Downs, terminates on the south coast at Eastbourne.

Another line of hills run like a giant eyebrow around the northern rim of the Weald. They extend in an arc from Guildford, passing south of Croydon towards the Medway Gap at Rochester, then on south westwards passing south of Canterbury to reach the coast at Dover.

If you look at the London basin itself, it is clear that there are more areas of higher ground to the north of the Thames than the south. Crooked ridges run south from the Chilterns. Around Stanmore, and Barnet, a snaking finger nearly 500' high extends down past Edgeware, to East Finchley and Hampstead Heath, which rises about 450' above sea level. To the north-east another thin line of hills points south-west from Epping to Woodford.

To the south though, the northern edge of the North Downs is much more clear-cut. In fact in south London, there are only three small isolated areas of high ground. A V-shaped ridge on which the Crystal Palace sits, running from Forest Hill in the north to West Norwood - a ridge which averages about 387' above sea level. There is another small ridge running north from the Downs at Orpington towards Chislehurst, where it reaches about 325'.

And then there is an isolated hill closer to the Thames, which reaches 423'. And this is Shooters Hill. And this is where we now are.

Shooters Hill is a London landmark, though it is not one which features in the guidebooks clutched by the millions of tourists who visit each year. It is not an 'attraction' like the Tower of London, or Madame Tussauds, or the British Museum.   It lies about ten miles out from Trafalgar Square, and just over 4 miles from Greenwich – which is the outer limit for most tourists when it comes to visiting London. Few overseas visitors find their way to it, and even fewer know about it. But it wasn't always so. In fact Shooters Hill was once famous or infamous! It was traversed by the vast majority of visitors from the Continent, and many people made a point of visiting the spot during their sojourn in the capital. In fact from the late 19th century onwards it became hugely popular with any Londoners who could manage a day away from the overcrowded 'urbs' of the Victorian city.

As you drive in towards London along the A20 from Kent, your first glimpse of the capital are the towers of Canary Wharf - that ongoing monument to 1980s mercantile capitalism and the materialism that it engendered. They appear in a gap between two low hills as the road twists in from the M25. I often wonder what visitors from the Continent think when they see this on their first visit by car. But the point is this. No sooner do you see the towers and think, erroneously, that you are on the verge of arriving in the city, than they are suddenly shouldered aside by something completely different. A stubborn, flat-topped wooded hillside, crowned with a gothic-looking steepled tower. This is Shooters Hill. It is natural and ancient, and its seeming dismissal of the modernity of London's latest financial emanation seems to signify its contempt for it. It is not just Shooters Hill's physicality, it is the fact that it is covered by woodland. And as you drive in closer to London, you see that that woodland is largely isolated. An island heaving itself up amidst the brick and tile and tarmac of the suburbs. Shooters Hill is marooned.

In some ways it is best appreciated from a distance, from whence it appears to be a ridge gradually descending from its highest point at the west and descending towards the east. Almost in the centre is the distinctive water tower which helps identify it – as if this were necessary. Seen from different angles, however, the profile of the hill is more complicated.

On the north side, the ground lifts steadily from the river at Woolwich and from the former marshland at Plumstead, and rises over a series of terraces to become Shooters Hill itself. The rising ground and terraces on the northern side were built-upon by the end of the 19th century. Because Woolwich was a garrison town, extensive barracks and military facilities were built there from at least the 17th century onwards, occupying large areas of ground. Along the river at this point too, there developed the massive estates of the Woolwich Dockyard and Arsenal and sundry other industrial establishments. Terraced houses for the workers and their families were thrown up in an extensive and complex maze that climbed up towards the hill. At some point, however, this sprawl came to a halt, leaving some woodland and pasture intact on the northern slopes.

Seen from above, Shooters Hill is seen to be a ridge which runs from the south-west to the north east where a partly wooded area survives as Shrewsbury Park. The plateau along the top of the hill was largely undeveloped until the 1930s.

On the southern side, however, the hill curls down to the south east in a giant crescent. The lower arm sweeps round towards another lower ridge on which sits the once Saxon village of Eltham, now a sadly characterless modern high street which, some would say, has seen better days.

Looking north from the ridge on which Eltham sits, if you can find a viewpoint between the buildings, the woods on Shooters Hill hunch over the nearest line of houses. In the summer, when the trees are thick with leaf, the woods look like a verdant tidal wave about to crash down on the puny red bricked structures below them. This illusion is even more pronounced from the east, where the open expanse Oxleas Meadow rolls down from the wooded hill-top. From the meadow, you can see along the lines of the back gardens of the houses closest to the woods, and when there is a strong breeze blowing, the foliage of the trees seems to be boiling with restrained hostility, thrashing about as though eager to crush the houses below.

The woodlands on the southern side of Shooters Hall fall within the parish of Eltham and in 1796, Daniel Lysons, in his *The Environs of London*, described Eltham as containing '*about 2,880 acres : of which about 360 are woodland; about 60 waste [either common land or wild uncultivated woodland]; about three fifths of the cultivated land are arable. ....This place had formerly a market on Tuesdays, and two fairs; one at the festival of the Holy Trinity, and the other at that of St. Peter and St. Paul; both of which have been long discontinued.'*

The markets are long gone, but the rural nature of the area in 1796 is clearly evident. Now, most of the area has succumbed to the growth of London, including the former arable land enclosed by the southern arm of Shooters Hill, now largely filled with Victorian and 1930s housing. The arms themselves, however, are wooded and collectively known as Shooters Hill Woods, Oxleas Woodlands – or, less accurately, as Oxleas Woods. In fact the woodlands consist of a series of woods and meadows covering around 133 hectares or about 330 acres. A considerable part of it is classified as Ancient Woodland, and it has several areas designated as having SSSI status (Site of Special Scientific Interest). The area has also been designated a Nature Reserve by the local authority who have responsibility for it, the Royal Borough of Greenwich - making it the third largest nature reserve in Greater London - and it is their Parks, Environment & Open Spaces Department who now manage it under the scrutiny of Natural England.

Shooters Hill. There is some ambiguity about the origin of the name. It is common to hear speakers make the claim that it derives from the fact that archery was practiced here from the late-Middle Ages until the Tudor period. Even the omniscient Wikipedia, gives a nod to this explanation. However there is no real evidence for this.

There are other possibilities. 'Shooters' may derive from two other root words. The Anglo-Saxons referred to a wood on a boundary as 'sceaga', which was pronounced more like 'Shaw', a word still in use in Kent. Even more likely as a candidate is the word 'Shote', the Middle-English word describing a clearing in woodland which was used for trapping game-birds – especially woodcock. And, as we shall see, the Oxleas Woodlands were once highly regarded for their game.

By the second half of the 14th century, the hill was, apparently, already known as *Shetereshelde* and was identified as such in a petition to King Edward III from around 1369-1375. Edward spent much of his youth at the royal palace at Eltham, and used it frequently once he had ascended to the throne. *Shetereshelde* would have been well-known to him.

The archery legend probably stems from a slightly later time and a much related event which was recorded in what various sources refer to as 'Hall's Annals'. One day in May 1515, while King Henry (the eighth of his name) was roistering with Catherine of Aragon and the rest of his court at Placentia, the royal palace at Greenwich, someone had the bright idea of taking the entire ensemble on an invigorating ride to the top of Shooters Hill several miles away, as we are told, 'to take the open air'. (It is amazing what the influence of a bucket of red wine can do).

A rather fanciful Victorian representation of Henry VIII's visit to Shooters Hill.

Upon their arrival, in what was clearly a bit of staged theatrical pageantry, they were accosted by two hundred of the King's archers, all hooded and dressed in Lincoln Green. Their leader introduced himself as Robin Hood and invited the royal couple to watch an archery demonstration. Upon the King's assenting, all two hundred archers loosed their bows en masse. We are told that *'their arrows whistled by craft of the head, so that the noise was strange and great and much pleased the King, the Queen and all the company.'* The demonstration was repeated. *'Then Robin Hood desired the King and Queen to come into the greenwood and see how the outlaws lived. The King demanded of the Queen and her ladies, if they durst adventure to go into the wood with so many outlaws. Then the Queen said that if it pleased him she was content.* (Wise decision!) *Then the horns blew till they came to the wood under Shooters Hill and there was an arbor made of boughs with a hall and a great chamber and an inner chamber very well made and covered with flowers and sweet herbs, which the King much praised. Then said Robin Hood: 'Sir, outlaws' breakfast is venison, and thereafter you must be content with such fare as we use'. Then the King and Queen sat down and were served with venison and wine by Robin Hood and his men, to their great contentation'.*

It's a delightful tale, and the outlaw's arbor, which we are told was erected in the wood under the hill, was probably erected, at no little trouble and pre-arrangement, somewhere in Oxleas Woods. And the arrows must have been loosed towards what is now either Castlewood Meadow or Oxleas Meadow. It would have to be, otherwise someone would have been given the un-enviable task of hunting through the underwood for all those missing specially-prepared arrows.

But, there, I have probably already caused confusion. Because, as I have already indicated, the woods which occupy the south of Shooters Hill, and which are often referred to as Oxleas Woods, are in fact a series of woods and former pasture land. So before we go any further it is probably best that I describe the layout of the woods.

The northern boundary of the woods lies in a straight west-east line along the route of the A207 – formerly the old A2 or Dover Road, although it has had various names in history. The line is straight because the Romans drove one of their deter-mined highways from the south side of Londinium Bridge, to-wards their original British bridgehead on the eastern tip of Kent. The road actually travels via river crossings at Dartford and Rochester, to Canterbury. The road became known, much later, as Watling Street, though in fact it predated the Romans by some considerable time. To the north of the road as it crosses the top of Shooters Hill, for example, is at least one Bronze Age burial mound. In many ways, the fact that it provided one of the main highways linking London with the Channel crossing ports, made it a highly important route and over time, it has had various names, Great Dover Road, Old Dover Road or simply the Dover Road, and now just 'Shooters Hill'. To avoid confusion, I'll refer to this road from now on as 'the Dover Road'.

The road climbs steeply from both east and west – and this has caused problems in the past, as we shall discover shortly. But its main significance as far as I am concerned is that it provides a clear and rather noisy northern edge to the woodlands. The road also marks the boundary between the parishes of Eltham to the South, and Woolwich and Plumstead to the north, a borderland which during the 18th and 19th centuries saw regular spats between the two Parish authorities regarding responsibility for road maintenance and drainage etc.

Housing crowds in on most sides of the woodlands. And where the southern boundary escapes suddenly from the entrapment of the housing, the busy Rochester Way divides it from its southern sister, Shepherdleas Wood.

Interspersed with the woodlands are the remnants of old pasture or arable land. In the north-western corner lies Eltham Common, which is now mainly wooded, except for the top-left corner which is still an area of mown grassland. It sits at the junction of the Dover Road and what is now the South Circular.

To the east and south-east of Eltham Common is Castle Wood and, on the southern slope below this, Castle Wood Meadow. On its eastern side, Castle Wood merges somehow with Jack Wood, which rolls along the undulating side of the hill to Oxleas Meadow. Oxleas Wood lies on the northern and eastern side of the meadow, and flows downhill in an easterly direction towards the borough boundary and the back gardens of the 1930s houses of Welling. To the south lies the already named Shepherdleas Wood and, to the south-east, a large meadow bounded on two sides by woodland, known as Falconwood Field. We'll explore these later, for once you take the time to get to know them, they each have their own individual character and story to tell. But for now I want to stay with the back story – if I can call it that.

Parts of Oxleas Woodland are designated as 'Ancient Woodland'. Technically, this means woods that have existed since 1600, since the deliberate planting of woodland only began some time afterwards. Therefore, anything which could be shown to have existed before must be natural woodland. And indeed, parts of Oxleas Woods are thought to date back to prehistory and it may even once have been a northern outpost of the great Kentish forest of Anderida.

Early maps are invaluable, if not always totally reliable, sources of evidence about the woodlands. Shooters Hill itself features prominently on those quaint old 'strip maps' which were produced for travellers from the late 17th century onwards. A typical early example of this is the map of the route from London to Dover produced in 1675 by John Ogilby Esq. – the King's Cosmographer. Like all the others, Ogilby's map was intended to assist the traveller by denoting significant landmarks along the route. For those travelling by the exhausting and uncomfortable coach of the day, the map probably served both to mark the progress of the vehicle and perhaps to assuage the boredom along the route. If the long-suffering traveller was unable to ask the perennial question 'Are we there yet?' – he or she could at least consult the map to see how much more of the wretched journey they had to endure. Ogilby's map not only features the towns and villages along the route, it counts down the number of miles from London to Dover.

But more significantly, the map also identifies the most significant hills and woodland along the route. There may have been a number of reasons for this. Hills meant a long slow climb and then a potentially dangerous descent – so the symbol on the map might have been a forewarning. But there was another hazard. Hills and woodland were also the haunt of highwaymen – but more of this later.

By far the biggest hill and woodland along the London to Dover road was that of Shooters Hill, which one reached 8 miles after leaving London and continued on for over two miles. The hill itself was followed by an extensive tract of woodland which stretched much further to the east towards the (then) hamlet of 'Wellen' (now Welling).

Until 1889 Shooters Hill lay within the County boundary of Kent, so it is to early maps of that county that we really need to look for evidence of the woodland. In Robert Morden's map of the county dating from the very end of the 17th – or perhaps the first couple of years of the 18th century, the woods are denoted as a round green blob on the landscape, which stretches much further to the east and south-east than the present woodland. In fact, according to Morden the woods stretched as far as the old Blendon estate, several miles to the east and encompassed the Danson estate, which later became the site of the grand Palladian mansion of Danson House, built in 1766 for Sir John Boyd, Secretary to the East India Company and major London slave trader.

In the maps produced to accompany Hasted's *History and Topographical Survey of the County of Kent*, from 1797, the woodlands are still depicted stretching continuously to the south-east, though the eastern parts of it have been named 'Runnet's Wood'.[2] In the early Ordnance Survey maps of 1806, the woodland is still depicted stretching several miles east from Shooters Hill towards Danson Park and south-east to the village of Blackfen though it is named 'West Wood'. However, the huge West Wood itself, which lay east of Oxleas Wood, was grubbed out from around 1862 and completely lost between the wars.

The great West Wood, from the OS map of 1806.

---

[2] This is a misnomer, as will be explained later.

Even as late as Bacon's *Street Map of London* 1912, a mass of woodland is still shown flowing south and east across the area now known as Falconwood to West Wood Lane, which marked its eastern boundary.

In all these changes however, the constant element is the woodland clinging along the southern side of the Dover Road as it crossed Shooters Hill. The fact that a lot of the woodland on and around Shooters Hill remained largely unchanged can probably be attributed to two factors. Firstly, part of the woodland clings to a steep hillside which is made up of thin acid soils. Up until the 1930s, the lower slopes of the hill were either meadowland or arable fields. But the steeper upper slopes and the heavy clay on the lower, made ploughing less practicable. In fact the heavy clay soils of this part of Kent led to the evolution of a special heavy plough – the Kentish 'turn wrest' plough – which required more horses than the standard plough and took significantly longer to work. So although farmland crowded up to the southern edge of the woodlands right up until the end of the 19th century with some remaining until the Second World War, the woods themselves remained. The second reason for the survival of the woodlands is that it belonged to the Crown. From the Middle Ages onwards, the land was part of the estate of the royal palace at Eltham. This placed a certain amount of restraint on the use or exploitation of the land – and woodland in particular.

In 1663 the Manor of Eltham was leased to the London wine merchant and Member of Parliament, Sir John Shaw. A strong supporter of the Royalist cause during the Civil War, Shaw was well rewarded after the Restoration of the Monarchy with a Baronetcy and a large range of lucrative posts and offices. One

of posts, incidentally, was Commissioner of Woods and Forests.
[3]

The Shaw family retained the estate until the late 1830s when their legal tenure expired following a dispute with the Crown Commissioners over the management of the woodland and their hunting rights. The ownership of the woodland reverted to the Crown Estate. This meant that it was managed directly by the Commissioners of Woods, Forests and Land Revenues, (hereafter referred to as 'the Commissioners') which had been formed in 1810. Although elements of the woodland were leased out to various individuals at different times, its status gave it a degree of protection which helped conserve it and preserve the woodland from complete deforestation. We'll find out a little more about this in detail when we come to visit the individual woods, but suffice it so say that from about 1800, in the middle of the Napoleonic Wars, there was growing concern about the supply of timber for the Royal Naval shipyards. As a result the Commissioners began to pay much more attention to the condition of the trees and woodland on the Eltham estate, and a series of reports were produced which are helpfully revealing.

In 1809 Sir John Shaw's leasehold (all of the first-born Shaws were called John – it's a failure of imagination in the British aristocracy resulting from years of in-breeding) came up for renewal. The Commissioners called on their manager, A C Driver, to survey the woods and, following his report, Shaw's leasehold was significantly reduced to exclude virtually all of the

---

[3] History of Parliament Trust Website.
https://www.historyofparliamentonline.org/volume/1660-1690/member/shaw-sir-john-1615-80 Retrieved 3 June 2020.

woodland. In fact the amount of woodland in his new lease-hold was reduced by a total of 280 acres, including 104 acres of Oxleas Wood and 49 acres of Shepherdleas Wood. The cause of this appears to have related, understandably, to a reduction in the income he expected from the woodlands. All woodland has some value, if properly managed. In the 18th and 19th centuries, this derived primarily from three sources. Firstly, the felling and sale of timber from the trunks of 'standards' or mature trees, especially oak trees. This was used in the form of beams and planks for ship building and other structures. Secondly from the sale of what was called 'underwood'. Underwood is less defined by a tree species than by the method of management. Whereas, in the case of timber, trees were planted and grown to maturity, in the case of underwood, trees and shrubs are cut at regular intervals, in a process known as 'coppicing'. This involved a tree being cut at a low-level, leaving the stump to regrow, producing a number of vertical shoots – a coppice 'stool'. This process allowed the underwood to be harvested on a regular cycle, while encouraging the tree to regrow. Coppicing is an ancient form of woodland management which ensures not only a regular income, but also a healthy woodland. Coppicing produced thinner flexible wood which could be used for a range of purposes, e.g. tool handles, hurdles, wattle, charcoal burning, and faggots for firewood. Thirdly, woodland can be managed in a way which makes it good habitat for game birds – thus income can be derived both from the sale of game itself and from shooting rights.

It was quite common for the same bit of woodland to be let and sub-let for different purposes. So, for example, one person could have the right to fell the timber, while another had the right to take the underwood. The tenants who held these rights were usually able to co-operate. Unfortunately, the same could not be true of the holders of hunting rights. Conflict between the different interests, and between the holders of adjacent shooting rights, were all too common. And, as any regular country walker knows all-too-well, the owners of hunting rights tend to employ a particularly belligerent type of person to protect their interests, commonly known as a gamekeeper.

Which brings us back to Sir John Shaw. When the Commissioners of Woods realized that they needed to manage their woodland in a more efficient way to produce timber for the Royal Navy, they insisted on a change which not only reduced Shaw's income from timber and underwood sales, but which also impacted badly on his hunting. In 1811, in preparation for this change in terms, A C Driver, the manager appointed by the Commissioners reported on the state of the woodlands. He noted that ten acres of Oxleas Wood consisted of 9 year-old trees, but that the majority of it was less than three years old. It was clearly going to be some time before these trees were going to be available for the navy. He noted that while the trees in the lower levels were thriving, those on the steeper slopes and on the top of the hill were rather stunted, *'the soil being very gravelly.'*

His summary makes interesting reading:

'The greater part of the soil in this wood is very poor and not well adapted for the growth of large timbers as it generally becomes very stunted and dead at the top, before it attains any size..10 acres are now cutting and the Men are in general careful in leaving the Tellers or any Shoots that are likely to become Timber.

In the Southern part of the Wood, and towards the West, the soil is deeper & produces good timber, and in some parts there is a tolerable succession of growing trees, but in other parts there are very few. I should therefore advise the planting young Oaks not less than 5 or 6 feet high as if they are of less size, they will be injured by the Underwood. As so small a proportion of the Wood is 4 years old, I should advise the cutting it early next year, and leave shoots from the stools, to become Timber, and then to fill up the Wood with Oaks & Acorns & to make a deep Ditch to enclose the same which will prevent the Cattle coming in, otherwise being so near the Turnpike Road great Depredation may be made.'

Shepherdleas Wood seemed to be in worse condition. *'There are but very few trees in this Wood but I hardly think it advisable to cut the Underwood as in that case the Shoots from the Stools are hardly old enough to leave for Timber and if left 2 or 3 years longer a great many be found sufficiently strong for that purpose, & the Underwood will be worth nearly double.'*

80% of the few trees he counted were less than 5-years old, and the remainder but a year old.

In fact, virtually all of the woodland on the Eltham Estate seemed to have been shorn of its mature trees, and it seems that Shaw's failure to plan for succession may have been part of the reason for his loss of holdings. In any case, Driver advocated an extensive planting program with either acorns or young oaks. He also recommended the appointment of *'some trust worthy labourer residing near the spot at a small Annual Salary, say ten guineas: who should at all times watch and prevent every sort of encroachment or depredation, which may be attempted to be committed in the Fences or otherwise.'* And more pertinently – *'that it will also be right that some proper person acquainted with the culture and management of Woods & cutting the Underwood, be appointed to have the general superintendence of them, with full power and control over the Woodreeve.'*

Driver's report also hints at some sort of previous malpractice. He noted, for example that in the past, Underwood had been sold at auction, and the buyers had been allowed to send their own men in to cut the wood itself. The suggestion being that, left unsupervised, they had not only cut more than they had a right to take, but had done so badly and in a way that damaged the coppice stools and prevented the vital re-growth. Apparently an eminently practical man, Driver had also pointed out the advisability not only of getting men appointed by the Woodreeve or the Commissioners' own agents to cut the wood, but also of providing them with some extra payment to ensure the recent regrowth and shoots were preserved in the process. He advised promising the men 'some trifling remuneration' as a reward. A generous suggestion which was slightly overshadowed, immediately after, by his offer to undertake superintendence of the woodland himself *'for the sum of fifty pounds Per Annum or such other Compensation as may be approved of by the Board.'*

Driver's proposals seem to have been effective. In 1848 the Commissioners requested another report on the state of the woodlands. Their surveyor this time was John Clutton, who appears to have been Driver's successor and who undertook a survey with the assistance of the Woodreeve. What it reveals is that some radical steps seem to have been taken after 1811.

In 1818 a very large proportion of the woodland on the south of the hill had been felled and replanted with 'red' or 'Scotch fir' and oak. Fir, of course, is very fast growing, and towards the end of the Napoleonic War, the Admiralty, to increase its production of frigates, had begun commissioning ships made of this timber. It was a short-term measure, as fir-built frigates had a short longevity (plus they were unpopular with seamen as wounds caused by fir splinters during an engagement, usually turned septic). With the surrender of Napoleon, the demand for frigates ended abruptly, and so did the demand for pine. Around 1832 virtually all of the fir trees - around 528 of them – had been felled, but those remaining in 1848 were having an undesirable effect. Clutton recommended they be felled immediately as they were now almost valueless and *'highly injurious to the underwood and timber.'*

The previous removal of fir trees had left some healthy stands of thickly growing oak. However, as before, it was remarked that those trees growing on the upper slopes or top of the hill, were slow growing. This must have been sour news for the Commissioners who had, after all, been charged with the task of maximizing income from the Crown's woodlands. Furthermore, Clutton considered that the oaks on both the hill and in the woodlands to the south, would not be ready for the Royal Navy for another 70-80 years – while the slow-growing trees on the top of the hill would not ready for another 120-150 years. In retrospect, of course, we know that the Admiralty were already planning the move from oak to iron-clad ship construction. With some prescience, Clutton drew attention to the fact that because of the poor management in the past, there was no timber in the woodland that was of any use to the navy.[4] Furthermore, the valuable 'compass timber'[5] that had been growing in the hedgerows around the field below the hill had been rooted out *"to enable the cultivator of the land to farm in profitably."*

Anything of value in the nearer future, he thought, would come from planting ash and chestnut in preference to oak, as these grew spontaneously in most of the woodland, and had a ready market in the form of hop poles for the Kentish hop fields. However, in a bleak conclusion, he pointed out that the value of the underwood was falling *"...as the effect of the railways has been to reduce the price of coals..."* especially in those areas where the poor used to be dependent on underwood for fuel.

In fact the value of underwood had been declining slowly since 1700. In 1724 in his *Tour thro' the Whole Island of Great Britain,* Daniel Defoe had remarked on the large stockpiles of faggots made from underwood, on the Thames quaysides at nearby Woolwich and Erith. They were awaiting shipment upriver for use as fuel in the city's taverns. But, as Defoe noted, coal from the north-east of England was now being shipped into London in such quantities it was becoming cheaper and more effective to use. *'What an alteration it makes,'* he lamented, *'in the value of these woods in Kent, and how many more of them*

---

[4] For example, Clutton drew attention to the fact that the woods suffered from inadequate drainage, and recommended that more open ditches be made and at greater depth. The result of this recommendation almost certainly accounts for the extensive network of old drainage ditches which can be traced today in both Oxleas and Shepherdleas Woods.

[5] 'Compass timber' usually came from tree like oak grown in more open spaces where the limbs could spread broadly in all directions, providing shipbuilders with naturally angled wood.

than usual are yearly grubbed up and made fit for the plough.'

A similar point, but with a slightly different conclusion, had been made at the end of the century by John Boys in his *A General View of the Agriculture of Kent* (1796). Boys was one of a number of surveyors who have been commissioned by the government to report on the state of British agriculture following food shortages in the first years of the Napoleonic Wars. Boys noted that in Kent many of the county's woodlands had survived, as Clutton later noted, because of the demand of timber for hop poles, but also because the regular maritime trade with the north-east of England provided transport for oak and birch timber for pit-props in the mines in the Newcastle coal fields. There was demand also for the underwood in Kent for making stakes and hurdles for the south-east's substantial sheep-farming activities, and more importantly, perhaps, for faggots used in the burning of bricks and lime in the building industry.

These factors may help explain why the woodlands survived. But other, more significant elements were about to come into play.

Chapter 2   The land around

Because the Oxleas Woodlands have been swallowed - but fortunately not digested - by the ever-swelling growth of Greater London, it is surrounded by roads or housing and therefore is easily accessed from almost any direction. This accessibility brings problems as well as benefits, which I will touch upon later. But it also means that there are various routes into the wood, and each of these is different. Many people arrive by car, and make use of the two car parks in the woods. They step out of their vehicles and are already surrounded by the trees. But in doing so there is a real danger that they miss something important.

I walk in the woods a lot. You've probably guessed that already. And sadly I don't have a dog for company or to use as an excuse. There is something about the woods that draws me again and again. And over the years I have become conscious of a change that takes place in the process of entering the woods. I am lucky in that our road borders the southern edge of Jack Wood and provides a pedestrian pathway into the bottom of Castle Wood Meadow (don't worry we are going to explore all of these locations in the course of this book). I leave my house, walk along a street of mainly 1930's semi's and turn north up a short cherry-lined pathway between houses, into the bottom of the meadow itself. At the end of the path, several oak trees mark the edge of the woodland itself and one in particular – a sturdy mature oak – stands like a sentinel. As you pass these trees, you are passing from one environment to another. From suburban London, to ancient woodland.

I had been using the woodland ('using' the woodland? - think about that phrase) for many years before I started to notice a change taking place as I entered it. And once I became aware of it, the more conscious I became of its effect and its meaning. It is something that practitioners of Shinrin-Yoku (Forest Bathing) call the 'Threshold of Connection'; because when we enter a woodland we are moving through a liminal space between the artificial existence that we have created in our modern everyday world and the real environment of Nature. Unless you insist on taking your mobile phone, tablet, MP3 player etc. with you, (and how sad is that) you are moving between worlds, where time and meaning is different.

As I walk past the line of cherry trees and reach the first of the mature oak trees I am crossing a threshold between one place and an 'other'. And once I became conscious of that moment of transition, I found that I always reflected on it as I enter the woods. It is a moment in which I become more aware of what I am doing and where I am. Over the past decade an increasing number of scientific studies have demonstrated that plants – including, obviously trees – have sentience. Peter Wohlleben in *The Hidden Life of Trees* (2015) points out that not only are trees conscious of their neighbours, they are conscious of us as well. It's a mind-blowing idea, and one which is, admittedly, greeted with skepticism from the more conservative elements of the scientific community. But the evidence for it is mounting.

And it has implications for me as I cross the threshold into the woodland. Not only am I conscious of moving through a liminal space, the trees might also be aware that I am doing so. Practitioners of Shinrin-Yoku make a point of recognising this and perform a simple ritual. It is important to them as the moment at which they immerse themselves consciously into the environment of the trees. And as I walk into the woodland, I am conscious of a change in tempo both in myself and in the world which I have entered. I walk at a slower pace, become more conscious of everything around me, the sounds, smells, movement, colour. And as I enter the wood I usually place the palm of one hand against the rough trunk of one of the oaks as a form of greeting, or mark of respect. The bark is hard under my skin, solid and real. It provides a sensory grounding into the place that I am entering; and that gesture creates a brief pause in which I consciously acknowledge the transition. And in doing so I have connected or re-connected with the woodland.

From this point of entry into the woods, Castle Wood Meadow opens up, climbing steadily and tilted slightly down towards the western side to where a thin screen of trees masks the backs of nearby houses. Of the two big meadows in the woodland, this one is the quieter. It is less manicured; the rough grasses allowed to grow during the summer months, so that butterflies dance in the sunlight and green woodpeckers hunch down over ants nests, launching themselves across the grass with a flash of red and green and that manic chuckle they have. Oaks line the meadow on all sides, and for most of the year the houses that border this corner of the woodland in the appropriately named Castlewood Drive, are screened by underwood of holly, hazel and blackthorn.

Tarmac paths skirt the meadow, meeting one another at the top where the hillside levels out below the terrace and rose garden that now marks the site of the old Castle Wood House. On the north side of this, steps climb steeply towards the tower of Severndroog Castle, a triangular tower that crowns the top of Castle Wood and gave the wood its name. Before reaching the foot of the castle itself, there are a series of iron park benches, positioned conveniently to give the breathless climber a reason to take a few moments to recover and enjoy the view. Because the view is a good one. Behind us stands the tower, and the woodland curls round comfortably, like a cowl, framing the view below – the falling meadow and the lines of houses dropping from left to right down into the valley and climbing up beyond to the Eltham ridge. And beyond, the brick red and tile grey blurs among clusters of trees to the mass of the North Downs in the distance around fifteen miles away.

Until the 1890s virtually all of the land south and west of the woodland was farmland. There is a particularly evocative photograph (see below) showing the hill from the west, looking up the slope towards the woodland. It must have been taken in the 1880s or 1890s. The top of Severndroog Castle is just visible amid the tree tops, so it is clear what we are looking at. Despite the sepia tinted monochrome, it appears to be high summer. The trees are in full leaf and a winding country lane leads from the foreground with a hedgerow to the right. It is a beautifully composed shot. The right-hand side is dominated by a large tree – an oak or possibly an elm, and standing in the shade of this is a man in a white hat, gazing out across what is clearly pasture land. Beyond another hedgerow which crosses the middle of the picture, the grassland rises up past some somnolent cattle, to the woodland edge. It is taken from the gravel lane which branched off of the winding Well Hall Lane and would, some years later, become the Westmount Road. It highlights the very rural character of the landscape below the woods right up to the end of the 19th century.

Shooters Hill from the west around 1880-1890. . (Greenwich Heritage Centre).

Well Hall Lane was then a quiet country lane that led up from Woolwich, where it crossed the Dover Road, and wound its way south past the hamlet of Well Hall and up to the village of Eltham itself. On the western side of the lane lay Kidbrooke Common, an area which, as its name indicates, provided communal grazing rights for the small population of the village of

Kidbrooke, a mile or so to the south west. As common land did not form part of the Crown Estate it lacked the protection of the latter, a situation which gave rise to numerous confrontations with the military authorities arising from the activities of the army at Woolwich. However, from our vantage point on the bench above Castle Wood Meadow, all this land to the west is hidden by trees and the shoulder of the hill itself. Below us the Eltham valley is now full of long lines of mainly Edwardian houses.

From our position on the bench though, it is almost possible to imagine the arable and pasture land that once filled the valley to the south of the woodland. Not that it was totally devoid of buildings though. In the bottom of the valley, midway between Shooters Hill and the village of Eltham on its ridge to the south, lay the substantial buildings of Eltham Park Farm. The farm buildings and fields, totaling nearly two hundred acres, occupied most of the land south of the woodlands. When the farm was put up for sale in April 1824, it was described in attractive detail as having ' *a substantial dwelling house and offices, enclosed yard, stables for six horses, a loft over a chaise-house, harness room, wood house and out buildings; a capital barn, and cowhouse for sixty cows, cart sheds etc.'* This was no peasant holding, clearly. And the size of the cow-shed emphasises the importance of dairy pasture hereabouts. In fact the farm was glowingly described as having *'capital rich productive meadow and arable land, divided in convenient enclosures, with most beautiful sites for building, and adjoining the high road from Eltham to Woolwich...only eight miles from London; plenty of fine water; very eligible for investment, and for the residence of a gentleman fond of agricultural pursuits.'* Even at this early time, though, we can see a certain speculative interest creeping in here. And just to re-emphasise the point, it was asserted that it would be *'A most capital property for Gentlemen in the building concern as the grounds are diversified, and well calculated for erecting villas, commanding extensive views etc.'*[6] The estate agents on this occasion may have been over ambitious – or at least, ahead of their time because it was the War Office who bought a substantial part of the land just north of the farm it-self, for a rifle range!

Beyond the farm, on the opposite ridge, screened by trees, stood the impressive house of Eltham Park. In the early 18th century it was the seat of Lady Mary Henrietta, the wife of Viscount Hinchinbrooke, but around 1775 it was purchased by Sir William James, the MP for West Looe. Sir William had made his name and his fortune in the East India Company. Born around 1721 into apparently impoverished circumstances, he ran away to sea and by 1738 was commanding his own vessel. In 1748 he joined the East India Company Marine – its powerful private navy – and rose to command its squadron based at Bombay (modern Mumbai). In 1755 he was instrumental in the capture of the fortress of Suvarnadurg located on an island between Mumbai and Goa. Depending on how old the source you refer to, the attack on Suvarnadurg was either part of a campaign against piracy – or a pre-emptive strike to protect the East India Company's ships as they went about their legitimate business. Neither is strictly true, as any of the more recent assessments of the history and practices of the East India Company explain. The 'Honourable Company', as it liked to be known, basically muscled its way into India and set about undermining the legitimate government of the Mughal and then

[6] *Morning Post* 3 April 1824.

the Maratha Empire. With their own private army and navy, the East India Company used a combination of force and devious practice to get what it wanted - trade, land and power. Although there were regular attempts to resist the onslaught, the Company got its way, plundering the India sub-continent until, ultimately, it ruled virtually all of India.

Back in Britain, there were huge misgivings about the Company's activities, but the fact is that they were hugely wealthy, wielded formidable political power and were virtually unassailable. They could also, when they were feeling co-operative, prove useful to the government – as indeed they did during the Revolutionary and Napoleonic wars. Not only could they effectively buy-off any criticism, they had hugely effective sense of what we would call propaganda. So, for example, until very recently, it was still accepted that Sir William James' attack on Suvarnadurg was an operation to prevent piracy – rather than a move to suppress native resistance to the Company.

Eltham Park from the south around 1790. Severndroog Castle can be glimpsed on the hill in the background.

James returned to England with sufficient wealth to buy the Eltham Park estate, rebuild the house and enclosed the land. He also became both a Director of the East India Company and a member of parliament – though not without some difficulty. In December 1783 he died during the celebration of the marriage of his daughter Elizabeth Anne to Thomas Parkyns, 1st Baron Rancliffe.[7] Ever loyal, Lady James commissioned the Severndroog 'tower' to be built – something which could clearly be seen from the north-facing windows and grounds of the house at Eltham Park. It served as both a memorial and a fashionable addition to the landscape – a picturesque talking point for guests taking an after-dinner perambulation around Eltham Park. (See Chapter 5).

After her husband's death, Lady James withdrew to their town house in Soho and rented Eltham Park to Sir Benjamin Hammett. Hammett was the Member of Parliament who campaigned to end the practice of burning women at the stake – a punishment which continued, shockingly, until 1789.[8]

In the early 1820s, Eltham Park was rented out to Frances Elizabeth Greville, Lady Crewe. Lady Crewe obviously valued her privacy and complained vociferously when the felling of some of the trees on the northern boundary of the Eltham Park grounds exposed the house to the view of the footpath which

---

[7] Rancliffe inherited the Eltham Park estate after the death of Lady James.
[8] The last woman to be technically burnt at the stake was Catherine Murphy on 18th March 1789. In fact, she was strangled half an hour before the fire was lit. But it was the threat of a similar punishment for another woman, Sophia Girton, which prompted Hammet to introduce *The Treason Act* in 1790 which put an end to the practice. Both Catherine Murphy and Sophia Girton had been found guilty of coining – creating counterfeit money by clipping legal coins.

ran alongside it. She did not occupy the house for long as she died in 1825. The house was then purchased by Benjamin Curry a solicitor and Clerk of the Parliaments – i.e. the chief executive of the House of Lords. When he died in 1848, the house was put up for sale. Once again the estate agents blurb (yes they had them even then), is very descriptive and gives us an interesting insight into the property at this stage. One of its main selling points was its location, described as '*a remarkably healthy part of Kent.*' [9] This is significant, because London was now growing rapidly and as it did so, was becoming increasingly undesirable as a residence for the wealthy. The draw of an attractive country seat which was still within striking distance of London was becoming stronger as the century progressed and rural Eltham Park offered an ideal opportunity for someone with the necessary cash. The property consisted of '*an elegant and substantial villa, with beautiful pleasure grounds, conservatory and hot-houses walled garden, &c., surrounded by a richly timbered park of a particularly dry healthy soil, skirted by ornamental groves and woodlands, and commanding on nearly all sides, extensive and rich scenery, being a finely wooded and highly picturesque country, and delightfully secluded, though in the midst of favourite neighbourhood , studded with gentlemen's seats : as a residence it comprises all that can required for a gentleman's establishment on moderate scale, excellent stabling, complete homestead, bailiff's home, and pleasurable park and farm, altogether above 130 acres, freehold ...*'

Shortly thereafter the house was purchased by the railway engineer Thomas Jackson. Jackson and his family were to have a significant impact on the area.

---

[9] *The Globe* Tues. 27th June 1848.

The landscape below Oxleas Woods remained virtually unchanged until the late 1880s, apart from the rifle range which was installed near the bottom of the valley for use by the army. However, things were about to change, as noted by the Suffolk *and Essex Free Press* in 1890:

"... the beautiful Crown Woods...stretch from Eltham to Shooters Hill and enclose several square miles of pleasant sylvan scenery. These woods, although so near the Metropolis, are almost unknown at present to Londoners, as they happen to be situated at an inconvenient distance from any railway station. The beautiful lanes and pathways in which they abound are little frequented except by Eltham folks and the sparse population of Shooters Hill. The Office of Woods and Forests are busy selling the neighbouring park land and meadow of the Eltham demesne for building sites. In course of time, they will, no doubt, do the same in Crown Woods, and London will be robbed of one of its outside play-grounds before public attention is called to the matter. The Woods and Forests Department want watching here and elsewhere."

At this point in the story we have to double back for a moment. As I mentioned earlier, when the Crown Commissioners for Woods etc. were reorganised in 1810, one of their tasks was that of increasing the revenues realisable from the Crown estate. Some hopes had obviously hung on the sale of timber to the Admiralty – but changing technology had put paid to that idea – and the advent of cheaper coal carried by the new railway system, undermined the former value of the underwood. Some hope had been pinned on the value of the agricultural land, though it is clear that Benjamin Curry, the owner of Eltham Park in the 1840s, found the adjacent land which he held under leasehold was very wet and difficult to work. He carried out extensive work inserting drainage and ditches to his fields, but then had to ask the Commissioners to repeat the exercise in their surrounding lanes, fields and woodlands, to prevent them flooding again. [10]

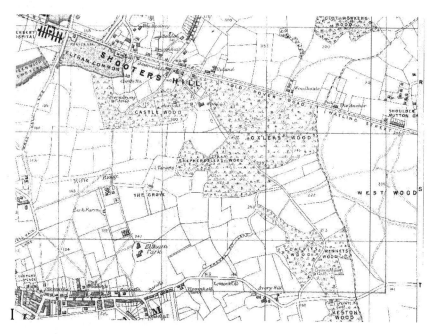

The Eltham Valley, from the from the George Philips & Son, Handy Atlas of London published 1873 (but map from c 1865)

In 1859 the Treasury asked for a review of the position of the Eltham Estate and received a rather despondent report from the Commissioners. They explained that of the 2138 Acres which constituted the Crown land in Eltham, about 271 acres was woodland still in direct possession of the crown, and the

---

[10] Curry to the Crown Commissioners. *9 March 1842.* TNA Crown Estate Records. CRES2/362

remainder had been rented out, producing £10,897. 7s 4d per annum. On top of this, the sporting rights were let separately, producing an additional sixty pounds a year.

Apart from the woodland under the Commissioner's control, and the farmland, there was a residue of land which had been leased out for residential villas, market gardens etc., and many of the leases on this were due to renewal. If the Crown wanted to consider selling the land, the time was imminent. However, there was a fly-in-the ointment, as the Commissioners observed rather pointedly:

'Up to the present time the Eltham Estate has not participated in the advantages derived by many other districts in the immediate vicinity of London from the extension of Railway accommodation. Several schemes have been introduced into Parliament for the construction of lines that would have intersected the Estate but all of them have failed and the distance of the property from any stations upon the subsisting lines of Railway will militate against the early appropriation for building purposes of the parts of the Estate which in other respects are best calculated for the erection of villas. Notwithstanding however the disadvantages attending the distance of the Estate from Railway accommodation, building operations are now going on in its immediate vicinity – It is necessary therefore that provision should be made for the future extension of building operations to the Crown Estate as well as for the possible construction of a Railway...' [11]

---

[11] Letter from Office of Woods to the Treasury. 23 Sept. 1859. TNA Crown Estate records. CRES 39/25

The Commissioners immediately began the process of taking re-possession of any land which might become suitable for the future building of roads, drains or railway lines. Any tenancies issued in the valley in the future would be of significantly shorter duration.

It was a prescient move. In the late 1880s proposals were drawn up for a new railway line to link Lewisham (several miles to the West) with the town of Dartford, thus linking up with the existing North Kent line. Two of the prime movers of this project were the railway engineers Thomas Jackson of Eltham Park, and his son-in-law Alfred Bean, owner of Danson House. Both men were well aware that the building of a railway line would vastly increase the value of their land – especially as Bean was also developing plans for housing development on the site of what had once been the great West Wood, adjacent to Oxleas Wood. It should have been no surprise that the proposed route not only crossed both their lands but also included stations at both Well Hall and Welling. In 1887, the necessary legislation was enacted and construction work finally began in 1891.

From the Crown Commissioners point of view, everything fell into place with remarkable convenience, because one man watching the developments with considerable interest was the wealthy property developer and MP, Archibald Cameron Corbett. By the 1890s Corbett had already been responsible for some major housing developments in south-east London. The estates built in his name were well-designed and the houses well-built, and they offered a range of designs and prices to suit different incomes. However – and I am probably courting controversy in making this observation – this doesn't entitle him to the claims of philanthropy which seem to have become the vogue. His houses weren't built for the poor and weren't built to replace slums. He ensured high prices by making sure the sites he selected for development were adjacent to new railway lines and had access to railway stations.

Corbett purchased virtually the entire Eltham valley for his new Eltham Park housing estate. (Shortly after the completion of Corbett's housing estate a station was added to the Bexley Heath line to serve it. Built more or less on the site of Eltham Park Farm, it was named, in wry acknowledgement, Shooters Hill & Eltham Park Station).

In truly Christian fashion (he was a strict Presbyterian), Corbett also insisted on the provision of churches of different denominations on the estate and forbade both public houses and the sale of alcohol!

Even at the time there were deep suspicions about what Cameron was up to, especially when the London County Council proposed installing a tram service from Woolwich to Eltham. As the radically minded *Suffolk and Essex Free Press* reported in April 1900:

"There is an extremely sore feeling in South-Eastern London about the light railways (i.e. trams) which the County Council intend running to Eltham and Shooters Hill respectively. The pleasant suburban roads which it is proposed to turn into electric tram lines are so quiet and so devoid of traffic that an infrequent 'bus hardly pays its way along one of the routes, and no public vehicle of any kind passes along the other. Why, then, do

the Council desire to force the obnoxious trams upon the neigh-
bourhood? Their scheme is perfectly insane except as it is con-
nected with the fact that Mr. Cameron Corbett, MP., has lately
purchased an enormous estate at Eltham – the most beautiful of
all the outer suburbs – which he is desirous of turning onto a big
working class district. He boasts of his intention of building elev-
en miles of streets of artisans' dwellings. Now this speculation
would be doomed to failure under existing conditions; for,
though the South-Eastern Railway runs to Eltham, it does not
connect it conveniently with any of the manufacturing districts
of London. But the two electric tramways are apparently de-
signed to tap the great manufacturing region of Deptford, and to
provide access from thence to Mr. Corbett's proposed artisan
streets. In other words, the ratepayers are being compelled by
the County Council to provide tramways in order that a Scotch
MP may make a big fortune out of his building "spec".

The area was, to put it bluntly being 'stitched-up'. With the arrival of the railway running east-west, connecting Eltham to
London, and a tramway connecting it to the industrial riverside
of the Thames from Deptford, to Woolwich and Plumstead, an
infrastructure was being put into place which could only encourage development. And with the 'help' of Corbett that development took place rapidly.

Also keeping a watchful eye on the railway company's plans
were the gentlemen of the Eltham Vestry committee – the organisation that came closest to a form of local government at
the time. The Vestry was charged with a range of local admin-
istrative matters including the protection of commoners'
rights, rights of way and sanitary issues. They were certainly
concerned that the route of the new line would sever a number

of tracks and pathways leading from Shooters Hill to Eltham, especially where the line drove through Park Farm. The railway company responded by suggesting they negotiate with existing landowners to see if they could negotiate right of way over their private bridge near Park Farm House. The railway company had already tried to divert an existing footpath but in the end had to compromise and provide a foot tunnel under the line instead. (It is still there and in use).

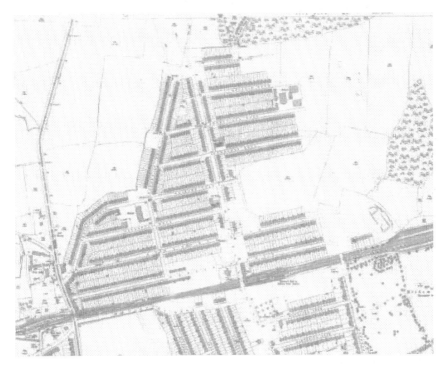

The extent of Corbett's Eltham Park Estate around 1914 from the 25 inch Ordnance Survey map. (Reproduced with the permission of the National Library of Scotland).

However, there was a limit to the impact of Corbett's estate and when worked stopped around 1908, a substantial amount of agricultural land still remained around the foot of Shooters

Hill. This was noted in February 1903 when a royal party made a formal visit to the nearby Herbert Hospital, beside Eltham Common. The hospital, a military hospital built in 1865, contained design elements contributed by Florence Nightingale (who was also the aunt of the hospital's architect Sir Douglas Galton). The route taken by the royal party from Well Hall station took them up the winding Well Hall Lane, which crossed the western flank of Shooters Hill to the hospital which was *'right out in the country, on a spur of gorse clothed Shooters Hill...a mile and a half's climb from the nearest station ...On this bright spring day the view from the hill had a charm of its own. The winding lane to Well Hall station was a zig-zag of colour.'* However the colour came not from wild flowers lining the hedgerows – it was too early in the year for that - but from the military uniforms lining the route and *'the jolly sailor boys of Greenwich School,'* who had no-doubt been marched all the way from Greenwich! [12]

If you look at a plan of Eltham around the time of the First World War, you notice something rather odd about the street plan in the valley below Shooters Hill. For a man so interested in regularity, Corbett's great new estate ended in a rather ragged and untidy manner. There is a great blank space in the centre, and Crookston Road, which runs along the southern edge of the woodland ends rather abruptly and is obviously incomplete. Further extensive vacant land, which Corbett had purchased from Colonel North, the occupant of the mansion at Avery Hill, remained undeveloped to the east of the estate and was subsequently acquired by the London County Council as a park. (Now Eltham Park South.)

---

[12] *Sheffield Daily Telegraph.* 17th Feb 1903

Corbett had obviously had every intention of continuing his development over the land, so what stopped him? It has been suggested that, true to his philanthropic nature, Corbett felt that he had done enough, and generously offered the land for use as a recreational park. But that doesn't fully explain the incomplete nature of the estate. In fact, Corbett's scheme almost certainly fell victim to what has been called the 'Edwardian Property Slump'.[13] Greater regulation of the rented sector – which benefitted the poor – reduced the demand for housing and prices began to collapse, reaching their lowest point around 1909; which is when work on the Corbett estate stopped abruptly. If he couldn't make a big enough profit from selling his houses, there was no point building them. Corbett seems to have abandoned the project.

Of course, from our vantage point above Castle Wood Meadow, we can see that the urban development resumed. The agricultural land is no longer there. The land is now full of houses, and Crookston Road now continues its eastward march along the edge of Jack Wood until it reaches Oxleas Meadow.

With the collapse in house prices Corbett sold the unused land below the woodlands.[14] In 1914, with a frantic acceleration of munitions production at the Woolwich Arsenal, the Government, desperate to find accommodation for the increased

---

[13] See *Indices of House Prices and Rent Prices of Residential Property in London, 1895-1939*. Luke Samy. Discussion papers in Economic and Social History. 134, April 2015. University of Oxford.
[14] Possibly to the Page-Turners (who may originally have been the owners of Wricklemarsh House near Blackeath.

workforce, began building a model estate to the east of Well Hall – the delightful Progress Estate. It was not enough. In October 1915, the land around Shooters Hill was requisitioned, and thousands of temporary hutments were constructed around the southern and western flanks of Shooters Hill. By the end of 1916 some 1,500 huts had been built, more or less obliterating the farm land. The huts themselves were of a relatively flimsy structure - wooden frames with creosoted weatherboard to the exterior, and slate rooves. Asbestos was also used in the interior construction. The huts were considered comfortable, but a failure to insert air bricks below the floorboard level, meant that dampness was a perennial problem

Those moving in to occupy the new huts met with a mixed reception. To start with, many of the existing residents of Corbett's Eltham estate were unhappy about at the loss of the remaining fields, and how they responded to the incomers was coloured by the condition of the hut settlements. With men and some of the women working twelve-hour shifts at the Arsenal and then queuing for ages to get on one of the crowded trams at either end of the day, there was often precious little time or energy for gardening or maintenance. Some of the hutments gradually subsided into near slum-like conditions, while others blossomed with neat vegetable and flower gardens. In a relatively short-time the settlement evolved into a community with a wide range of shops and services. It is possible now, reading the memories of those who lived as children in the hutments, to see the community as a very successful one. That would be, however, to overlook the regular complaints. The dampness has already been mentioned. But the government's agents also failed to keep up with the general maintenance, especially of the roads. Following an enquiry in January

1919, Sir Kingsley Wood, the MP for West Woolwich, agreed that conditions on the estate were 'wholly unsatisfactory' and, as a result, the rents being charged were unfair. An official survey confirmed the poor conditions, especially in the houses built on the lower slopes, where dampness and poor drainage rendered some of the huts actually unsafe.

One would have thought that, given the reduced demand for munitions and munitions workers after the war, the need for such accommodation would have declined. But something unpredictable happened. As a rather value-laden Ministry of Munitions document reported: *'...After the Armistice the better type of tenants tended to move away as they found work elsewhere, leaving a very rough element in possession.'*[15]

This was a slightly unfair assessment of the situation. With huge numbers of men being demobbed there was huge competition for jobs, and the country was sliding into economic depression. The Ministry of Munitions view might also have been coloured by the fact that in February 1919 a number of the residents formed themselves into a 'hutments protection league' and organised a rent strike to try and effect both a permanent reduction on the rent, and ongoing repairs to both the huts themselves and roads and paths in the estate. The strike ended at the end of March, following a permanent reduction of 2s 6d in the rents.

New housing was being built along the Well Hall Road by the early 1920s, but the end of the hutments was really signaled in 1927 when the Ministry of Transport issued instructions for the building of a 'Shooters Hill bypass'. The route of this – now

---

[15] See *The Eltham Hutments*. John Kennett. Eltham Books. 1985 p27

known as the Rochester Way – had been covered by the hut-ments to the north of the Corbett estate.

In the autumn of 1928 the War Office sold off its land on the slopes of Shooters Hill – the land on which the hutments were located – for approximately £50,000. This put the future of the remaining 700 huts, with their 3,500 residents in some doubt. The huts and land adjacent to them were sold off to private de-velopment companies, Eltham Park Estates Ltd, and Castle-wood Estates. According to the deal, as it was reported in *The Scotsman*, the residents were supposed to be offered the chance of renting the new houses at the same level of rent has they were paying for a hut. [16] There is little evidence that any of the residents were able to take up – or even offered – this opportunity. On the contrary, the new landowners, keen to get rid of both huts and sitting tenants, offered the huts for sale at ten pounds each. The only catch was that the purchasers had to dismantle and remove them under their own steam, which some managed to do. Some ending up as holiday huts at places as far away as Camber Sands and Clacton.

By 1935 new houses were being built on the site of the hut-ments, filling in the areas once occupied by farmland on the western and southern flank of the woodlands.

One of the developers, Percy Bilton Ltd, made maximum use of the land available, erecting new semi-detached houses as close to the woodland edge as possible. It was a move which might have seemed commercially advantageous at the time. But an-cient woodland and houses make for uneasy neighbours, and years later, residents (or their insurance companies) began

---

[16] *The Scotsman* 15 October 1928.

demanding that trees pay the price for land subsidence on the now unstable hillside.

Bilton and the other developers simply carried on where Corbett left off. Their new 1930s model houses were simply bolted on to the truncated streets, or filled in the gaps left by their Edwardian predecessor. Almost seamlessly, after the turmoil of the First World War, London convulsed again and spread over more of the landscape. And as it did so it flowed around Shooters Hill like a slowly surging flood water. Fortunately, in July 1934, the London County Council had decided to purchase all of the remaining land on the southern side of Shooters Hill – a total of just over 212 acres. The urban tidal surge swept round the hill, but did not engulf it completely.

The 380 acres of ancient woodland that had once formed the great West Wood, stretching from Oxleas Wood to Alfred Bean's Danson estate, had been felled in 1862 and the woodland grubbed up completely in the following year. Its farmland too now disappeared and as the fields of Eltham and Welling filled with new housing, the development moved on leaving the woodland marooned in a suburban sea.

The development on the farmland around the southern side of Shooters Hill, however, was not the only catalyst in bringing change to the landscape. Around the middle of the 19th century, just as the Commissioners for Woods were exploring new methods of raising income from the Crown Estate, another factor came into play. Between 1800 and 1850 the population of London had doubled to two million. It may have been the wealthiest city in the world, but it was also one of the most overcrowded and insanitary. The Thames itself was disease ridden and noxious, and the increasingly unhealthy state of the capital prompted radical action. While this was going on, those who could afford to, started moving away from the centre towards the leafier, better-smelling suburbs. In 1865 the arrival of the railway at Denmark Hill on that other area of south London high ground, the Norwood Ridge, initiated a Victorian house-building boom, making better housing available for a wide range of middle income earners. Lesser white-collar workers and the better paid artisan class began moving out with their families. (As Cameron Corbett had anticipated)

The very wealthy too wanted to escape from the squalor of the inner city – or at least – wanted a country bolt-hole within easy reach. In the late-18th century, several attractive houses had been built alongside the Dover Road as it crossed Shooters Hill. But in the mid-19th century the attraction of Shooters Hill with its fabulous views across the still unspoilt rural landscape of Kent, did not escape notice. Nor did the fact that the Dover Road, once trampled by Chaucer's raucous pilgrims, was within visual travelling distance of both the industrial Thames riverside and the centre of the capital.

By the 1850s, the Commissioners of Woods, Forests etc. began leasing out portions of the woodland to wealthy individuals with a desire for a convenient country seat. And over the next twenty years several of these were to build themselves substantial country houses near the crest of the hill and, having secured an exclusive location, they guarded their holdings tenaciously.

For just as the hill was attractive to the wealthy, it also provided a focus for the attention of the less affluent who also wanted a break from the city. Although the May Bank Holiday wasn't formally recognized until 1871[17], the arrival of spring had long been celebrated in an ancient tradition, and those who could now poured out of the city to enjoy the return of finer weather. The development of the paddle steamer on the Thames, and the growth of the steamer companies, soon provided cheap and easy access to the countryside for millions of poorer Londoners. The growth of the railways soon added to this facility. In May 1845, for example, the *Morning Post* noted that it was now the habit of vast numbers of people to leave London by rail and paddle steamer to escape *'the smoky atmosphere of the capitol'*. While the main attractions were Rosherville Gardens near Gravesend, or Greenwich Park, *'the country in and about Woolwich, Blackheath, and Shooters Hill, was thronged with visitors.'* [18]

The clean air, tranquility and fine views of the Kent countryside from the top of Shooters Hill, attracted the poor as well as the wealthy, and led to growing hostility as the former began to wonder through the woodland and 'trespass' onto the private estates.

In 1897, the effect of weekend visitors to the area prompted a formal complaint from the members of the Eltham Vestry to the Chief Commissioner of Police about the nuisance being caused by *"by pleasure parties and others, who in passing through the main streets of the parish on Sundays, are in the habit of using musical instruments, and making other noises, detrimental to the peace of the neighbourhood...".* [19]

---

[17] Though the Bank of England staff had enjoyed a holiday on 1st May for much longer.
[18] *Morning Post* 12 May 1845
[19] Eltham Vestry Minutes. Nov 2, 1897

Three years later further complaints were prompted by the arrival of shows, steam-powered roundabouts and 'powerful organs' on Woolwich Common, not far from the foot of Shooters Hill. [20] The disturbance was too much. Many of the wealthier residents of the hill began to decamp to quieter countryside.

---

[20] Op Cit 3 July 1900

Chapter 3. The Dover (Shooters Hill) Road

It may seem a little odd, in a book about a woodland, to be referring quite so much to a road. But the road variously known as Watling Street, then Great Dover Road and now as the A207, occupies an important place in the history of the Oxleas Woodlands. Firstly because, today, it lies as a clear northern boundary to the woodland. Secondly because the use of the road had important and frequent implications for the history and use of the woods. Thirdly, because it is probably the route that most people take today when travelling to the woods.

If you want to want to visit Shooters Hill, there is no escaping a climb – even if you do it on wheels! Approaching from the west, the hill starts to climb from the junction of the south circular road with the A207. If you look at a map you can see the course of the old road from Tabard Street in Southwark, where Chaucer's pilgrims began their journey. A road follows an almost arrow-like course across south-east London to climb onto the Blackheath plateau, where the Kentish peasant army camped before being betrayed and overwhelmed during the Peasants revolt in 1381. Once you've climbed that hill, Shooters Hill looms up in the distance, and the continuation of the road you are standing on is clearly visible as it climbs.

At the junction with the south circular at the foot of the hill is a former police station. The first police station was built here in 1829, but the present building was converted into private flats some years ago. It's a four-storey building in terracotta brick with white horizontal banding. On the corner that overlooks the road junction, there is a window-filled circular bay. Whichever road you took from the crossroads, the eye of the law was watching you. Or at least, that is how it feels. Perhaps intentionally so.

It is appropriate that one of the main approaches to Shooters Hill is marked by something associated with the law or rather, lawlessness. Some of the earliest official references to Shooters Hill arose because of the activities of unsavoury characters who lurked in the adjacent woodland, waiting for the unsuspecting or unarmed traveller.

One has to use quite some imagination to recreate the experience of the weary traveller making their way up the steep ascent, as the woods crowd in close on either side. Some of the earliest references to the hill relate to its danger for the traveller. Edward Hasted in 1797,[21] commented; *'It was always a place of much danger and dread to travellers, from the narrowness of the road over it, and the continual lurking nests of thieves among the woods and coppices, with which this hill, especially towards the south and east, was much overspread.'* The Crown took regular action to clear the woodland from either side of the road to make it safer for travellers but *'Notwithstanding*

---

[21] *The History and Topographical Survey of the County of Kent.* Vol 1. 1797.

which, this road continued so hollow, and narrow too, on the eastern descent of the hill, that it was impossible for a passenger, if way-laid, to escape falling into the ruffian's hands, which gave occasion to continual robberies being committed here, even at noon day.'

Up until the 18th century it was certainly an isolated spot. To the south of the road, just below the crest on the western side stood an inn, The Catherine Wheel. Excavations carried out in 1977 indicated that the inn had been in existence before 1640, and may have survived until about 1760-1778 when the building was demolished and replaced by Hazelwood House. [22] Tentative plans drawn up by the archaeologists suggest that The Catherine Wheel featured a long, single-storeyed building facing the road, with courtyard to the rear surrounded by two stable blocks and a coach house. A tiny illustration on John Holmes' map of 1749 seems to indicate that there might have been a tower or two-storey section. Tantalisingly, in his novel *Roxana*, Daniel Defoe has his heroine visiting *'the best house of entertainment on Shooters Hill'* (which could only really have been The Catherine Wheel) where, ascending a tower or upper floor, her party are able to view the recently completed dome of St Paul's Cathedral. This suggests that Defoe visited the inn itself between 1710 when the cathedral was completed, and 1724 when *Roxana* was published. By 1760, it seems that The Catherine Wheel had been eclipsed by a newer and better equipped inn further up the hill, The Bull.

The hazardous nature of the road over the hill is amply illustrated by the tactics of Col. Nathaniel Rich, in 1648 during the

---

[22] The site lies under the Oxleas NHS Trust's Highpoint House. Hazelwood House was, in turn demolished in 1816.

Second Civil War. In May of that year, Royalist sympathisers at Canterbury commissioned Col. Francis Hammond, a professional soldier of considerable experience, to raise a force in rebellion against the Parliament. Hammond's force of both foot and horse, marched on London, using Watling Street as their route. Having taken Dartford and the river crossing there, they marched westwards until they reached the eastern side of Shooters Hill, where their advance guard encountered as troop of New Model Army cavalry. A brief engagement followed, during which one the New Model Army troopers, Sgt. Lobb, was killed. The Royalist force appears to have withdrawn, leaving Lobb's comrades to bury his body somewhere in either Oxleas or West Wood.

Parliament responded to the uprising by ordering Col. Nathaniel Rich to lead a force out to meet them. One of the reasons for this may have been that Rich had just purchased the Eltham estate, including Eltham Palace, and therefore probably knew the area quite well.[23]

Rich's career was even more interesting than his opponent, Francis Hammond. Rich became a lawyer three years before the beginning of the First Civil War and, at the outbreak of war, volunteered initially for the Earl of Essex's regiment of Lifeguards. He fought throughout the war, surviving both the Battle of Edgehill (the first major engagement of the conflict), and

---

[23] He kept Eltham Palace until the Restoration in 1660, when it was taken from him and given to Sir John Shaw. In 1656 the diarist John Evelyn, who lived a few miles away in Deptford, visited the palace and described the palace as being in 'miserable ruins, the noble wood and park destroyed.' The description of the condition may have been accurate. Though as Evelyn was hostile to Rich, the cause of the state of palace and park may have had more to do with neglect over a long period of time. Before the war, the palace had been used as a residence by the painter Van Dyck.

then the decisive final engagement at Naseby. Appointed to the New Model Army as Colonel of a regiment of horse, he supported his men in the quarrel with the Parliament, and then became an active supporter of the Levellers. [24]

Rich's force appears to have assembled on Blackheath to meet the Kentish Royalists and then, move on Dartford. Following the news of the skirmish on the eastern side of Shooters Hill, Rich decided to advance to meet them. The most direct route for him would have been to march over Shooters Hill. But the surrounding woodland offered an all too obvious location for an ambush; on top of which, the steepness of the hill would have made it difficult to move both baggage train (and artillery if he had any). Wisely, Rich decided to circumnavigate the hill. He advanced to Eltham, where his force camped for the night, and then advanced along the ridge on what is now the Bexley Road.

Hammonds force retreated and Rich advanced into Kent where he joined up with a force under Sir Thomas Fairfax, finally storming Maidstone after heavy fighting on 1st June.

If Rich's military force managed to avoid ascending the hill, another, more sombre procession arrived there on 18th November 1758. On the previous day, the corpse of Charles Spencer, the third Duke of Marlborough had been landed at Dover, where it was met by a hearse and three coaches carrying several of the Duke's retainers. Like his more illustrious predecessor, John Churchill, the First Duke, Spencer's body was des-

---

[24] Curiously, John Lilburne, one of the greatest of the Leveller leaders, and one of the main authors of *The Agreement of the People*, died in Eltham, where his wife was living, in August 1657. Lilburne's career during the First Civil war shadowed that of Rich

tined for burial in the family vault at Blenheim Palace. Also like his predecessor, Spencer was commanding British forces overseas in wartime. On this occasion it was the Seven Years War – mainly fought against France (as usual) – and Spencer died of a fever while leading a force against St. Malo. As protocol demanded, a suitable overnight resting place had been organised for the corpse. A room hung with black and *'properly illuminated was prepared for the reception of the corpse; upon which was placed his Grace's heart, embalmed and wrapp'd in lead, and afterwards inclosed in a case of wood resembling the form of it.'* [25]

Unfortunately, no record survives of the location of this event, but since the Earl of Shrewsbury's house [26] on the top of the hill was not built until 1789, it is possible that the substantial Bull Inn was requisitioned for His Grace.

On a dark winter's night it is possible to imagine the arrival of the procession making its cautious way down from the summit of the hill; the flare of the torches guttering in the November wind, the stamping of the horses still steaming from their climb, and the black crepe drapes and plumes giving the whole a dramatic if gloomy cast.

Indeed, a winter's night is the best time to recapture the atmosphere of the old road. It is best to start from the old police station, heading eastwards, leaving the South Circular Road behind you. At a late hour in winter, the old road becomes much quieter. Traffic, usually fairly regular during the day, diminishes to an occasional trickle. On the left hand side, the

---

[25] *Oxford Journal* 25 November 1758.

[26] Now the site of the Shrewsbury House Community centre. Because this lies some way north of the Dover Road and away from the woodland, it is not covered in this book.

road is lined by a mixture of old and new buildings. At first these are screened by trees and hedges. On our right though, behind the police station and a small block of flats, is the open grassland of Eltham Common with its wood beyond. The grassland is faintly illuminated by the orange glow of the street lamps, but beyond it the thick dark belt of trees stand watchfully. As you climb, that belt of woodland gradually moves closer to the road, until you are walking beside it as it hangs over you (unless you decide to walk on the north side of the road, that is!)

Opposite the woods, an eclectic mix of buildings moves closer to the pavement. A Turkish restaurant with large, brightly lit windows, shines momentarily onto the woods opposite. Then the Red Lion, a rambling Victorian pub set back from the road; next the simple Georgian architecture of Albion cottages whose front doors step right onto the pavement. Larger, later houses, set back in deeper gardens. On our right the trees of Eltham Common give way to a small modern development of quiet town houses, set back in a cul-de-sac. The wide openness of the Memorial Hospital grounds follow, and then trees close in again upon our right.

By this point something interesting has happened to the gradient of the road. Something which you could never notice if you travelled by car or bus today – though you might have noted it a couple of centuries ago. The road appears to have sunk some five feet. To the left, the pavement has lifted – while to our right the ground level is above shoulder height. A section of the hill has been carved away to reduce the steepness of the gradient.

In December 1816, the Trustees of the New Cross Turnpike Roads met to consider necessary repairs and improvements to the various routes under their care. One of their main concerns was that of the difficulty caused by the road over Shooters Hill. They had accepted the task of finding work for some of the large number of men who found themselves discharged from the army and navy following the final defeat of Napoleon at Waterloo. In fact, the country was awash with men who found that after years of service to their country, their livelihoods had been usurped by machines or the enclosure of agricultural land – a situation exacerbated by an economic decline after the war. The Trustees of the New Cross Turnpike had pledged themselves to finding work for an extra one hundred labourers – so they set them to work reducing the gradients on Shooters Hill, a task which they considered would be *an object of great and lasting importance to the constant and immense traffic between Dover and the Metropolis.'* [27] So, in the depths of winter, these hardy labourers were set to work scraping away the road surface as it climbed towards the summit, and barrowing the spoil down towards the lower part of the hill, where it was spread on the existing road surface to smooth out the slope.

Even today, the climb up the hill takes a bit of effort, so it is not hard to imagine what it must have been like before 1816! As we continue to climb, the lights of The Bull can be seen on our left at the crest of the hill. As already noted the Red Lion existed before The Bull, though it has a less interesting history. By the 19th century it included both a detached house and a cottage which was rented out to produce extra income. In 1870, when it was put up for sale, it was described as *commanding extensive views of the charming scenery that abounds in this locality'* and offered both stabling for horses and a large tea garden for visitors. The main building, which gave its name to the adjacent Red Lion Lane, was an attractive white stuccoed building with large windows and an attractive coach-like entrance. This was, however, replaced by the current red-bricked Victorian-gothic structure, in 1902.

---

[27] *Report of the Committee of the Trustees of the New Cross Turnpike.* 28 December. 1816.

The current Bull inn which dates from 1881, replaced an earlier and more extensive establishment which may have dated back to 1749 or a little later. The original Bull Inn stood a little further to the east, and OS maps from the 1860s show that it was a sizeable establishment. A photograph from shortly before the demolition of the original building, shows that it had a rambling stuccoed frontage, consisting of at least three adjoining buildings of differing heights. It certainly seems to have been the main facility for refreshing or resting horses in the 18th and 19th centuries. According to the local 19th century historian, W T Vincent, at the height of its glory, the Bull had a grand salon which attracted people from far and wide to the many balls and public dinners held there. The buildings which housed these facilities appear to have been demolished between 1820 and 1849, leaving a rather diminished inn in its place.[28] Nevertheless it continued – and continues to be – a popular local establishment, if you are not deterred by the ghostly footsteps at night!

The water tower around 1935.

Continuing eastwards beyond the Bull, the hill climbs to the summit of the hill, now crowned by a distinctive water tower which cane seen clearly from the North Downs Way some 15 miles to the south. The

[28] Records of the Woolwich District Vol II. 1890. W T Vincent.

tower is a mock-gothic octagonal structure[29], with a steeply-pitched tiled roof and medieval looking dormer windows. The tower was built in 1909-1910 by the Metropolitan Water Board to meet the growing demand for water from the housing development to the south of the hill. The design, though, gave rise to something of a dispute between the Works Committee, tasked with the building project, and the trustees of the Water Board itself. A budget of £5,000 was allocated for the project, however the Works Committee felt that the sum was insufficient to do justice to what would become such a prominent landmark. A more elaborate design, a cross between a lighthouse and a church steeple, was therefore presented to the Board for approval, even though it would increase the building cost to £7,000. An apoplectic Charles Fitzroy Doll [30] – himself a famous architect – derided the design as *an egg boiler on stilts* and the more elaborate design was rejected – losing, presumably, the lighthouse element.

As we approach the water tower, though we realise we are on the gently rolling crest of the hill. If the road is quiet, as it is now, something starts to feel different. We can now see that the water tower itself is beyond the crest, just down the eastern side of the hill, its base hidden in foliage. On the right hand,

---

[29] Incidentally, the Shooters Hill water tower is often confused (especially in internet references) with the earlier Brook Hospital water tower on Shooters Hill Road, about a mile to the west. That tower was built to supply water to the Brook Fever Hospital which opened in 1896. The hospital was built to a new more open design. Rather than standing as a monolithic structure, it featured a range of smaller buildings connected by covered corridors. For better or worse, the design was intended to facilitate access to sun and air for its 500 fever patients.
[30] Charles Fitzroy Doll (1850-1929) was mainly known for designing grand hotels, but perhaps more famously for designing the dining room of the *Titanic*.

a lane leads off into the woods. This is Crown Woods Lane, once an important track leading south towards Avery Hill to join the road along the opposite Eltham ridge.

Half hidden behind an ivy-clad fence on our right, is the white faced façade of Holbrook House, erected between 1780-1805 and therefore one of the oldest surviving houses on the hill. The simple and elegant Georgian frontage is now clumsily dwarfed by a less attractive late-19th century extension at the rear. But in the muted light of the street lamps at night, the uglier element fades into the background, and Holbrook recovers some of its original elegance.

Beyond Holbrook, though, Oxleas Wood reclaims its territory, crowding close upon the road on the right-hand side. To the left, a string of unattractive modern houses clings on for a while, and then the land abruptly falls away leaving us alone with the woods. Even in winter when the branches are bare, the light from the street lamps seems diminished as the trees crowd in on either side. If you walk here alone at night, it can feel as though time has shifted backwards. No houses, no vehicles. The road stretches away into the dim distance and the trees and underwood stir and rustle on either side. As the road begins to descend at a steeper angle, there is a deeper darkness on either side. In the fields of the Woodlands community farm on the left, a sheep moans in response to the wind.

At this point where the woods press closest to the road we are isolated from company, from help. The woods are closeted and unfathomable. This part of the hill was renowned as the haunt of robbers and it is easy to understand why.

We have already noted the poor reputation of the hill during the Middle Ages. But that notoriety continued for centuries. The hill is the scene of a notorious murder depicted in the Elizabethan play *A Warning for Fair Women*. The play was performed by Shakespeare's company, The Chamberlain's Men, in 1599 and although the author is unknown, suggestions have been made that it might have been the bard himself. The plot of the play is based on a real murder which took place in 1573 when a London merchant, George Sanders and his servant John Bean, were attacked on their way back towards the City. Sanders died at the scene and Bean died of his wounds three days later. The murderer was Sanders' wife's lover, George Browne. Sanders was very highly connected. His cousin was Chief Justice of the Queen's Bench and the Chief Baron of the Exchequer. Retribution was swift and merciless. George Browne was arrested and tried, then executed at Smithfield a month later; but the execution of his accomplice, Anne Sanders, was delayed when it was revealed that she was carrying his child. She was executed shortly after giving birth.

From the mid-17th century onwards, the lonely road through the woods was a notorious haunt of highwaymen. The earliest recorded of these appears to have been Captain James Hind who was finally captured and executed in September, 1652. Born in Chipping Norton, Hind served two years as apprentice to a local butcher before abandoning that trade and fleeing to London. There he rather predictably fell into bad company – in particular that of an experienced highwayman by the name of Thomas Allen. Allen took the young Hinds under his wing and gave him his baptism into a new life of crime on Shooters Hill, where the newly initiated highwayman robbed a gentleman and his assistant of fifteen pounds (then returned 20s for their travel expenses!). It sounds like a typically romantically-tinted story: but then it is recorded in *The Newgate Calendar* which loved to spice up and romanticise its villains. [31] Hind's subsequent activities were located further away and so the rest of Hind's career is of little relevance to our story. Later authors embellished his career slightly by claiming that he was an ex-soldier in the Royalist army, and that he repeatedly robbed or attempted to rob both Cromwell and high-ranking parliamentarians. This may explain why he was, apparently, finally executed for treason rather than robbery – and why some seventeen pamphlets were published outlining his career as some form of latter-day Robin Hood!

But it was really during the 18th century that the woods became the haunt of highwaymen. Contemporary newspaper accounts are peppered with reports of such robberies. Here is one of the earliest, as reported by the *Stamford Mercury* on 23rd February, 1738.

'On Tuesday last at 5 O'clock in the evening, Mr Phillips of White-chapel, coming to town from Dartford, was stopped at the bottom of Shooters Hill by two footpads, pistol in hand; and Mr Philips refusing to stop they swore they would shoot him if he did not deliver, upon which he gave them about 15s in silver, and they thanked him very friendly and wished him well home. He had a watch in his fob but they did not search him.'

---

[31] There was no single volume known as *The Newgate Calendar.* The 'calendar' really consisted of a series of stories or biographical accounts which were published in various combinations from 1705 onwards. Many of them originated in popular broadsheets and chapbooks which were sold by itinerant street-sellers. Some were even produced for sale at the execution of their subject. The contents of the 'calendar' are still being reprinted in various combinations today.

The casual tone of this report, together with the polite behaviour of the robbers, is typical. Some of the robbers, like Hinds, became famous. In April 1742 the highwayman William Piggott was condemned to death, having been captured in a wood near Farnham some months previously. Piggott had lately been committing highway robberies in Sussex, but this was not where he made his name. As the *Derby Mercury* reported to its eager audience, *'He is the man that so much infested the Kentish Road chiefly about Shooters Hill last summer.'* [32]

Not all victims got off so politely. In June 1750 a rope-maker by the name of Jackson was attacked on his way back from Dartford. At 9pm as he reached Shooters Hill two footpads attacked him, stealing 10s , beating him severely and leaving him lying beside the road with his hands and feet bound. He was found at four o'clock the next morning by a gentleman's servant out on an early morning errand. Perhaps the fact that Jackson was the victim of footpads rather than highwaymen – surely a higher class of criminal? – determined the severity of his treatment.

These encounters did not always go the robber's way, nor were they entirely without an element of farce. Such was the unfortunate experience of the (one suspects) rather inexperienced highwayman who attempted a robbery here on the evening of 16th January 1748. The would-be robber had secreted himself in trees beside the road awaiting an opportunity, when a lone horsemen began plodding his way up the long hill. The robber rode out onto the road and drew his pistol, bidding his intended victim – in the time-honoured phrase – 'to stand and deliver'. Under normal circumstances, this might have been enough - as was expected - to render the intended victim incapable of fight or flight, or even intelligible speech. Not so on this occasion. Unfortunately for the highwayman, (name unknown) the

---

[32] *Derby Mercury.* 1st April 1742.

intended victim was actually a sailor – more specifically a hoary tar from the frigate HMS *Hastings*.

From 1708 onwards, sailors involved in the capture of either an enemy warship or a merchantman, were entitled to a share of the value of either the vessel – or the vessel and its cargo in the form of 'Prize Money'. The disadvantage of this arrangement was firstly that the shares were often not paid out for years, and secondly that recipients often had to travel to either London or one of the naval ports to collect their money. Prize money was frequently not collected because the sailor concerned died or was killed before it was paid out – or because it was impossible to collect because of the difficulties of getting to the specified prize pay office. In this particular case, the sailor had travelled from London to Chatham to collect his pay, and was merrily making his way back with his pockets full.

Having made his demand to 'stand and deliver', the highwayman was startled and perplexed when the sailor shrugged and confessed that he didn't understand what that meant. The robber attempted an explanation to the effect that he wanted the tar's money, and if he did not deliver it up, *'he was a dead man'*. This was probably not the wisest thing to say. The sailor pointed out that he had already risked his life fighting for his money and that he wasn't going to surrender it now without receiving some 'broadsides' first! Somewhat alarmed, the desperate highwayman fired his pistol. The shot missed its target, and Jack calmly rode up to the robber and struck him from his horse with a single blow to the head. Before the highwayman could recover, two men who were conveying straw to Wricklemarsh, (the country estate of Sir Gregory Page a few miles west at Blackheath) arrived on the scene. They helped bind the robber who was then arrested and dispatched for committal at Maidstone gaol. [33]

---

[33] *Daily Mercury* 20 January 1748

There is something wonderfully Fielding-esque about that incident (or is it Smollett-like) but there is a more modern element to a later incident, in 1776. On this occasion the robbers were two highwaymen with crepe masks over their faces who were clearly of the more experienced and better equipped variety. They lay in wait at the foot of the hill until a carriage, driven by a single and apparently unarmed man, began to climb the hill. Riding out into the roadway, they stopped the carriage and made their usual demand. However, on throwing open the carriage door, they found themselves facing not a terrified and wealthy gentleman, but a calmly composed, glamourous-looking and fashionably dressed woman. Their victim was actually the **actress Susan Greville, well known at Drury Lane and the Haymarket, as well as other London Theatres. In 1776 she had been playing in** *The Suspicious Husband.* Though the part for which she was probably most well-known was in the title role, Martha Brady, in David Garrick's play *The Irish Widow* at Drury Lane in 1772. A contemporary described her as having 'a smart figure, a lively countenance, a very pleasing voice and an easy manner.' [34] She was obviously also extremely canny and not at all what the highwaymen had been expecting. As she went to hand over her purse, she affected some distress and asked the two men to put away their pistols, as she hadn't been able to bear the site of loaded pistols since she had worn them herself in *The Irish Widow.*

It was at this point the penny dropped and the highwaymen suddenly realised who they were dealing with. Obviously terminally star-struck, one of them was suddenly overcome and proclaimed that he would rather give her ten guineas than take a single one from her. Making the most of her obvious position

---

[34] *A Biographical Dictionary of Actors, Actresses, Musicians, Dancers, Managers.* By Philip H. Highfill, Kalman A. Burnim, Edward A. Langhans Vol 6. 1976

of strength, the actress insisted that, on the contrary, they must take her purse. At which point the leading highwayman was overcome, grasping her hand and bursting into tears. Pressing home her advantage Mrs Greville offered her watch instead. It was tearfully refused. And instead of robbing their victim the bold robbers actually handed half a crown to the coach driver with instructions to see her safely home! [35] One hopes that the wily Mrs Greville did complete her journey in comfort and safety. Sadly, she disappeared from the stage in 1778, the rumoured victim of an unhappy and brutal marriage.

Continuing down the hill, moving away from the lights of houses or other buildings, the woodlands to our right seem to take on a wilder, more brooding character, as though something is lurking in there. Something, unseen, watching and waiting. Strangely, this seems stronger when the night is still. When the wind is blowing strongly, the sound of the trees stirring fills the air with sound. In summer, when the canopy is full, the sound is a full, ululating hissing sound, almost like waves being driven onto a beach from unrelenting cross-currents. But in winter, when the trees are bare, there is a hollow, haunted sound in the air. It's as though a wildness is creeping closer to the road. It hasn't changed much since 1866 when a journalist for the *Illustrated London News* described Shooters Hill as *'a miserably bleak place, as one who has driven up and down it on a cold spring night might well know.'* [36]

This wildness is certainly a hangover from the past. The woodland used to be thicker and apparently impenetrable in places. Twice in 1827 convicts bound for the prison hulks on the Thames managed to escape from the wagons carrying them and make their way into hiding in these woods. In May 1827,

---

[35] *Ipswich Journal* 20 April 1776.

[36] *Illustrated London News* 5th May 1866

four of them hid themselves in the dense underwood and furze hoping to evade capture. Unfortunately they were seen by two boys who gave them away to the pursuing troops. Possibly more successful in his attempt was James Hawkins, who attempted a similar escape on 23rd December of the same year, and who was still at large a week later. [37]

Violent robberies on this road continued sporadically for most of the 19th century. The culprits were clearly undeterred by the fact that gallows were situated beside the road on both sides of the hill – unlike Samuel Pepys who noted in his famous diary the ghastly state of a corpse still hanging in one, months after execution. In what seems to have been an attempt at consistency, a number of those so treated were displayed near the scenes of their crimes. In March 1801, for example, a gang of three named Morley, Seamonds and Shepherd were sentenced to be hung at Shooters Hill, close to the scene of their robberies. Even as late as 1834 the woods had an unsavoury reputation, as a rather dismal report in *The Morning Advertiser* noted: *'It is at present worse than useless being a harbour for vagrants and dangerous characters'.* [38]

In 1865 workmen excavated a skeleton on the site of the gallows at the junction of the Shooters Hill Road/South Circular Road, a site later covered by the surviving police station building. The discovery prompted an elderly local resident by the name of George Bym, to recall witnessing the execution of four men in March 1801- three for a burglary at Charlton, and a soldier *'for a more heinous offence'* which prompted his subsequent interment in the unhallowed ground in the shadow of the gibbet itself.

---

[37] *London Courier and Evening Gazette* 29 December, 1827
[38] *The Morning Advertiser* 18 November 1834. The paper suggested that a solution might be to cut a new public highway through the wood from Welling, in the east, to Well Hall in the south-west, creating a new route to London via the hamlet of Kidbrooke.

But robbery continued. In 1880 a messenger of the Greenwich Burial Board was robbed by two men who attacked him at *'a portion of the road which is very lonely, with extensive underwood and bushes on either side'.* [39] He had been carrying cash from the Board to the Superintendent of the Cemetery at Shooters Hill, but as he had not long passed the Herbert Hospital when the attack took place, it must have been on the western side of the hill.

Continuing our way down the eastern side of the hill, with Oxleas Wood still pressing in against the southern side of the road, a curious thing happens if you are paying attention. The woodland suddenly drops below the level of the road. Not many yards further on, the grounds to the north also drop away into the darkness, and we are walking on what is, to all effects, a raised causeway.

In December 1816, the worthy gentlemen of the New Cross Turnpike Trust, while endorsing plans to shave off some of the steepness on the road as it climbed the western side of the hill, also considered plans to improve the road on the opposite side. Initially it was proposed that the four-hundred yard stretch of road descending from the crest down the east slope, should be excavated to create an easier gradient for travellers climbing towards the top of the hill, while several acres of land to the north of the road should be purchased to facilitate a diversion of the road itself onto a gentler slope. Unfortunately, the tenant occupying the farmland to the north of the road demanded such exorbitant compensation for the loss of his grazing land that the plan got nowhere. The Trustees resorted instead, with the agreement of the Crown's Commissioners for Woods and Forests, to fell a number of the trees in Oxleas Wood to the south of the road, and excavate the soil to build the existing road up into a gentler ramp. The soil thus excavated left a

---

[39] *Yorkshire Post and Leeds Intelligencer,* 28 December 1880

great hollow which can easily be seen today when exploring Oxleas Wood itself.

The improvements had limited effect. In March 1823, the driver of the Swallow – the London to Dover Coach – lost control of the vehicle as it came down the slope when the reins broke. The horses, unable to slow the weight of the coach, panicked and fled down the hill at full speed until the coach overturned crushing one of the passengers, a French woman. She was carried to the nearest Inn but, as a newspaper dolefully recorded, was not expected to survive. Less than four months later a more serious accident occurred on the eastern side of the hill – despite the enormous efforts taken to ease the descent. In July, the 15th Hussars had been ordered to Canterbury and were in the process of making their way there when one of their baggage wagons ran out of control down the slope and overturned. This time, the daughter of one of the regiment's sergeants was killed, and two of the soldier's wives were seriously injured. [40]

In October, 1879, a Metropolitan fire engine overturned near the police station after its brakes failed coming down the hill. The firemen were thrown violently into the road and the captain had his leg broken. One of the horses had to be killed as a result of its injuries. [41]

While the steepness of the hill continued to cause accidents, some of them very serious, [42] it also attracted problems from

---

[40] *Kentish Weekly Post or Canterbury Journal* 25th July 1823.

[41] *Wrexham Guardian & Denbigh & Flintshire Advertiser* 18 October 1879.

[42] On Easter Monday, 1920, three people were killed and 31 injured when a bus overturned after the driver swerved to avoid two dogs who ran into the road in front of him as he drove down the western slope.

thrill-seekers. And, because it is, frankly hilarious, I beg no forgiveness for including the following report in full, entitled *'Scorchers' and the Police* from *The Globe* on Wednesday 24th August, 1892: (modern cyclists beware!)

'The cycling "scorcher" is, undoubtedly, an unmitigated nuisance. Cyclists of the better sort admit that freely enough, and right glad would they be were some means discovered to suppress the baser species. But, if, the "scorcher" does not quite deserve capital punishment when caught in the act of furious riding, some constables appear, however, to take the other view, judging from what came out at the Woolwich police court yesterday. The defendant, a young man, was charged with riding his safety [bicycle] down Shooters' Hill at a furious rate, the police estimate being from fifteen to twenty miles an hour. As he had his feet off the pedals and did not put on the brake, it may be accepted that his speed down the sharp declivity was not far short the higher figure. Clearly, therefore, his life would be brought into imminent jeopardy it the machine upset. That is precisely what two policemen in succession endeavoured to compass. One of these too zealous champions of order deposed that "he tried to stop the defendant by putting his rolled-up cape in front of the machine"; another lower down the hill seized the handle bar, suddenly stopped the safety, and, of course, sent the rider flying through the air as if discharged from a catapult. Not without complete justification did the stipendiary remark that "such methods of stopping cyclists appeared to excessively dangerous." More than dangerous—one might almost call them murderous. The only excuse is that, unless the police proceed in that summary manner, the "scorcher" is out sight in few seconds. How would it answer to give cyclists the option of either taking out licences or having their names and addresses legibly painted some prominent part their machines. The quiet riders, who form the more respectable moiety, would as a rule elect for the former alternative, while the other sort could be quickly identified without risk of manslaughter.'

Happily the local constabulary soon had a more worthy opponent, as the local *Kentish Independent* noted in July 1907, they were continuing to prosecute *"speed loving motorists who apparently imagine that Shooters Hill was made especially to drive down at a break neck pace."* This because a man was summoned to Woolwich magistrates court for travelling downhill at 25mph.

The Dover Road looking west towards Shooters Hill, around 1900. The eastern boundary of Oxleas Wood is on the left, with Woodlands Farm to the right.

Cars travelling down the hill nowadays certainly exceed the outrageous 25mph, especially at night when the road is quiet. On a wet night though, even the motorists seem deterred by the loneliness of the road. At the bottom of the hill the road levels out on its way to its first Kentish 'village' – Welling - now a suburb of the Borough of Bexley. On our left as we continue, the fields of the Woodlands Farm follow us still, behind a hedge and the dim outline of the old farmhouse. On either side of the road now, the woods and hedgerows start to give way to houses. More street lamps. Lights behind curtained windows. A car speeds past and is gone, swallowed by traffic lights in the distance. At the eastern end of Oxleas Wood I stop and look back up towards the top of the hill. The air seems to thicken and haze over, and a shower crawls over the hill and rolls down the slope towards me. The thin claw-like reach of the winter trees stretching out from the woodland is tinged with orange, as they gather the droplets from the drizzle. I remember that in 1924 there were several reports of the ghostly figure of a bearded man seen on the road at this point – and pulling up the hood of my jacket. I turn and head back for home.

Chapter 4 Eltham Common.

In my haste to climb the Dover Road, I really missed Eltham Common. It is the large area on the south side of the road be-hind the police station. It looks like a large meadow area, but the common itself extends up under the thick woodland above it until it reaches Castle Wood. Up until the middle of the 19th century, it was a largely an open area of rough scrubland with scattered trees, climbing up the western side of Shooters Hill. In maps of the area (or Google Earth) it occupies the top left or north-western corner of the Shooters Hill Woodlands, spread-ing in a south-easterly direction from the old police station mentioned in the last chapter. In total it occupies about 25 acres, or just over 10 hectares if you prefer that.

The common is an anomaly in the woodland because, as com-mon land, it never came under the jurisdiction of the Crown Commissioners – and was managed instead by the gentlemen of the Eltham Vestry. As far as Eltham Common was con-cerned, the Vestry's main duty was to protect the rights of the commoners to graze livestock or take wood for fires etc. from the land. In doing so they had to try and ensure not only that there was equitable use of the land, but also that it was used in a way that conserved it as a common resource for the future. Their task was not made easy by the presence of two powerful neighbours – the Commissioners for Woods and Forests, and the military.

The relationship of the locals to the army or its masters at the Board of Ordnance and War Office, was not always easy, especially with such a large military presence at Woolwich, with its multiple barracks and horse artillery stables. In the 1840s, the Eltham Vestry had to write to the Board of Ordnance reminding them of their parishioners' long-standing right to cut timber, furze and underwood on the common. In September 1861, the Vestry members received a complaint from one of their parishioners that he had been prevented from grazing his cattle on the common by representatives of the military authorities at Woolwich. The War Office issued a muted apology, but problems rose again in 1864 when the War Office began the building of the military Herbert Hospital on the other side of Eltham Lane (now the Well Hall Road). Plans for the hospital were developed in the aftermath of the Crimean War as part of the health care reforms for the army. The architect, Captain Douglas Galton, designed it in a style which included 'pavilions' which provided more air and natural lighting to fight bacteria, and was approved of by Florence Nightingale.

The contractors building the hospital began excavating reservoirs as part of the water supply to the hospital, but in doing so encroached onto Eltham Common, possibly because the reservoirs needed to be on higher ground. On this occasion the Eltham Vestry were helpfully cooperative and agreed to take an equal area of Kidbrooke Common (which the War Office had already acquired) in exchange for the lost land. Unfortunately, the War Office then reneged on the agreement and refused to hand over their portion of the land.

The dispute rumbled on until 1877 when the army probably thought it better to settle the issue, as Kidbrooke Common and the lands around the south of Shooters Hill were being used for manoeuvres by the Royal Horse Artillery. Moreover, the army had installed a rifle range in the bottom of the Eltham valley. It was situated immediately adjacent to the largest farm in the area, Eltham Park Farm, whose fields survived until the end of the century. There is a Stanford wall-map from the 1870s which shows clearly the layout of the fields and woods at this time. There are few buildings in the area – the only other significant structure being that of Well Hall farm with its (still standing) Tudor barn.

The area was sparsely populated too. In 1881 there were only 859 inhabited homes in the whole parish, and even less in the neighbouring parish of Kidbrooke (257). This compared with 5248 on the other side of the hill in Plumstead. Fifteen years later, the population of Eltham (5911) was still small compared with the other side of the hill, where industrial growth and the development of both the army facilities and munitions works had helped increase the population of Plumstead and Woolwich to more than one hundred thousand.

The building of the Royal Herbert Hospital nearly sparked a further development. In early 1868, the Board of Guardians for the Woolwich Union discussed the possibility of acquiring part of Eltham common behind the police station, for the site of a new workhouse. What the Vestry's response to this might have been doesn't seem to be recorded, but the idea was dropped following an investigation which surprisingly found the site to be too damp for such an institution.

The Eltham Vestry might have had more than just their commoner's rights in mind when they made their complaints to the army. At the end of the 19th century, the area south of Shooters Hill was still an attractive stretch of quiet countryside - when, that is, the horses and gun carriages of the Royal Horse Artillery weren't thundering around.

There was due cause for alarm. By 1897 the War Office was looking for a larger area to acquire for military training, and the area they had their sights on included the sparsely populated area south and south-west of Shooters Hill, including the little farm at Well Hall and the hamlet of Kidbrooke. The *Kentish Independent,* reported that the area had once been *"attached to the princely residence known as Wricklemarsh, and much of it was a beautiful park, but, by the folly and extravagance of its last occupant, it was brought to the hammer and returned to the more useful service of agriculture. The Eltham side of the property...is that which would be the greatest service to the military, for attached to this are not only the rugged uplands of Eltham Common behind Shooters Hill police station, but the very extensive Crown Woods which stretch over the hill down to East Wickham. The uplands and woods are already government property."* [43]

In fact the *Kentish Independent* considered the area ideal for bush training - but then the paper was a keen supporter of military intervention in South Africa against the Boers – perhaps

---

[43] *Kentish Independent* 23 October 1897

imagining that Shooters Hill resembled one of those rugged South African 'kops' which were soon to become so notorious. Not everyone could have been so sanguine about the loss of the 'rugged uplands' of Eltham Common and the woodlands that lay beyond it.

The defence of Commoners' rights on the common was not always a straightforward issue, especially when the Vestry tried to balance that with their own attempts to raise income from the common to support the local poor fund. In the early 1870s a local resident by the name of Haworth had applied for and, for a fee, been given permission to extract loam and turf from the common for resale. When he subsequently received legal advice that he could be in trouble because what he was doing technically conflicted with the commoners rights to pasturage or cutting brushwood on the same land, he became alarmed. Hastily trying to rectify the situation, he restored the ground that had been disturbed by his extraction work, filling in the pits and levelling the embankments. He also contacted the Vestry and suggested making a retrospective donation of a proportion of his profits to the local poor fund. That all seemed very generous. But when the Vestry attempted to find out just how much of a profit he had made from selling the loam and turf, the proverbial shutters came down. Haworth became unusually coy. In the end, following an appeal to the Charity Commissioners for help and the appointment of trustees to pursue their claim, Haworth paid the sum of £25 into a newly created 'Loam Fund', for redistribution to the poor of the parish (that's about £2,700 at more recent value).

Haworth may have given up on his loam extraction but it appears the Vestry itself did not. In July 1888 it was actually the

Royal Engineers at Woolwich who protested about the damage being done by continued loam extraction from the site. With some foresight, their Colonel, R W Stewart, wrote pointing out that the grazing land was being damaged, and urged the sewing of seed to renew the grassland. Although responding in rather a defensive fashion, it appears that the Vestry agreed to his suggestion, and this may account for the acres of grassland which cover the north-western part of the common to this day.

By the 1880s, the Vestry committee were probably finding the task of managing the parish's common land a little too onerous anyway. The committee members discussed the idea of assigning the land over to the Metropolitan Board of Works as a public recreation ground. However the idea was rejected because, apparently, the wild nature of the woodland that covered much of it, together with its steep gradient, made it unsuitable for proper recreational purposes. This is not altogether unsurprising. At the time, the popular concept of public recreational areas took the form of neatly manicured and formal parks, rather than naturally wild areas. It was also objected that local parishioners would not make use of it as it lay a mile and a half from the village. Six months later, in January 1886, the idea was obviously floated with the Metropolitan Board of Works itself, but even the inclusion of Severndroog Castle in the offer failed to attract them. In the view of the Board, there was already too much open space in Eltham - an extraordinary response given what was shortly to happen. The decision was also a little surprising as support for it actually came from further north, in the more crowded and industrialised Plumstead, where the local Board of Works had urged the acquisition of the land – which it thought would be easy – and '...*would make a splendid open space as the view from the summit was magnifi-*

cent...' [44]

The occupants of industrial Plumstead could apparently appreciate something which was lost on the residents of rural Eltham.

The Eltham Vestry relinquished its control over Eltham Common in 1900 and it seems to have been taken over by the local Board of Health, whose management certainly left something to be desired. Certainly that was the view of the local historian Col. A H Bagnold, who lived on the top of the hill (See Chapter 12). In the late 1930s he recorded that *'Rubbish of all sorts has been dumped and turf has been removed, leaving hollows which become filled with stagnant water.'* [45] The neglect was also evident in the area behind the police station which had been requisitioned inappropriately as a depot for storing material for mending roads.

From the bottom of the hill there are two routes to take when climbing up through the woodland. From the former police station on the corner of the Shooters Hill Road, there is a pleasant and easy walk across the rising grassland, following the woodland edge as it rises beside you. Half-way up the hill, the grassland meets the busy Dover Road,[46] but a few yards further on you can escape this by turning up a stepped path that climbs gradually through the wood towards the small car park in Castle Wood. It is the easiest route, but it is rather unsatisfying.

---

[44] *Kentish Independent* 29th November 1884
[45] A H Bagnold. *Shooters Hill.* 1937. P41
[46] Officially named, of course 'Shooters Hill'.

The best way to explore Eltham Common is to plunge in through one of the footpaths that lead through the thick hedge of bramble and thorn that mark the western boundary of the wood, close to what is now the busy Well Hall Road and was once the quiet Well Hall Lane. Admittedly it is not an immediately attractive prospect. To start with you begin next to the busy south circular road. Traffic thunders beside you during the day and the air is tainted with that faintly acrid smell of metal and petrol. There are two bus stops in close proximity and their accompanying litter bins are frequently overflowing. The prevailing wind, from the south-west, picks up the lighter material and flings it into the grasping mesh of the nearby undergrowth where the paper and plastic is torn into fluttering rags. There is worse. Deeper into the undergrowth there are caches of domestic waste. Faded carrier bags gradually deteriorating into shreds, spilling empty plastic bottles of household cleaning products, containers, toothbrushes, sponges – literally every sort of stuff that goes into the landfill bin at home. There are dozens of these little caches scattered along the perimeter of the wood, partly submerged in the leaf litter and entwined in the stems of plants as nature tries to swallow this outrage. Wherever the litter has come from, it is an almost constant reminder of the sometimes damaging interaction between the urban population and natural spaces. Something that seems depressingly inevitable in a woodland that is surrounded by a human population, besieged by suburbia and its often unsympathetic practices. [47]

In places the understorey in the lower part of Eltham Common Wood is so dense it seems almost impenetrable. It is perhaps

---

[47] The Friends of Oxleas Woodlands regularly dispatch work parties to clear this mess – but it seems to be renewed frequently.

why, occasionally, lone itinerants set up camp here. Their camps are not like the dens created by adventurous young explorers, which tend to be more natural, made of woodland material and built for temporary fun. The itinerants camps seem have more purpose to them, and have a more permanent quality. There is also something slightly strange about the way they appear. It is as though they are created overnight, materialising out of some other space. I have never found them occupied, but there is usually clear evidence of occupation. Unlike other similar manifestations on the woodlands, those in Eltham Common tend to seem well organised. A camp discovered recently had a shelter made from an old tent, with a wooden shelf unit and a car seat rescued from a dump somewhere. Clothing had been left to dry on a line suspended between two hollies, and there was a pile of dirty food tins and plastic containers.

In some ways I can understand why people might want to camp here. I too would much prefer sleeping in a wild woodland to a harsh, uncomfortable and considerably more vulnerable doorway in the local high street. But in truth, Eltham Common is not a spot I would want to sleep in. Especially in that thickest part of the wood where the itinerants camp. It has a history and a very bad one. It was the site of a brutal murder.

As mentioned in Chapter 2, during the First World War, much of the land around the south and western edge of the woodlands was requisitioned by the Ministry of Munitions to erect hutments for the accommodation of workers at the Woolwich Arsenal. Just below the reservoir beside Eltham Common stood a row of hutments named Juno Terrace. One of these was the home of Alfred and Selena Trew with their sixteen year-old daughter Nellie, who was known affectionately as Peg.

Alfred worked as an overseer in the cartridge factory at the Arsenal and it was probably through this connection that Nellie got a job there as a junior clerk. She was a bright girl. She had won a scholarship to the Old Mill Secondary School in Plumstead and was an avid reader. To satisfy her hunger for books, she regularly walked from her home to the public library in Plumstead – an impressive round trip of nearly six miles, including a formidable and lengthy uphill return journey. On Saturday 9th February 1918 she set off to change a book at the library, but never returned. At midnight her father notified the police that she was missing.

Her body was found the following morning, just 150 yards from the police station, in the bushes near the Well Hall Road. She had, to use the language of the time, been 'outraged' and strangled. A button and badge torn from an army greatcoat were found at the scene and led to the arrest of a 21-year old former solder, David Greenwood. Greenwood had been a near neighbour of the Trews, though he claimed never to have met or spoken to Nellie, and denied any involvement in her murder. He was nevertheless found guilty. The jury recommended clemency due to his distinguished war record – he had served with the Royal Army Medical Corps until 1917 when he was discharged suffering from shell-shock. Then, bizarrely, despite his continued protestation of innocence, Greenwood begged the judge to inflict the maximum penalty on him – death. When the judge complied, Greenwood had a sudden change of mind and appealed for clemency. His sentence was commuted to penal servitude for life.

Without the certainty of the DNA evidence which we are now accustomed to, it would be hard to know for certain whether

Greenwood was guilty or not. The circumstantial evidence was certainly compelling – the button and badge had come from his coat, though he claimed he had sold the badge a day or two before the murder! However, other people were convinced of his innocence and a petition eventually resulted in him being released in 1933. Where or not Greenwood was the murderer, Nellie's death on Eltham Common was brutal and savage. Her final moments must have been full of fear, anger and resentment. Many people believe that emotions so powerful are sometimes absorbed into the place where they are created. A place can become tainted and, if anyone had a right to haunt a spot in the woods, it would surely be the spirit of Nellie Trew. But the violence committed on Nellie was not just committed on her personally, it was also an outrage against Nature, against the beauty of the place in which it was committed. And even on the best of days it can be hard to walk in this part of the woodland without remembering her. Perhaps Nature too remembers. The footpaths through this section of the wood are narrow and crooked, the bushes which crowd in on either side are tangled and ragged and full of tearing, angry thorns. It's not somewhere I would choose to walk at night. But perhaps it's best not to dwell too long either on the subject or on this spot.

Following the narrow paths which wind through the shoulder-high bramble-brakes, we pass through holly, hawthorn and even clumps of gorse. Gradually the woodland opens up as we climb. Each of the woods on Shooters Hill has a different character. Eltham Common is on the western side of the hill, so in the afternoon it catches the light in a different way. This is particularly so because on its southern edge lies the site of the 19th century reservoir built to supply the nearby Royal Herbert and Brook Hospitals. It is now a large open area of bright grassland, protected by an ugly metal barrier topped with wicked looking rotating spikes. But despite the barrier, that grassland is a boon. It provides clear access for the sunlight and in spring and summer the grass seems to reflect the light up under the canopy of the trees in this part of the wood. Elder, beech, sweet chestnut, silver birch, hazel and more grow here. And despite the thickening clumps of holly which seem to be trying to swallow the light, the sunlight seems to reflect up to the leaves of the beeches and flutter back down with the gentle movement of the breeze.

When you have climbed some way up the hill it's a good idea to stop and have a good look behind you, because it is surprising how much of a hill this is. Looking back, the ground drops away markedly. In the autumn, this wood becomes one of spectacular beauty. It contains more beech than any of the other woods and the ground is covered with a coppery red carpet of fallen beech leaves. These seem to come first from the older trees, which by late November seem to have lost most of their leaves. For there is something quite eye-catching that is not obvious at any other time of the year. The wood is full of young beechlings. In November, their leaves turn to a bright gold, and as the skies darken under the lower skies of the season, these little trees seem to take on added energy and bring an incandescence that contrasts starkly with the oaks and hollies and the odd rhododendron and laurel. It is as though someone has ignited roman candles randomly across the slope below us, each one of them a frozen spray of gold.

Turning to climb further, we find the hill dropping away to the north. Here stands the remnant of a massive old beech grove.

The trees here are among the oldest and most majestic of the trees on the Shooters Hill. Being part of the common, it is possible the standards here were never harvested for the use of the navy or anyone else for that matter. There is an old feeling to this spot, as though the beeches stood sentinel to some sacred site now long forgotten. There is stillness here, and longevity. I am not the only one to notice this. Sometimes when I walk here, I have noticed that I am not alone. Sometimes there is someone sitting against one of the trees, nestled in a yogic position amidst tree roots that erupt anarchically from the soil. Keeping a discrete and respectful distance I skirt their space, not wishing to intrude or break the spell they have cast around themselves. Sometimes I lean against a distant tree myself, close my eyes and try to capture something of what it is they have found. At first, the most noticeable thing is the sound of the traffic. It is, after all, closer here than in most other parts of the woodland, and vehicles accelerating to climb the Shooters Hill Road emit a rising howl that is inescapable. Yet, the mind does slowly absorb all that. It doesn't filter the traffic howl and rumble out completely, but it does make space for other sounds. The openness of the woodland seems to encourage the blackbirds. Their liquid piping seems best suited to this sort of woodland, the notes flung out and around the columns of the beeches and high into the canopy. And when the breeze lifts the tops of the trees, the leaves hiss a gentle chorus as accompaniment.

With the sunlight flickering through the canopy at midday or the early afternoon, there is a dancing quality to the light as it flickers across the eyelids and, if you sit down, the soil is soft and warm to the touch. It is easy to understand why someone would find this spot a suitable place to meditate.

But the Beeches are dying. In the winter of 2018 one of them collapsed, its broad branches sweeping down and shattering to lie like the broken and crooked limbs of some weird beast. Fungi sprouting from the thick columns of several others pronounce a slow death sentence. In time they too will give way, and who knows what will grow in their place, how the nature of this spot will change.

I am startled by a sudden metallic clank. I turn in time to sidestep a cyclist clad in orange lycra hurtling down the path, bouncing wildly over the roots and uneven ground. His eyes glance at me momentarily through goggles, but there is no expression in them. His mouth is stretched wide in what I assume to be a mixture of fear and exhilaration as he wrestles his machine over a jump, skids sideways across a patch of grass and crashes through the undergrowth further down the hill. In the shocked moment that follows I hear a tit calling te-te-te from somewhere above me, and then an outraged squawk from a parakeet. As the wood settles again, I notice a movement out of the corner of my eyes, and see a pair of song thrushes dropping down to pick delicately through the leaf litter. They are an unusual sight and very welcome.

Past the beech glade, the reservoir to my right gives way to woodland on high ground buttressed by an old brick wall. It marks the boundary between Eltham Common and the higher ground level of Castle Wood which was part of the former Crown Estate. There are young yews here and the trees of Eltham Common are now overshadowed by those of their southern neighbour. Near the top of the path a young oak has grown tall and thin, sparing no energy for useless side branches in its desperate fight to reach sunlight. It is a struggle echoed in many parts of the woodland. As the path reaches the top of the wood it is joined by the stepped path coming up from the Dover Road. The two paths converge at the Castle Wood car park which is often busy because of the proximity of the tower of Severndroog Castle. Two women are standing at the top of the path, their dogs circling in a bored fashion sniffing here and there. Both dogs and women eye me with a hint of suspicion. A single man in the woods without a dog – odd! I give them a cheery greeting and stroll past wondering just when and how the pleasure of walking in woodland became a deviancy.

Chapter 5 – Castle Wood

It is January and the air is heavy and grey. On a whim I walk up
the Dover road to access the woods, rather than make my usual
entry from the south. There seems to be a post-New Year haste
to the cars climbing the hill, and even those gliding down at a
lower gear seem to be moving faster than usual. Across the
grassland of Eltham Common the woods look black and
stretched. The trees reduced to a thin tracery against the low
weight of the sky, thickened only by clusters of holly. Past the
Victorian Christ Church I turn into the narrow, pitted lane that
leads into Castle Wood. Most visitors, when they come to this
part of the woodland, whether travelling on foot or by car, take
this route to the small car park to the north of the Severndroog
Castle.

By the late-18th century, several large houses had joined the
taverns on the Dover Road as it crossed the hill. These included Hazelwood House (c 1773) and Holbrook (c 1780-1805),
both located beside the road as it approached the summit of
the hill. Lower down, on the western side of the hill, and on the
corner of the lane leading into Castle Wood, stood a pretty

white-stuccoed, bay-fronted Regency villa known as 'Bankside'. This had been built in the late 1830s to replace a late-18th century cottage. The upper floor of the west-facing bay, which featured the lady of the house's boudoir, offered a fine view across to the City itself – or at least that is how it appears in a watercolour from about the same period.

Severndroog House, around 1839. (Image - Greenwich Heritage Centre).

In 1874 the house was let to the City tea merchant Henry Stuart Bartleet who, in addition to being a great collector of books and prints, was a keen gardener and a member of both the Rose and the Royal Horticultural Societies. He built extensive greenhouses, and regularly won prizes for the flowers he exhibited at various shows. When the freehold for the house came up for sale in 1891, he purchased it from the Crown and changed its name to 'Severndroog House'.

Bartleet was well known to the local historian A H Bagnold,

who lived at the top of the hill (see later) because, following the former's death in 1929, Bagnold described him rather affectionately: *'His portly figure, his somewhat slow but genial and kindly manner, his sense of humour, his love of music and of other arts, and his great knowledge of horticulture made him a very charming companion.'* [48]

In 1930, the house was purchased by the Ecclesiastical Commissioners as a vicarage for the nearby Christ Church but, in the end, it probably proved too large and costly to maintain and it was demolished to make for new housing in 1969.

As we walk into the lane off the Dover Road today, the site of 'Severndroog House' is obscured behind a dilapidating wooden fence and a plot of land rapidly succumbing to hazel bushes and sycamores. A few yards into the wood and we pass the single storeyed Castle House Lodge. The name features on the small lead-roofed porch which shelters the front door and is perhaps the only distinguishing feature of what is really a rather plain looking building. But then it was never meant to be glamourous – it was simply the lodge guarding the entrance to the formal driveway leading to Castle House itself. Castle House, named after the nearby Severndroog Castle, was built in 1829 by Thomas Lingham who, at the time, was living in Hazelwood House a little further up the hill.

Lingham acquired the lease of Hazelwood in 1810 when Sir John Shaw relinquished it following his dispute with the Crown Commissioners. The site was occupied by a very dilapidated

---

[48] *Shooters Hill.* A H Bagnold. 1937. p45

school building, and in 1816 Lingham replaced it with a new building, Hazelwood House itself. Shortly after that he acquired more of the land known as Hazelwood Fields to the south and west of the house, and because the building of a house on this land was a condition of the lease, he built Castle House there in 1829. [49] Castle House was approached by a long carriage drive which started by the lodge and wound through woodland and a plantation of rhododendrons and laurels to reach the house itself.

Castle House, around 1890.

A photograph of the house survives, taken from the end of the shorter service driveway (now the site of the Castle Wood car park). It shows that the house was stone-built and ornamented with a circular tower on the southwest corner surmounted by an ornamental cupola. At the entrance to the shorter service drive, stood another lodge – a two-storey structure which

---

[49] A H Bagnold states that the house was built in 1839, but this is incorrect.

with its jetted upper storey, pantiles and timber beams looks contrastingly mock-Tudor in comparison with the main house.

The house, together with its outbuildings, lodges and gardens, cost Lingham £2000, but he didn't live long to enjoy them. In 1831 he died and his widow Elizabeth decided, with the agreement of the Commissioners, to sublet Castle House and leave. Unfortunately the income from the sub-letting was poor and by 1840 she had to plead with the Commissioners to increase the rent they were charging for the house. [50] The reaction of the tenant - by this time the Rev. J S Ruddach - to this plea is not recorded. He himself was involved raising funds to alleviate the poverty and suffering of local families following the laying-off of men at both the Arsenal and the Royal Dockyard at Woolwich. Ruddach was one of several people to take on the sub-lease to the house during this period creating a sense of impermanency which may have related to uncertainty about the future of Castle Wood itself.

It was already clear that the Crown Commissioners were looking to increase their income from the woodlands – both by retaining the timber and underwood rights, and by leasing off parcels of the land itself. This probably encouraged the sense of uncertainty and might have deterred anyone from committing themselves to either a longer-term or more expensive leasehold. The situation was exacerbated in the autumn of 1847 when the former Prime Minister and Commander-in-Chief, the Duke of Wellington, proposed the area be acquired

---

[50] The National Archive. Crown Estate Records. CRES2. Report by A C Driver to the Crown Commissioners. *10 Feb 1840*

for a vast military mausoleum.

This startling proposal was the result of the Duke's long-standing grievance that the men who had served and died in the long wars against Revolutionary and Napoleonic France, had never received the recognition rightfully due to them. He was, of course, thinking primarily of the officer class and his proposal included the army, navy and East India Company forces. By November 1847 a plan had evolved and discussions were underway with the Crown Commissioners for the compulsory purchase of land to create 'The Shooters Hill Necropolis and United Services Mausoleum.'

On the 5th November, Goodwin, Partridge, Williams & Edwards, Solicitors, proposed an Act of Parliament to establish a new Company to undertake the project. A week later, *The Kentish Mercury* published the full details of the proposed site. It would occupy both Eltham Common and Castle Wood (including Severndroog Castle) and all of the land leading down to what is now the Well Hall Road (what was then the main road leading from Eltham to Woolwich). It would cover Jack Wood to the east and extend southwards to occupy over 36 acres of agricultural land. All existing paths and rights of way, streams and watercourses, would be closed or diverted, and a formal entrance avenue would be opened across Eltham Common.

The site would be filled with monuments, tombs, mausoleums and chapels, set in lawns, dotted with yew trees and cypress. Those who have visited any of the older early-Victorian London cemeteries will easily conjure up how this might have looked. Whether or not one shudders or delights at the prospect that the proposal offered, one thing is certain, the landscape of Shooters Hill would have been radically different than it is today.

Fortunately, the scheme appears to have been abandoned very quickly and this may have been because it was overtaken by a much more general crisis – that of finding burial sites for the rapidly increasing number of London dead. The existing cemeteries were already horrifically overcrowded and by 1850 new legislation had been passed relating to the burial crisis in the metropolis. Other proposals were to create a huge new cemetery for the East End at Abbey Wood (a few miles north-east of Shooters Hill), and to extended the use of the Kensal Green Cemetery in the west. There was even a proposal to use corpses as land-fill in land reclamation in the Thames estuary! In the end the famous London Necropolis Company was formed, with its famous Necropolis railway to a new cemetery at Brookwood, north of Guildford.

The Necropolis wasn't the only threat to the wood. In fact a much more serious danger surfaced in 1860 and one which would have completely devastated the whole of the top and south face of the hill. In the 1850s there was growing concern about the growing military strength of France and its imperial ambitions, and a Royal Commission was convened to review the state of British defences in the event of a potential French invasion. The Commission's report recommended a complete overhaul of defences, especially in relation to naval dockyards, arsenals etc. The total cost of the proposed work amounted to a staggering sum – nearly £12M pounds. Amongst the proposals was a plan for a fort to be built to defend the Woolwich Arsenal and naval dockyard from any attack from the south. And the ideal location for this defensive work was on the south side of Shooters Hill.

In June 1860, plans for the requisition of the Crown Land on Shooters Hill were made public. A massive new fortification was to be built and armed with new Armstrong guns.[51] Anyone who has seen the Palmerston forts in areas like Portsdown Hill overlooking Portsmouth, will be aware of how massive these structures are, and the enormous impact which they have on the landscape. Gigantic moats are excavated and ramparts are built to house guns. Every tree in the area has to be felled so as to keep the field of fire clear and to deny cover to any approaching hostile force. Shooters Hill would have been stripped of its woodland. Completely. Fortunately for us, the plan for a fort on Shooters Hill was abandoned.

But other changes were to take place on the hill. By the early 1850s Castle House had a new tenant. This was the railway contractor, Alfred William Bean. Born in Yorkshire around 1825, Bean seems to have trained with the railway engineer Thomas Jackson. By the 1840s, the two were working together on the Caledonian Canal and other projects. When Bean moved into Castle House, Jackson (as we have already noted) had occupied the James's old residence at Eltham Park. In 1852, Bean married Jackson's daughter Annie and the two of them lived in Castle House until the 1860s when they temporarily moved to the south coast.

Once again Castle House passed through a number of hands until 1883 when the Commissioners put the lease up for auction. It was purchased by (or in the name of) Emily Phillips the wife of Samuel Edward Phillips, of Holbrook House, the 18th century house further up the hill. Samuel was a pioneering telegraph engineer and electrician who, with partner, Walter

---

[51] *Army & Navy Gazette* 30 June 1860.

Johnson, had founded a large factory on the Thames riverside at Charlton just a few miles to the north-west of Shooters Hill. The company developed and manufactured a wide range of electrical engineering components and were probably most closely associated with the production of submarine telegraph cables. In its secluded wooded location, Castle House would have been hugely more attractive as the residence for a wealthy industrialist and his family, and Samuel and Emily consequently vacated Holbrook, leaving it empty for the next ten years. In 1891 Samuel also purchased Hazelwood House, together with the fields which lay between it and Castle House.

In July 1893, Samuel died suddenly leaving Emily as the sole beneficiary of an estate worth a stunning £87,995 3s 4d. (about £11.3 billion at 2020 values). Emily was something of a philanthropist and President of the Brabazon Scheme – a fund which provided craft materials for elderly men and women in workhouses, which could be sold to raise income.[52] She was also ap-

parently a gifted musician who performed on piano, organ and harpsichord and encouraged her son Charles to learn the piano.

Charles Phillips

---

[52] The scheme was set up by the Countess of Meath in 1882 and seems to have been initially aimed at elderly women. Later men were also encouraged to produce basket ware, rugs etc. and were paid in tobacco!

Following her death in 1902, Charles as eldest son, inherited Castle House.[53] As a biographical essay in *Historia Medicinae*[54] rather snootily pointed out, Charles had little formal education but benefitted from being the son and grandson of wealthy industrialists: '*It was during this 19th century that what can be termed the amateur gentleman scientist of independent means appeared within the scientific spectrum. These wealthy scientists, often with little or no formal education at a university or college, could afford because of their inheritance, to set up and fund their own laboratories and study whatever took their fancy.*'[55] And this appears to have been what Charles did. He became fascinated by the possibilities of using X-Rays, and set up his own laboratory in the garden at Castle House. He studied briefly at the Central Technical College, South Kensington, and by the age of 23 was inducted into the Royal Institution (later part of Imperial College). On one occasion he and a student colleague set up an early public demonstration of X-Ray photography in the Town Hall at Kensington, in the presence of the Mayor. The demonstration – which was more like a fairground act – involved taking an x-ray photograph of a woman volunteer from the audience, rushing it to a local photographer for development and then displaying it to the audience before the end of the show. The whole thing was apparently a sensation success. Phillips sat on the door taking the money as people entered, and between them the two students raised a princely £25.

---

[53] There were other children, including William Charles Owen Phillips, born in December 1882 and killed during the retreat from Mons on 24 August 1914. He was a Captain in the Royal West Kent Regiment.

[54] Published in *Journal of Oncology*. 2011 volume 61 Number 5, pp 66e–80e

[55] Ibid.

In July 1896, there was a three day charity 'Fair and Grand Bazaar' in the grounds [56] of Castle House with funds raised being donated to organisations like the RSPCA, the Royal Society for the Prevention of Cruelty to Children, The Waifs and Strays Society and the District Nursing Fund. Attractions included a 'Grand Hippodrome' in the grounds in which entertainment would be provided by clowns and boxers, a phenomenal 'Lady Champion Boxer!!'; Mademoiselle Springhette 'the admirable Equestrienne' who apparently was going to recreate Dick Turpin's ride to York. A 'High Class Melodrama' would be performed every evening in the tent, followed by 'fire balloons and illuminations in the grounds. Mr. H C Donovan promised to give Phrenological advice every day from 5pm (each character written for the sum of one shilling); and Samuel Phillips offered to photograph hands with 'the New Rontgen Rays' for two shillings. All this for an admission price of 6d, payable at the Castle House lodge.

By 1896 Charles had in fact become one of the pioneers of X-ray photography and his career attracted a wide range of honours and appointments which really fall outside the scope of this book. He was appointed as a consultant at the Royal Marsden Hospital and, apparently, rode there daily on horseback from Shooters Hill. (How commuting has changed!) However, much of his research was undertaken in his laboratory in the garden at Shooters Hill. In one of his surviving letters to a colleague, dated June 1899, it is clear that the location of the laboratory was one of the big attractions. He pointed out that Shooters Hill was less than an hour from Charing Cross; 'thirty

---

[56] There was a large lawn beside the driveway to the north of the house, but it is likely that the large tent was set up in Telegraph/Hazelwood Field to the east of the house.

minutes to Blackheath and then a twenty minute drive' and 'the trees are in full leaf & the country around looks perfect.'[57]

During the First World War, Phillips worked for the War Office advising on the use of X-rays and lecturing at the nearby Royal Herbert Hospital, for which he was commissioned with the rank of Major.

All this however offers a rather monochrome portrait. In 1945 when Sir Henry Hallett Dale, President of the Royal Institution, gave a memorial lecture about him, he revealed that Phillips had had three ambitions in life. Firstly to be elected to the Athenaeum Club, secondly to own a Stradivarius and thirdly to have a picture exhibited at the Royal Academy. Astonishingly, he achieved all three in the same week in 1925. In fact he was apparently a rather good violin player, and one of his other scientific interests involved the analysis of violin tone to try and understand what it was that made the Strad so superior. But it was not all science. As a boy he apparently made himself a fiddle from an old cigar box, and also learned to play the banjo and the bagpipes. He also did a good comic turn playing the bones or spoons. He was perhaps better known though, as a keen painter in oils. His paintings appeared in the annual exhibition of the Royal Institute of Oil painters every year from 1924-1938, with titles which clearly indicate a love of landscape. Subjects included scenes 'Near Winchelsea' (1924), The Quarry, Lewes' (1925) , Piddinghoe, Sussex, (1926) Marshide, Kent, (1933), and even 'On Shooters Hill' (1926). He had two paintings exhibited at the Royal Academy of Arts, including 'On

[57] Referenced in article in the *Journal of Oncology*. http://docplayer.net/42094510-Historia-medicinae-major-charles-edmund-stanley-phillips-x-ray-radium-pioneer-artist-musician-secretary-of-the-royal-institution.html#show_full_text Accessed Jan. 2020.

the Purbeck Hills' in 1938. Although he also painted other subjects, his entry in the Dictionary of British Artists 1889-1940, lists him as a 'landscape painter'.

Following the end of the First World War a trust was established to create a new hospital as a memorial for the war dead of Woolwich and the surrounding area. When the Trust's committee approached Charles with a view to acquiring Hazelwood and its accompanying fields for the site of their new hospital, he agreed to sell for £3,500. However, a short while later he generously returned the money as a donation to the building fund. In the mid-1930s Charles retired to Lymington in Hamphire where he died in 1945, leaving a staggering £1.25M to the Institute of Physics.

Castle House was put up for sale and became the home of the Economics Journalist Douglas Jay. Soon after the beginning of the Second World War, Jay joined the civil service in, firstly, the Ministry of Supply and then the Board of Trade. Something of a rising star, he was elected as Labour MP for Battersea North in July 1946. He later held various posts in the Treasury and became President of the Board of Trade for a while before being appointed to the peerage in 1987. By this time Castle House had probably been abandoned. It was certainly demolished, though I haven't been able to ascertain the date of this.

Today the site of Castle House has disappeared under the woodland which lies on the east side of the Castle Wood car park. Strangely enough, although the demolition rubble must have been taken away, the yawning hollows of the cellars are still evident amongst the trees, now masked by ivy and cluttered with rubbish. The Memorial Hospital is, of course, still very much active, and Hazelwood Field still belongs to the

Trust.

From the Castle Wood car park it is possible to glimpse the top of Severndroog Castle ahead of you through the trees at the end of a winding driveway skirted by ivy clad oaks and chestnuts on one side, and a sloping grassy meadow on the other. On the right, behind a metal gate, a tarmac drive leads off round the far side of this meadow, to disappear in the trees and wind round the west side of the hill. This was the formal carriage drive to Castle Wood House, which we will encounter in a while. But for now, we'll take the other path leading straight towards the castle itself.

Many of the people who visit Castle Wood do so specifically to see Severndroog Castle, the 63' red-brick tower built in 1784 by Lady Anne James as a memorial to her late husband, Sir William James who, as already mentioned, died the previous year. The architect was Richard Jupp, who may well have been known to Lady James as he was the Surveyor to the East India Company. Although it has been nominated a castle, it is really no such thing. It is crowned by crenulations, true; but is a more akin to the type of tower-follies which were very popular in the 18th and 19th centuries. There are at least thirty of them scattered throughout Britain and they come in a wide range of different styles and building materials. The two things they have in common is that a) they are towers, and b) they have no real practical use.

Initially the Severndroog tower seems to have been used as some form of museum – somewhere to store Sir William's collection of 'trophies' from his Indian campaigns. (One is tempted to think Lady James may have been tired of them cluttering up the house).

Severndroog Castle and Flint Lodge, an engraving by Hassell. 1801

It was certainly an early visitor attraction. Contemporary engravings show sightseers standing near the base of the tower, clearly enjoying the view of rural Kent and, presumably, the distant prospect of the James' house, Eltham Park, behind its screen of trees.

Modern visitors, however, find the tower surrounded by trees which have matured during the course of the 20th century, partially obscuring the view towards Kent. In the late-18th century there were fewer trees on the top of the hill, partly because of the presence of an admiralty telegraph 'station' in what was then called Holbrook Field, to the north-east of the castle. The building was part of a network of semaphore signaling stations built to link the Admiralty in London to naval bases at Chatham and Portsmouth.

John Blades, owner of Castle Wood between 1816-1829.

There had to be clear sight lines between the stations, so part of the top of the hill was kept clear of trees and under-storey. The telegraph lines were created around 1795 and the station on Shooters Hill remained in position until 1816.

Following the decease of Lady James in 1798, the castle suffered a period of uncertainty. After the closure of the telegraph station, the estate was acquired by the famous London glass and chandelier manufacturer, John Blades, who had been Sheriff of London in 1812. Blades carried out repairs to the stonework and steps in the tower, and in 1824 drew up a proposal to convert the tower into a 'Gentleman's residence'. The plans for this, including an attractive watercolour of the proposed elevation, survive in the Historic England archive.[58] The architect for this was the celebrated John Papworth, who had also designed elaborate light fittings and wall brackets for Blades' company. Just a few years previously, Papworth had published a book of designs for model rural residences. It had the rather snappy title *Rural Residences, consisting of a Series of Designs for Cottages, Decorated Cot-*

---

[58] Historic England Ref: PB1320/Pap[155].3

tages, Small Villas and other Ornamental Buildings; Accompanied by Hints on Situation, Construction, Arrangement and Decoration, in the Theory & Practice of Rural Architecture; Interspersed with Some Observations on Landscape Gardening. 1818. In spite of the heavyweight title, the book is actually rather delightful, containing a series of designs ranging from 'modest' cottages for labourers, to lodges, villas and even ornamental gates for a country estate. The book probably inspired Blades to consider a more practical use for the Severndroog folly.

Papworth's design involved a two-storey addition to the eastern side of the castle – effectively adding wings to the side of the tower. On the ground floor these housed all the essential elements of a Gentleman's residence – study, book room, breakfast room, dining room, kitchen with beer and wine cellars, dairy, knife and shoe store etc. Bedrooms were located on the first floor, including those for the maids and manservant. While the main chamber on the ground-floor of the tower was retained as the entrance hall, the first floor room was to become the Drawing Room. Needless to say, the new extension closely followed the mock-gothic style of the original tower.

Notwithstanding the qualities of Papworth's design, the plan was not implemented and following Blade's death in 1829, the castle, lodge (see below) and 70 acres of Castle Wood were again put up for sale.

Papworth's design for extending Severndroog Castle. (RIBA Collection).

I haven't been able to find out who purchased it, but in 1835 another plan was prepared for the castle. This time, the aim was to turn Severndroog Castle into either a tavern or hotel; one suspects that at a certain level these two facilities were pretty much interchangeable. In this case the tower was to be converted into 'a spacious hotel' and fourteen acres of the surrounding woodland were to be converted into gardens. The spur for this development was the continuing popularity for 'taking the waters' – that is either bathing in, or drinking, spa mineral water. A mineral spring had been discovered on the hill in the previous century and several schemes had been proposed at various times to exploit this – including, in 1766, a grandiose plan for an entire new town to the north of the Dover Road. This was to consist of 1,500 new houses with crescents and circuses around a 'noble Assembly Room' – a development which the *Bath Chronicle* reported with particular interest.[59] The scheme's proposers even came up with a name for the development – the rather unimaginative 'New Plumstead'. But in this instance it was obviously easier to come up with the name than the financial backers and the scheme came to nought.

The fact that the mineral water spring had never been known to freeze, even in the severest of winters, may have encouraged the scheme's proposers to consider Shooters Hill as some sort of winter resort or, at least, something which might encourage all-year-round customers. However, the *West Kent Guardian* sounded a slightly sour note in observing that '...*Few sites near the Metropolis are certainly more improvable.*' For better or worse, these 'improvements' all came to nothing.

In August 1845 the tower was visited by the London diarist William Copeland Astbury. Astbury had long wanted to visit Severndroog castle, having come upon a reference to it in the

---

[59] *Bath Chronicle and Weekly Gazette* 6 November 1766.

poet Robert Bloomfield's *The Farmers Boy.*[60] He arrived on foot, having taken the railway to Blackwall and then the increasingly popular steam-boat service to Woolwich. Never having been to Shooters Hill before, he was uncertain how to gain access to the tower itself, but coming across a gentleman with two ladies walking in the field to the north of the tower, he discovered that although they had gone to the trouble to obtain a 'ticket' there had been no-one in attendance in the building itself. Perhaps rather cheekily, Astbury decided to pose as one of their party and made his way into the unlocked, unsupervised building. Climbing to the top he found he had a very clear view towards the City, and of the Kentish countryside towards the south – 'The *site is very high. At the distance of about 10 yards the ground gradually commences sloping down to the wood on the South West & North. And within its own enclosure there are many large trees.'* He was less impressed with the interior of the building. The ground floor hallway was furnished with two mahogany benches and several chairs bearing the arms of Sir William James. There were also '*a few ancient Indian weapons, & coats, a round shield etc.'* [61] But he was struck by the general air of neglect and hinted that the building had been uncared for since the death of John Blades sixteen years previously.

Despite the various plans put forward, Lady James' tower remains more or less untouched. It faced a more serious threat of dereliction and abandonment in the late 20th century, after

---

[60] Bloomfield was one of the artisan poets of the Regency period, often likened to John Clare. Bloomfield knew the Woolwich and Greenwich area very well. He married the daughter of a shipwright and the naval dockyard at Woolwich. His first published work, *The Farmers Boy* was published in 1800.

[61] *The Astbury Diary.* https://www.astburydiary.org.uk/

the local Council was forced to close it following budget cuts in 1986.[62] After years of neglect, the castle is now in the hands of the Severndroog Castle Building Preservation Trust.

If the castle has survived, the lodge which once served it was less fortunate. The building, known as Flint Lodge, stood on the eastern side of the drive up to the castle. It was a simple flint-built box structure, with small dormer windows set on either side of a low-pitched roof. However, this simplicity was disguised by a sturdy and disproportionate neo-classical portico which may have been considered fashionable at the time it was built, but was somewhat out of keeping with its surroundings. It was presumably used by one of the retainers employed on the Castle Wood estate, and survived until sometime during the Second World War when it seems to have been demolished. The site was quickly forgotten, lost amidst a bank of bramble and holly and then locked behind a fence erected by the Memorial Hospital Trust to deter people from walking across Telegraph Field.[63]

Just south of the castle, the hillside drops away suddenly to the large grassy oval of Castle Wood Meadow. From the top of the hill visitors can enjoy one of the panoramic views for which Shooters Hill was once so famous.

Today the view is misty. But pausing here for a while I notice a phenomenon which I have been aware of before. Below me the valley falls away into the Eltham valley only to rise towards the Eltham ridge, approximately a mile to the south. In the distance, the North Downs can be seen as a purple-grey back-

[62] Happily the tower was reopened following the formation of the Severndroog Castle Building Preservation Trust in 2003.
[63] Now known as 'Hospital Field'.

ground against the horizon. In between the Eltham ridge and the Downs, a series of ridges can be seen like serrated waves frozen in mid-motion as they wash towards me. The low January sun and the moist air gives it all a soft wash as though a water-colourist had run a brush over the entire scene. Houses, trees, distant church spires all become insubstantial and shimmering. As I gaze at the view, the houses of suburban London lose their form and rigidity, and dissolve. It's a visual phenomenon I usually associate with the Weald, though in that case the buildings are absent, replaced by clumps of woodland. The effect is strangely ephemeral, but it helps generate the illusion that the natural world could wash over the urban landscape, given time; and that liberation is not far away.

From the tower a path descends steeply here in a series of broad, uneven steps, where the Council have been considerate enough to place several benches on either side for people to rest and admire the view.

Overhead there is a delicate twittering and a small flock of long-tailed tits dodge through the branches of one of the trees beside me. They are delicate, pretty birds, grey with a black streak to their cheeks and tiny bright black eyes. At the same time, they have that comic toffee-apple shape: little fluffy round bodies stuck on a long, stick-like tail. Then they are gone again, busy in their winter search for food.

At the foot of the steps is a broad terrace with a series of beds laid out in a symmetrical pattern as a rose garden. The right-hand or western half of the garden has more or less been abandoned. The beds there are overgrown with a mixture of naturally sewn flowers and grasses, their outline rapidly disappearing as the turf surrounding them overwhelms the wooden border edging. A thin layer of long red needles covers everything. The cause is a huge mature redwood tree standing at the west end of the garden. Slivers of fibrous looking bark hang from it and litter the surrounding grass, which is parched-looking despite the wetness of the season.

The eastern side of the garden offers a different prospect. The beds have been restored recently by volunteers from the Friends of Oxleas Woodlands, and new roses planted, awaiting their first prune in the coming spring. On the far side of the terrace, a set of steps leads down a bank towards the meadow itself. To left and right, formal driveways lead onto the terrace from the surrounding woodland. We are looking at the site of another of the houses that once stood in the woods – Castle Wood House. I realise at this point that you might be wondering why a book about a woodland is paying so much attention to houses and their occupants. The reason is that the houses all had an impact on the landscape and environment of the woodland. They and their former owners, have left a ghostly presence whose existence forms part of the experience of the woodland itself. To fully appreciate the woodland on Shooters Hill, it is not enough just to know and understand the flora and fauna.

Castle Wood House was built shortly after 1869 and featured a double bayed frontage to the south elevation, designed to take advantage of the position and view. Architecturally, the house was elaborately styled with Dutch style gables and baroque – almost Rococo - dormers, while the chimneys were topped by tall barley-twist pots. On the west side of the house stood a sturdy, square entrance porch and a four-storey square tower with an Italianate balcony and cupola roof.

Castle Wood House seen from the south. Around 1900.

Against the east side of the house stood a large glass 'winter garden' and a more conventional lean-to conservatory. On the ground floor, the southern side of the house was dominated by the morning and drawing rooms. Between these was a study with doors opening onto steps leading down to the garden. All of the rooms lay round a central atrium with marble columns and a glass lantern-roof giving natural light to the interior. A photograph survives from 1903, showing that stairs led up round the central atrium to upper floor galleries with elaborate gilt cast-iron bannisters and mahogany rail. Potted palms and ferns, a patterned-tile floor and oriental rugs all demonstrate that this was the house of someone wealthy and conscious of high-Victorian taste.

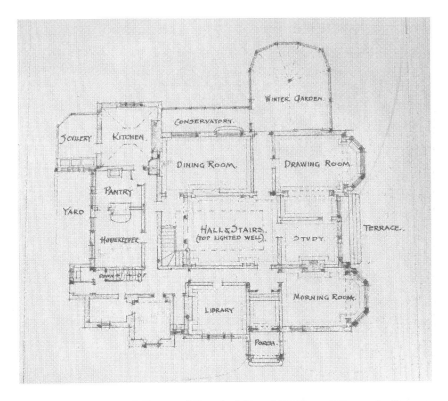

Plan of the ground floor of Castle Wood House. (Historic England Archive).

The Castle Wood estate stretched from the top of the hill right down to the Eltham-Woolwich road (now named Well Hall Road). Visitors arrived at the house via the ornamental drive mentioned earlier. This started at what is now the site of the Castle Wood car park, and wound its way along a more-or less level terrace along the western shoulder of the hill. They were brought this way to be impressed by the size of the estate and its stunning views towards London and the south-west. At the last minute, the drive swung to the south-east revealing an even more impressive view of rural Kent and the house itself. From the main entrance, another driveway wound round the north side of the house to the stable block, discretely hidden behind a high bank topped with trees and rhododendrons.

There is something of a mystery surrounding the origin of Castle Wood House. A H Bagnold, the local historian (who lived further up the hill between 1903 – 1944), thought that the house had been built around 1869 by an Eltham ship-owner by the name of Barlow.[64] This story has been repeated without question ever since in a range of sources. The problem is that there appears to be no trace of such a person. Likewise there is no record in the Crown Estate records at The National Archive of the lease or sale of any property on Shooters Hill to anyone called Barlow. However, there is an entry in the Register of leases to the letting of 44 acres of Crown Estate to Thomas Jackson from the late summer of 1869.

Now, as we have already seen Thomas Jackson, the railway contractor, had purchased Eltham Park at some point between 1861 -1871. But the 44 acres he leased from the Crown could not have been part of the Eltham Park estate, since he had purchased that outright. 44 acres, however, is the size of the remnant of Castle Wood excluding the land that accompanied Severndroog castle. We also know that the Crown retained much of Castle Wood itself because it was still selling the underwood there in 1853. [65]

---

[64] For some time I thought the only possible contender for this might be the more famous William Henry Barlow who , although not a ship owner, was a civil engineer and worked on a number of local projects including the London Docks and St Pancras Station. Indeed he was born in Woolwich and had a house at Charlton. However my friend Barbara Holland, who has carried out detailed research into this Barlow found no evidence that he built or owned another house so near at hand.

[65] *Kentish Mercury.* 5 & 12 November. 1853.

In other words, it seems more likely that Castle Wood House was actually built on land leased by Jackson. This idea is supported by the fact that according to Bagnold, the mysterious Barlow never actually moved into the house. Its first occupant was actually Thomas Jackson's son John, who was not only another civil engineer but also in partnership with both his father and Alfred Bean who had lately been living next door at Castle House.

Castlewood House would have made another perfect home for a wealthy industrialist and his family. It stood on elevated ground and dominated the view of Shooters Hill from the south. Photographs which were taken from further south in the 1880's-1890s show Castle Wood House as a major landmark clearly visible in the woodland.

Castle Wood features in the novel *A Flash of* Summer by Mrs. W K Clifford, published in 1896. The story is a bit of Victorian romance fiction: the heroine, Katherine Kerr is an orphan who lives with an elderly uncle in 'The White House' on Shooters Hill. This actually turns out to be Severndroog House. Katherine, whose life is pretty miserable – this is a romance after all – finds solace by wondering through Castle Wood and in sitting, reading, on the steps of the abandoned Severndroog Castle. She also wanders regularly around Eltham Common – *"...a wide expanse of gorse and blackberry bushes, the great trees of Severndroog and its ruined tower showing above them...on the right, beyond the Scrubs, as the tangle of bushes was called, a narrow road that led to Eltham went across the landscape, and beyond again stretched the open country, showing Crystal Palace in the distance.'* [66]

It is clear that Clifford knew the area well, as the following extract illustrates. Here, several years later and after a voyage to India, the heroine of the story decides to visit re-Eltham:

'...there was the Palace and the moat, and the way through the church and across the cornfield to the woods that led to Shooters Hill. So she walked through the quaint old place that day and stood before the palace, and saw the moat, and the little bridge and the gnarled trees that looked as if centuries had passed since they were saplings..She went across the corn-fields, brown and bare in the winter sunshine, and over the stile to the woods. A wooden hoarding had been put on one side of them: someone had enclosed half the ground...She trod the leaves under foot, and looked up through the brown boughs and twigs at the winter sky. There were hips and blackberry briars trailing on either side of the pathway with scarce a leaf upon them; but the holly-bushes looked green and sturdy. A thrush flew overhead, giving out a sweet, fresh note, while a robin hopped along the ground as though it were a bird of lowlier degree. She sat on a tree that had been felled...She was afraid to go out of the wood by Severndroog Tower...she took the narrow path that led to the high road opposite the Bull, and walked slowly down Shooters Hill till she came to the turning with the well at the corner. The White House was only a step beyond. A high fence, through which she could not see...She turned back swiftly past the post office and the Red Lion...' [67] and thence to Woolwich Station.

---

[66] *A Flash of Summer.* Mrs W R Clifford. 1896. P6-7.
[67] *A Flash of Summer.* Mrs W R Clifford. Ch. XXI. Clifford, real name, Lucy Clifford (1846-1929) was a successful novelist and playwright. Her friends included Henry James and George Eliot.

Clifford gives us an interesting glimpse into the scenery at the end of the 19th century, including its interesting reference to the hoarding and the partial enclosure of the woods. This may have been a reference to Castle Wood House's next resident. For by 1891 Castle Wood House and its estate had been leased by the wealthy barrister, Edmund Probyn Godson. A 41-year old bachelor, Godson came from an affluent Worcestershire family. Two of his brothers were Members of Parliament and one of his ancestors, Sir Edmund Probyn, was both a lawyer and Chief Baron of the Exchequer in the 1740s. Godson himself built a successful legal career, with a house in Shinfield in Berkshire and an apartment in central London. By the 1890s his practice had expanded, taking on business on the continent which required him making regular visits to Brussels. This may have contributed to his decision to move to Shooters Hill which might have been more convenient than a small village south of Reading, for the trains to the Channel ports.

By 1907 Godson had been able to acquire the freehold of the estate (including Severndroog Castle) but it would appear that within a few years he was finding the cost of maintaining it too expensive. He tried to let the place but, as he lamented, the location was not what it once was: 'There is but little if any probability of being able to let Castle Wood on account of the great alteration of the view caused by the building in the valley and on the opposite rise and also on account of the domestic difficulty on account of which it is almost impossible with facility carry on large establishments...' [68] The former is a clear reference to the impact of Corbett's new estate, while the latter is an echo of that old bourgeois complaint about the difficulty of obtaining

---

[68] Codicil to E P Godson's will. October 1907. The National Archive.

good servants!

In 1911 he tried to sell the freehold of both the Castle Wood Estate and Severndroog Castle, and the sales material produced for this gives us a more detailed picture of the house and its estate. It is clear, for example, that the major selling points included the views still to be had, which were described as both extensive and distant – ignoring, of course, the fact that Corbett had filled in much of the valley below with his rows and rows of red-bricked terraced housing. In the space of twenty years the view from Castle Wood House had changed dramatically from one of idyllic Kentish farmland to that of suburban town-scape. Sure there were trees aplenty, as the woodland still stretched extensively in an arc around the top of the shallow valley to the east and across towards the Eltham ridge. But even there, what had been arable or pasture-land had been converted into a more formal park. And, to the south-west, the Bexleyheath Railway Line could be seen on its embankment before it disappeared into a cutting to run through the bottom of Shepherdleas Wood. London had arrived.

We read that, closer to hand, the house was set in 'well-timbered pleasure grounds...delightful woodland and park-like paddocks'. There was stabling for four horses, both cinder and grass tennis courts, a 'well-stocked kitchen garden' and, in one of the aforementioned paddocks, a 'capital swimming bath with dressing lodge'. Gazing round the site now it's hard to work out where some of these facilities were. I turn to the surviving photographs of the house, which were probably taken in 1911. One of these was taken from the east end of the path which runs along the south side of the house. To the left of the path is a bank topped with evergreen trees, which is still easily identifiable today. From the house another set of ornamental steps led down to another level grassy terrace which looks very much like a tennis court. Once again it is still identifiable, though the laurels and the rhododendrons which must have been planted so deliberately to provide spring colour, have now run rampant, choking the once well-kept beds. Enlarging this photograph one morning to get a better look at it I noticed that at the far (western) end of the terrace is a charming look-ing thatched summer-house. The sun is highlighting the thatch and someone has left a garden chair in the sunshine just out-side. It is a small detail, but it adds life suddenly to what is otherwise a static image. Someone was sat there enjoying the warmth and the view before the photographer arrived. It is a tantalising connection with one of the former residents.

Shooters Hill from the south-west in around 1900, with Castle Wood House prominent.

The sale of Castle Wood House was put in the hands of Deben-hams who pitched the sale of the house as an attractive gen-tlemen's residence. But, it is as though even they recognised that both the time and the locale were changing. Even the sales literature acknowledges that, if no longer attractive to a gentleman of means desiring a near-country estate, the house and its grounds would be 'very suitable for an Institution or school'; the fate of many such large Victorian houses of this period. Even more foreboding, they acknowledged that the site was also 'rapidly growing in value for building purposes'.

Fortunately it was not yet Castle Wood House's fate to be turned into either a school or small, modern housing estate. Godson could not get a buyer.

Chapter 6 – Saving Castle Wood

It was fortunate that Edmund Godson was a wealthy man. He spent in the region of £32,000 on leasing and then acquiring the freehold of the Castle Wood estate, and on what he described as improving and putting the place in order. He also purchased a villa in Linkebeek in Brussels and added an acre of garden to it. On the surface it seems that the villa was acquired as a convenience, given that much of Godson's legal work required him being in Belgium. But in fact there is a more complicated explanation and since this was closely bound up with the fate of Castle Wood, it is perhaps better to step aside for a minute and outline the tale. All of what follows is derived from Godson's will, which is unusually detailed.

By the mid-1890s Godson's health had declined. He rather candidly attributed this to his bachelor life-style, hinting that the unremitting company of fellow males had had a rather deleterious effect upon him. As he became almost bed-ridden he realised that he wanted female company – whether this was because he actually wanted a woman's companionship or a convenient nurse might be open to speculation were it not for

what actually happened. For the fact is that he did meet someone and does appear to have developed a deep and genuine
affection for her. Sadly we never learn this woman's name
though we do learn quite a bit about her. It seems most likely
that she was someone he met in Brussels, where she owned
property in her own right. She also owned some property in
England. We also know that she was a spinster, having – like
Godson's sisters, Mary and Alice - given up hope of a family in
order to care for her parents. She had had a hard time of this,
as her mother suffered a long illness which culminated in a difficult operation, which she doesn't seem to have survived.
Then her sister and her brother-in-law, with whom she was
very close, died suddenly or were killed, leaving two orphans.

By this time she was caring also for Godson and became so
anxious about him that her own health began to deteriorate.
Finally she seems to have been defrauded out of a substantial
sum of money by someone she trusted, and had to sell some of
her property to cover the consequent debts. The result was a
nervous breakdown. By 1907 Godson had been forced to accept the fact that his intended had tragically, to use his own
words, 'lost her reason'. Marriage was impossible, at least for
the foreseeable future.

To secure his fiancé's future he added a codicil to his will.
Three hundred pounds per annum were to be paid for a nurse
or carer to be employed to look after her for life. The villa at
Linkebeek in Brussels was purchased for her use, and the acre
of garden had been added to it. Now she was to have villa and
garden, with all its fittings and effects. And in the event of her
mental health getting so bad that she had to be sent to an Asy-
lum, Godson left funds to ensure that it would be a first class

establishment. In that eventuality, £100-£120 pa was to be paid as a fee to some 'reliable lady' to make fortnightly visits to her and send written reports to Godson's Trustees after each visit.

It's a sad little tale. But the end is perhaps even sadder. Godson was in the villa in Brussels in 1914 when the German army invaded. He may have been kept there under house arrest, or he may have been in a nearby prison of some sort. Either way, his health being already weak, he died there on 4th January, 1918.

Godson's absence left Castle Wood in a state of limbo. Fortunately there were gardeners and labourers resident in the lodges and at least one servant retained to maintain both house and grounds, though we should bear in mind Godson's reference to the difficulty in obtaining staff. [69] It was not until March 1919 that Godson's Will cleared probate and there could be some clue as to the fate of the Castle Wood estate.

Godson came from a large family, and most of his siblings had pre-deceased him. Of those that were still alive, two older sisters, the previously mentioned Mary and Alice, remained unmarried, probably because they had sacrificed their chance of family life to care for their mother, who died in 1895. Godson made them the chief beneficiaries of his will. Following their decease, the main beneficiary was his sister Jessie, who had married the lawyer Henry Bohn in Jamaica in 1874. By 1891 the Bohn family were living in the Netherlands. Godson's surviving brothers were excluded from the will, probably because, if they weren't dead, they had already established themselves

---

[69] In the case of the gardeners and labourers, it's probably safe to assume these were of senior age.

in wealthy careers.

Godson directed that after the death of the three sisters, 20 acres of the estate was to be conveyed to the Corporation of London for the purposes of a public park. The Corporation were also to be secretly given first refusal on the rest of the estate, again as a public park, with the hope that they might also be induced to purchase an adjoining 25 acres which, although it did not belong to him, might be available for purchase.

By the time Godson came to draw up the Codicil of his will, the corporate beneficiary had changed from the City of London Corporation to the much bigger London County Council. He also now specified an asking price for the remainder of the Castle Wood estate, to be put in secret to the LCC: £21,000. Godson had calculated this to be a fair price compared with other land which the LCC had purchased. The proceeds of this sale were to go to his sisters, and if they had deceased,[70] to a nephew and niece. (Interestingly, there was a warning in the codicil that if any of his other relatives contested any part of the will, they would be cut out completely – suggesting that the family were not altogether happy with his former marital intentions. And even then, no capital [71] was to be distributed until after his fiancé's death).

An approach was duly made to the London County Council. Although the records of the discussions do not appear to have survived, it does appear that the LCC's land acquisition committee were very reluctant to either take on the extra commitment or commit the funds to purchase any of the additional

[70] They were in fact alive at the time of Godson's death, but Alice died in 1920.
[71] Godson's estate was valued at over £32,000 (Gross)in 1919.

land. Discussions certainly dragged on for the next couple of years. Meanwhile an interesting parallel situation had evolved on the other side of London.

In the early 1920s the Earl of Mansfield decided to divest the family of Kenwood House and much of the land which surround it on Hampstead Heath. A very prestigious preservation group – The Ken Wood Preservation Committee - was quickly established under the presidency of the Rt. Hon. Earl of Plymouth, to try and save the area from building development. Appeals, including a poster for distribution on the London Underground, were sent out for funds to enable them to purchase the land. By August 1921 the borough councils of both Islington and Hampstead had each pledged £20,000 towards the cost.

South of the river, things did not go so well. The LCC's Parks Committee had finally agreed to contribute towards the purchase price of Castle Wood. But they expected nearly half of the funds to be raised from elsewhere. The task of raising this clearly fell beyond the remit of Godson's executors. Fortunately, at this point, someone more local stepped into the action. This was Charles Herbert Grinling.

Grinling is a fascinating and sadly, now largely forgotten character. He had originally trained for the church and was actually a curate when he arrived in London from Nottingham in 1889. Grinling's aim in coming to London was to work at Toynbee Hall, a 'settlement' institution primarily set up to work with the poor of the East End. Its proponents aimed to get educated, middle-class volunteers to work alongside the poor to help them in community-based activity. The emphasis was more on reversing the social effects of industrial urbanisation than seeking to blame individuals for their social poverty. In this its proponents leant decidedly more towards socialism than Conservatism.

Charles Grinling from a portrait by Francis Dodd. 1920. (Courtesy of the Estate of Francis Dodd)

By the turn of the century Grinling had become an open agnostic and had moved to Woolwich to work with the poorer communities in southeast London where he very quickly became active in the local Labour Party. He was editor of the local party newspaper *The Woolwich Pioneer*, and seems to have managed the General Election campaign of 1902 which saw his close friend and colleague Will Crooks elected as the first Labour MP in the traditional Tory seat of Woolwich. At Toynbee Hall, Grinling met another young socialist, Gilbert Slater, who, impressed by the social work Grinling was doing south of the river, came to work with him. With Grinling's support, Slater became the first Labour mayor of Woolwich and later, in 1909, Principal of Ruskin College Oxford.

Grinling was also a close friend and mentor of Harry Snell, who was elected to the London County Council in 1919 and later became the Labour MP for Woolwich (and in 1931 Baron Snell of Plumstead). Both Grinling and Snell met whilst working for the Woolwich Charity Organisation Society – an early form of social work organisation.

We get an attractive glimpse of Grinling from the journal of Ray Stannard Baker, an American journalist who was sent to London at the beginning of 1918 to report back on Britain and its people's attitude to the war. In March, 1918, Stannard visited Grinling at his home in Rectory Place, Woolwich, and found him *'in the midst of a vast forgotten population of more or less depressed working men...He has been in Woolwich for thirty years, serving every kind of democratic cause without salary of any kind.[72] He lives with the severity and simplicity of a monk. There is a quaint little garden behind the house with rock-fringed beds, an old cedar tree, and vines along the wall. He has all sorts of scholarly and scientific interests...is a keen botanist and zoologist; has portraits of the great democrats of the world around him: Mazzini, Whitman, Tolstoy, Ibsen, Edward Carpenter, William Morris, and Prince Kropotkin. [73] ...He has toiled all the years to inspire "the first principles", the "faith" of democracy, in the great crowded districts around him. He has the manner of a priest, and the eyes and lips of a saint. He told me at length of the labour situation in England and of the democratic revolt from the old, hard, red-tape trade unionism. It was a fine human experience for me. I would rather any day meet such a man than to meet the King – for I believe him to be more useful.'* [74]

---

[72] According to Baker, Grinling had inherited a 'considerable fortune' from his father who may have been a brewer.

[73] Baker noted that Grinling knew Kropotkin well.

[74] *A Journalists Diplomatic Mission. Ray Stannard Baker's World War I Diary.* Ed Hamilton & Mann. Louisiana State University Press. 2012.

Stannard liked Grinling very much and visited him again a month later for a meal of 'bean and onion stew, without wines or coffee or tobacco.'

By 1921 news about the proposed sale and purchase of the Castle Wood estate had spread quite widely round the country and it was picked up in particular by the *Diss Express* a paper which often displayed a left-leaning tendency. In August 1921, the paper carried an article from its London correspondent expressing a degree of outrage at the imbalance in wealth in London demonstrated by the situation. The more affluent areas of north-west London were going to be able to benefit from access to additional green space, while the poorer citizens of the industrialised south-east were not because of the relative poverty of its local authorities.

In fact, action was already underway to rectify this. The prime mover was Charles Grinling. With his involvement a Shooters Hill Preservation Committee was established to raise public awareness of the issue and encourage donations towards the balance of funds. Grinling himself appears to have launched into a personal crusade to persuade the south-east London borough councils to contribute towards the fund.

By 21st October 1921 the *Diss Express* correspondent was gleefully reporting: *'Less than £300, I learn, is now required to save one of the chief beauty spots in South London. That success is so near is due largely to the public-spirited attitude of various local authorities in the immediate neighbourhood. For example, Woolwich Borough Council has contributed £2,000 to the fund, the three Councils of Deptford, Greenwich and Lewisham £500 each, and that of Bermondsey £250. These are, respectively regarded, handsome contributions, and amply indicate the spirit that animates the metropolitan bodies where there is at stake anything in connection with civic welfare. It is a sign of a united community determined to make the best of things in circumstances in which...it is a credit to be cheerful.'[75]*

Weeks later the London County Council's Parks Committee formally recommended the purchase of the Castle Wood Estate and, by the end of November, all of the required funding was in place. A further £800 p.a. was committed towards the upkeep of the grounds and castle, but the LCC balked at the cost of maintaining Castle Wood House itself. At first it was thought that the house would be kept as part of the public amenity.[76] Indeed, Grinling wanted it to become a museum. But the LCC was adamant and the house was demolished in 1923 or 1924.

There can be no question about the popularity of the acquisition of the estate as a public park. Shooters Hill had long since become a popular spot for public recreation. In fact, as one correspondent rather grumpily observed as early as August 1883 when Castle Wood House came up for sale *'there are splendid views of London...as well as of the Kentish and Surrey scenery..[but]...The erection of the huge military hospital in the close vicinity, and the prevalence of the cockney element in the neighbouring woods on Saturdays and Bank Holidays, have perhaps rather spoilt what was one of the finest sites for a gentleman's mansion near London."[77]*

---

[75] Incidentally the paper's adjacent column carried the news of the release from Holloway prison of three female Poplar councillors who had been imprisoned for five weeks for refusing to levy increased LCC rates on their desperately poor borough residents. See *GUILTY AND PROUD OF IT! Poplar's Rebel Councillors and Guardians, 1919-25.* by Janine Booth

[76] See report in *The Gloucester Citizen.* 10 August 1922.

[77] *Walsall Advertiser.* 14 August. 1883

The Castle Wood estate may have been acquired for the public, but it was to be some time before it was formally opened to the them, as we shall see later.

Of course, when the estate was acquired by the LCC the view from the site of Castle Wood House would have been different than it is today. If the panorama had been changed – even damaged by Corbett's big housing project - at least some of the meadowland still survived to the south of the hill because his housing had stopped half way up the hill. The eastern side of Corbet's estate, as viewed from Castle Wood House, was still bounded by fields and hedgerows, filling in the valley as it climbed towards Shepherdleas Wood and the Eltham ridge. It's very different now, of course. In the 1930s urban London gave one of its massive periodic spasms and expanded rapidly, filling the area below Castle and Jack Wood.

The site of Castle Wood House survives as the aforementioned rose garden, and the terraces which ornamented the formal part of the grounds are still there. You can descend the steps from the house and walk down across the meadow, much as I imagine Godson did to his bathing pool in the early morning. The site of the pool is still detectible. Near the bottom of the meadow there is a rectangular depression in the grass, bounded on one side by a course of partly buried stonework which must have been the north side of the pool. In summer it's still a lovely spot, surrounded by oaks and serenaded by blue tits. I have sat there imagining what it must have been like, sun-warmed water up to the chest, with the shadows of the branches flickering across closed eyelids.

But London closed in. Between the trees now you can't mistake the houses pressing close against the woods, especially in winter when the leaves have been blown away. By 1939, Castle Wood had been hemmed in to south and west. London's grip had tightened again.

Chapter 7 Jack Wood.

Jack Wood is a triangular-shaped wood that spreads across the southern face of Shooters Hill and, to my mind, it is the most attractive of the woods. To the north-west of the wood lies the area of grassland often referred to as 'Hospital Field', though its historic name is Hazelwood Field.[78] When Charles Phillips sold much of the grounds of Castle House to the Memorial Hospital Trust just after the First World War, the deal included this large area of meadowland between Castle and Jack Woods. The hospital itself occupies over half of the land, but the south-western part of the strip remains as open meadow. In summer it is a brightly lit and tranquil space; an almost secret haven for butterflies and the green woodpeckers who skim undulating over the tufted grass, leaving their delighted chortle in the air behind them.

When viewed from above (try Google maps) the field is really seen to be a continuation of the Castle Wood Meadow referred

---

[78] See Chapter 5

to in the last chapter, a broad diagonal of grassland and wood-pasture that runs from the site of the hospital fronting the Dover Road, down to the south-west corner of the woodland.

The left-hand edge of Jack Wood follows the line of an old road that crossed the hill from Plumstead to Eltham. The route, later known as Stoney Alley, is very clearly marked on the 1862 Ordnance Survey map, though its origins apparently date back at least to the Middle Ages. It was a significant route because until the 20th century, Plumstead was the largest and most important settlement in the area and the smaller village of Eltham was connected to it via the most direct road over the hill – Stoney Alley. The best way to explore this ancient lane, is to find where it intersects with the Dover Road, opposite The Bull. The pub, which was mentioned earlier, is located quite significantly at the crossroads – for Stoney Alley crosses the Dover Road and continues northwards down Shrewsbury Lane on its way to Plumstead.

From the Dover Road, the entrance to Stoney Alley looks like an insignificant and somewhat uninviting patch of overgrown driveway – as though it once led to somebody's garage, now long abandoned. It's a sad introduction for such a venerable local trackway. At first, heading south, the old lane is now squeezed between an annexe of the hospital (formerly the site of Hazelwood House itself) and the back gardens of much more recent houses. If the lane was once wide enough for the passage of a cart, it is now barely wide enough for a single walker – a narrow footpath squeezed between wooden garden fences on one side and the concrete perimeter wall of the hospital grounds. It is a bramble-bounded path which is made even more hazardous later in the year when bramble and nettle add to the foliage, and it feels like you are wading through a hostile stream. The alley's attraction is also undermined by the black plastic sacks of household refuse which are regularly dumped in the undergrowth to one side of the path, inevitably spilling their ugly contents of plastic bottles, food packaging and cans.

Nevertheless it is worth persevering with this route. A hundred yards further on and the pathway widens as Jack Wood opens up on the left. The lane marks the boundary of the former Jackwood estate, which we will talk about shortly, but then swings suddenly to the west to follow the edge of Hospital Field. Over the years, the trees have slowly sewn themselves closer to the old road so as to gradually encroach upon it. But the lane pushes on levelly along the hill until, after a while, the ground falls away to the left as the route continues along an old terrace. Actually, you can miss this feature because the woodland here is now thick with dark clusters of holly which obscure the shape of the land and make the route quite gloomy in places. Eventually the old road crosses the upper path through Jack Wood and begins to drop downhill beside the old cob wall that hides what was once the kitchen garden of Rose Cottage – formerly the stable block to Castle Wood House. The lane, which becomes noticeably wider as it makes its way along the terrace through the wood, narrows again as it drops down beside the garden wall, hemmed in between the high wall on one side and yet more holly. The old wall continues beyond the grounds of Rose Cottage, but as it is hung with a curtain of ivy it is often overlooked, and from the other side the combination of ivy and rising banks of bramble hide it completely.

That Stoney Alley was once a significant route is proven by the fact that, as we follow it downhill through the trees, we pass several gas-lamp posts remaining in situ. The more ornamental tops with their gas cowling have long since disappeared – as one hopes has the gas supply – but the posts remain as one of several relics of the past to be found in the woods. Half way down, the hill the route becomes ill-defined and seems to disappear under bramble and underwood. But it was still important in the early 1900s because, when Corbett extended his building project up the hill to Crookston Road, space had to be left where the old track exited the woods. In fact, up until then, the route had continued straight down through the fields for some distance before eventually striking south-west towards Eltham village itself. Corbett got permission to divert the route of ancient Stoney Alley, providing Westmount Road as an alternative. It always strikes me as a little weird that whenever I drive up Crookston Road, Stoney Alley appears on my car Sat-Nav, as though its ghost has insinuated itself unbidden into modern technology.

As I said at the beginning of this chapter, Jack Wood is the loveliest of the woods which make up the Oxleas Woodland. There are several reasons for this. Firstly, being on a south facing slope, it presents itself to the sun unimpeded and there is much less shade than in the other woods. Secondly, the hillside is gently undulating. Were there no trees here, it would be seen that the hillside features several small vales or hollows which disappear as the hillside evens out under the houses to the south. This gives the woodland a rolling character, and an attentive walker will notice how the woodland seems to shift its perspective according to the viewpoint – but of this more in a while.

It is possible that the vales were created in some distant past, by springs, because the narrow line of a watercourse can be seen in the bottom of each of them. One of them - named on the 1807 Crown Estate map as the 'Arundel Spring' - actually makes an occasional appearance as a 'winterbourne' or seasonal spring in the wettest winter months. In fact the little watercourse seems to consist of several springs – the most prolific of which, secretly seeps from the ground in a rather magical manner, half-way up the hill. In 2019, the little stream stayed with us into the early spring, and, curious to know more about it, I scrambled alongside the little channel which it has carved for itself, to find the source. It was not the easiest of tasks as the hillside at this point, while still a gentle slope, is thick with clumps of bramble and low hanging holly. But, mainly on hands and knees, I crawled alongside the chuckling little spring as it bubbled on its way. To my surprise, where the little channel deepened into a narrow basin deep underneath a particularly dark patch of underwood, I found that, far from rising at the top of the hill, the spring appeared about two-thirds of the way up the slope. The little gulley continued up past this spot, and although choked with leaves, it was clear to see that very little water came from higher up. The spring itself could be clearly seen here bubbling into the side of the gulley. Watching the bright, clear water pushing its way through the humus made it easy to understand why people attributed such springs to some supernatural agency. Having made this discovery, I followed the course of the gulley up to the top of the hill, but there was little sign of another spring, apart from an area of waterlogged grass. Between May and July, the pretty little yellow flowers of Yellow Pimpernel can be spotted along the course of the spring. A low-lying, plant with green, oval leaves, the flowers are canary yellow with four or five petals and about 1-1.5cm across.[79] It thrives in damp areas – unlike its cousin the scarlet pimpernel, which loves dry, sunny spots - and is one of several indicators of old woodland.

Jack Wood is the most popular with walkers, partly because of the more interesting terrain and partly because it links the main car park in Oxleas Wood with Severndroog castle. Apart from Stoney Alley, which we have previously explored, there are three main paths running west-east through the woodland. The Upper and Middle paths are now broad tracks which ramble unevenly and make for a relatively easy circular stroll, which is probably why they are so popular – especially at the weekends, so it is best to explore them during the quieter weekdays. Oak predominates here – as indeed it does in all the other woods – partly because of the more acidic soil on the upper part of the hill where gravel layers lie not far under the soil. In fact these stony layers can actually be seen while walking along the Middle Path through the wood, as on steeper parts of the path, winter rain and heavy footfall have eroded the surface badly. The oak mainly found here is the sessile oak, recognised by its acorns which cling closely to the branch rather than hanging on stalks as in the pendunculate oak which is found elsewhere in the wood.

The Lower Path through the wood runs along the backs of the houses and gardens in Crookston Road. I have often envied the lucky householders who have the wooded hillside as the backdrop to their garden. In summer the woods here are lovely and the shifting light and bird-song invite you to drop whatever

[79] It is often mistaken for a similar plant, the creeping jenny which has larger flowers and rounded leaves.

you are doing and just ramble. Lower Path meanders slightly, so that the walker is offered slightly different prospects along the route. Because the path lies along the southern edge of the woodland, on bright days it is flooded with sunlight and, in spring, the woodland is filled with sparkling light. In places the view through the wood is extended as though a powerful torch was being directed in and up through the trees and under-wood, highlighting the patterns of trees and bushes, under-lighting the higher foliage. To a lesser extent this effect can be seen on the north side of Middle Path as well, though here the sunlight is already muted by the trees to the south.

Much later in the year, the low sun highlights the autumnal colours of the bracken, fern and leaf carpet. So much so that, in places, the gold and copper leaves of beech and oak look like a molten golden stream frozen in its course down the hillside. To my mind this sight is one of the secret treasures of the wood-land and every year I welcome it as one of the sensory high-lights of the autumn, though I suspect many people probably tramp over it without noticing it.

The lower path has the added attraction of greater numbers of song-birds. The wood is popular with the harsh-voiced para-keet which began to make its presence felt in the later 1990s, but the woodland edge and the nearness of so many gardens, also makes it attractive for the smaller birds. Tits of all variety, finches (though in fewer numbers now than a few years ago) blackbirds, robins, goldcrests and the larger birds – Jay, Mag-pie, green and lesser-spotted woodpecker – will all soon make their presence felt.

At various points along the route, inviting looking side paths lead up the hill to the higher paths, which is convenient, because during the winter months and especially after heavy rainfall, the lower path accumulates water on its clay surface and becomes extremely muddy. Unfortunately this is leading to a problem which is beginning to impact on the longer-term conservation of the woodland and especially its flora and fauna. It is a problem which is having an impact on other parts of the woodland too, so it's best to highlight it at this point.

Besieged as it is by suburban London, this precious area of woodland is accessible to large numbers of people who live locally and who, quite rightly, are attracted by the opportunity of spending time in relatively fresh air and enjoying the beneficial environment offered by the woodland. It means that, in addition to the dutiful dog-walkers who tread the footpaths on a daily basis, there is great pressure from weekend visitors who generally arrive by car to explore the woodland or the castle, and enjoy the excellent refreshment offered by the cafes. These weekend visitors – if they decide to go beyond the café (and not all do) – generally plunge into the woodland, often preceded by understandably excited children (and/or dogs), and lose themselves in exploration for an hour or two. Unfortunately, during the winter months, these forays soon encounter a woodland path slippery with leaves and deep in soft, very squidgy mud. More often than not, at this point, the inadequacy of somebody's chosen footwear will become apparent, and the party will leave the pathway to find an alternative route to one side or the other. In a very short space of time, parallel paths are created, trampling whatever was growing or dormant to the side of the main path and paring down the habitat required by wildlife. As the main paths become increasingly damaged through erosion they grow wider and the foliage which holds the soil in place disappears.

The result is, in several places, especially in Jack Wood, wider and wider paths detrimental to the adjoining natural habitat. The situation is made worse because quite often walkers abandon the main paths entirely and push their way through the woodland in an attempt to escape from a difficult route. Areas which had been left quietly for the benefit of nesting birds and small mammals are interrupted in a process which conservationists call 'fragmentation'. Some nesting birds, for example, need an undisturbed surrounding area at least 50m away from any passing human traffic. Studies have also shown that in many woodland plant species, footfall has a major impact on the plant's ability to either grow or reproduce. It only takes two hundred walkers to tread the same spot before the colony of a plant like the bluebell becomes weakened or fails. Soil becomes compacted and resistant to plant growth in the spring; and bulbs and leaves created for the following spring become damaged – to the extent that it can take years to recover, if it does at all. Bluebells in particular rely on the ability to produce seed for reproduction. But this ability is so badly damaged after just 200 passes that it can take many years for the plant to recover.[80] Once this area is disturbed, for example by dogs or walkers following a new trail, the habitat becomes less viable for wildlife; woodland flowers and plants are trampled underfoot – and the bio-diversity of the area declines.

The Shooters Hill Woodland Work Party – which for decades has carried out conservation work in the woods, together with the Friends of Oxleas Woodlands – regularly erect barriers known as 'dead hedges' to try and deter the creation of new

[80] See for example: *The ecological response of forest ground flora and soils to experimental trampling in British urban woodlands.* James Littlemore & Susan Barker. Urban Ecosystems, January 2001.

footpaths through the wildlife habitat, but sadly these are frequently ignored.

Most visitors to Jack Wood, though, tend to take Upper Path, which meanders in a pleasant fashion through the wood, linking Severndroog Castle and what is now known as the Jack Wood rose garden. Upper Path has its own attractions. From Rose Cottage it becomes a generally well surfaced path – so is more accessible in winter. It undulates across the top of the two vales mentioned earlier – though these are largely disguised under a woodland of oak, sweet chestnut, holly, hazel and blackthorn. On the northern side, the ground rises towards the rampart supporting Stoney Alley, itself hidden by dark thickets of holly and piles of bramble; while below, sunlight fills little glades and hollows.

After a while the path climbs to one of the woods large oaks, planted sturdily at a junction of a path which slowly drops downhill and marks the western boundary of what was once the Jack Wood estate. For, like Castle Wood, Jack Wood had its house and an even more interesting history.

Continuing eastwards along the path we have just been following, a knowledgeable observer will notice that the trees on the north side of the path feature a much more diverse range of species. There are several different types of deciduous and even some more ornamental varieties. Beyond these, walls appear on the bank above us, an ornate wrought iron gate hidden amidst a curtain of ivy; a little further on and what appears to be the remnant of a formal garden terrace with steps and wall-set arbours appears to the left. The back of the terrace features a long ornamental wall built of gently-faded red brickwork. What appears to have once been a balustrade is hidden behind uncontrolled sprays of honeysuckle, jasmine and wisteria. Beyond this again, another small formal rose garden.

This feature in the woodland is one of its most popular attractions. In summer the creepers provide a scented backdrop to the terrace, along which lavender and rosemary shrubs predominate and wash the lower part of the old wall with a soft blue-grey-green haze. But, once this was a very well-stocked formal garden, and in summer the balustrade and terrace beds were ablaze with masses or orange, red and yellow flowers - probably of stocks, wallflowers and snapdragons. In all the area of natural woodland this remnant of a formal garden is the only significant relic of the large houses that were built here in the 19th century. Here perhaps more than anywhere in the woodland, history pushes up to the surface and impresses its presence on the passer by.

Chapter 8 Jackwood House

Around 1861 a very successful 45 year-old Barrister by the name of James Plaistead Wilde, submitted an application to the Commissioners of Woods to lease part of the woodland on Shooters Hill. Tall and slim with beefy sideburns and a penchant for natty chequered trousers, Wilde's career had definitely been on the up. A graduate of Trinity College, Cambridge, he was called to the bar in 1839 and became a Queen's Counsel in 1855. He was knighted in 1860, following his appointment as a Baron of the Exchequer. In the same year he married Lady Mary Pleydell-Bouverie, daughter of the 3rd Earl of Radnor. It should have been no surprise to anyone that he felt himself entitled to acquire a moderate country seat within easy travelling distance of the Inns of Court.

In April, 1861, the Crown agreed to let him have just over of 21 acres of land to the west of Crown Woods Lane and issued a 99 year lease starting from April 1862. The rent started at £20 for the first year, rising to £75 in the second year and £150 for each year following. [81] The reason for the cheap starting rent reflected the costs that would be incurred by Wilde in clearing part of the woodland and building his house.[82] The architect chosen by Wilde to design the new house was the 47year-old Architect to the Ecclesiastical Commissioners, Ewan Christian.

James Plaistead Wilde, Baron Penzance

Christian, who was distantly related to Fletcher Christian, the officer who led the mutiny on board HMS Bounty, was one of the most prolific architects of the Victorian period. He was commissioned to build or 'restore' a large number of churches round the country. His work was, at best regarded as 'competent'. In reviewing some of it, the esteemed Pevsner architectural guides accused him of being callous in his approach, leaving a church 'maimed and lifeless' and attacking windows with real 'hatred'. Startlingly, even William Morris dubbed him a 'great criminal'.

By the 1860s Christian was also receiving commissions to de-

---

[81] There was an additional 4% per annum charge relating to payments for the redemption of tithes by the Crown Estate. Crown Estate Records. The National Archive. CRES2/362

[82] In some similar local cases the building of a house of a specified quality on the site, within a certain period of time, was one of the conditions of the granting of the lease.

sign private houses for the wealthy, completing over 160 during his life time. One of the earliest of these was, of course, the house he designed for James Plaistead Wilde, which was originally called 'Mayfield'. It was completed between 1862-1863 and stood at the eastern end of the surviving rose terrace.

Several photographs of the house have been available on the internet for years. I was therefore really excited when during the course of my research, Pauline, the archivist at the Greenwich Heritage Centre, emailed me to say that she had found several new images in their collection. The photographs were contained in one of a number of 'scrapbooks' assembled in the late-19th century and early-20th centuries by W T Vincent, a journalist and local historian. Amidst hundreds a press cuttings and illustrations cut from publications like the *Illustrated London News,* Vincent had acquired five photographs of the house and had thought fit to include them in his collection.

The best of these, taken from the north-east, shows the house in clear detail and amply illustrates what came to be Ewan Christian's trademark design for many of his houses. Mayfield was built in a mock-Tudor style, with steeply pitched roofs, tall and sturdy brick chimneys, jettied upper-storeys and large stone mullioned windows.

The exterior was decorated with timber framing and hung with terracotta tiles. The main entrance was via a Tudor-style doorway. Perhaps it is the soft sepia tone of the print, or perhaps the fact that the photograph was taken in bright sunshine in high summer, but the house seems soft and mellow, as though long settled into its landscape.

Jackwood House from the north-east around 1890. (GHC Collection)

Which would indeed be an achievement for which Christian should have been proud. But, as in the photograph of Castle Wood House, it is the detail which catches the imagination; the ivy or Russian vine established and climbing up to the first floor of the front elevation, the exterior blinds which the housemaids have pulled down in front of two of the windows to keep the interior cool.

The ground floor entrance led into a large entrance hall lined with pitch pine panels and a matching staircase. There was a bright morning room looking out onto the driveway in front of the house, a study with private staircase leading to a library on the floor above and a dining room. Tucked behind the scenes were a surprising number of service rooms - the butler's pantry, china closet, housekeeper's room, lamp room, large kitchen, scullery, cook's pastry room, servant's hall, dairy, larder, beer and wine cellar, knife house, coal store etc. On the first floor were the two principal bedrooms with associated dressing rooms; and a library of 'noble proportions'. This latter benefitted from folding doors which gave access out onto the garden terrace on the west side of the house – and must have made it a delightful room in which to work in fine weather. The upper floor accommodated five servants' bedrooms plus presumably a smaller one for the housemaid (which lacked the luxury of its own fireplace!), and two large bedrooms.

Throughout, (presumably with the exception of the servants quarters) the ceilings were decorated with plaster moulding and walls lined with pine panelling. The ground floor rooms, study and library featured large open stone fireplaces, while the bedrooms had stoves installed. Hallways were warmed by an early form of central heating provided by a system of hot water pipes, and there was gas lighting in the hall and corridors. To ensure there was an adequate water supply, Wilde quickly acquired additional land to the north of the house and had a reservoir excavated to provide fresh water.

Meanwhile a number of ancillary buildings were added to the north of the house; stable, coach house, wash house with accommodation over for bachelors (!), a chemist's laboratory (?), carpenters shop and cart shed. The house was accessed by a driveway leading off of the existing Crown Woods Lane, where a double lodge was built to accommodate the gardener and groundsman.

Wilde paid as much attention to the grounds as he did to the house itself. On the west side of the house he built the ornamental ballustraded terrace with a matching brick wall on the north side to catch the warmth of the sun. This was the terrace which could be accessed directly from the library. At the western end of the terrace a small arbour was set into the wall to catch the sun in the mornings. Behind the ornamental brick wall, lay the kitchen garden, with its orchard and greenhouses. An ornate iron gate (still in existence) gave access to the orchard and, following his elevation to the peerage as Lord Penzance in 1869, this was surmounted with a representation of a baronet's coronet.

The reason Wilde chose this site for his house becomes apparent in another of the photographs in the Greenwich Heritage Centre. Taken from the western end of the terrace, the image shows the west elevation of the house with the windows of the library looking over the terrace. The folding doors mentioned earlier are located at the back of another arbour, this time set into the elevation of the house itself.

In the photograph we can just make out a number of comfortable-looking whicker chairs placed there to catch the afternoon or evening sun. The more one gazes at the house, the more the charm seems to grow. What the photograph also shows is the view from the front of the house. For looking beyond the building itself, we can see that there is a large open area in what is now deep woodland.

Part of the hillside was clear of trees, and the house enjoyed a view across the top of the Eltham valley with its farmland and Shepherdleas Wood to the south, and to Elmstead Woods, Chislehurst and the distant North Downs in the south-east.

Jackwood from the west end of the terrace. (Greenwich Heritage Centre)

Closer to home, Wilde had the hillside below the house turned into a picturesque landscape with lawns, woodland walks, an ornamental stream and pond. With its secluded walks and carefully designed glades, he had replicated a romantic garden which was widely admired. Ornamental trees and shrubs (some of which are still there) were installed to give variety to the natural fauna, and beds of roses were created, for Wilde was passionate about them.

Professionally Wilde was associated with some important cases. He was appointed as the first judge of the new Divorce Court established in 1863, and sat on a number of high profile divorce cases; and, as Dean of Arches, presided over a number of cases arising from the 'ritualist' [83] controversies of the later 19th century.

In 1872 Wilde retired and moved to Godalming where he and Lady Mary [84] (who was also a renowned gardener) spent the remainder of their lives cultivating new varieties of roses – some of which were named after characters in Wilde's favourite Walter Scott novels. When not gardening, Wilde also spent his time being controversial about the authenticity of Shakespeare's plays! [85]

Having no further need for the house, Wilde relinquished the lease and in 1874 the leasehold was put up for sale by the Commissioners. Unfortunately, its fate now became rather uncertain, and a series of unsettled leaseholds followed.

Initially, the lease was purchased by Lady Mary's nephew, William Pleydell-Bouverie, the 5th Earl of Radnor, who held the courtesy title, Viscount Folkstone. He had just been elected to the House of Commons as MP for South Wiltshire, and the location and nature of the house suited his new position. His tenure of the house was brief, but long enough to enable him to carry out some improvement works, including a new fountain in the centre of Wilde's rose terrace, which is still there today,

---

[83] The ritualism controversy revolved around attempts to introduce much greater ritual into the services of the Anglican Church. The introduction of 'wafers' in Communion, candles, incense etc. caused huge controversy at the time.

[84] There were no children from this marriage.

[85] Wilde was a noted 'Baconite' who argued that Shakespeare could not have been the author of the plays attributed to him because of the deep knowledge of the law which they displayed. Wilde' and his fellow Baconites' argued that the plays must have been written by Sir Francis Bacon.

though in a dilapidated state.

A year later the house was leased to John Harvey, one of the Directors of the Borneo Company whose headquarters was in Mincing Lane in the City. He appears to have used the house for a couple of years, but in 1877 he also relinquished it and the lease again came up for auction. There appears to have been no immediate takers, but in 1880 it was acquired by Sir Charles Edward Hamilton, who at the age of 35 had had a varied career as Liverpool city councillor, army officer and senior partner in the London-based printing firm of McCorquodale and Co. In 1880, the partnership of the company was dissolved, and this may have been why Hamilton took on the leasehold of Mayfield. Five years later he was elected as Conservative MP for Rotherhithe.

In 1888, Hamilton decided to leave the house, which by this time had been renamed 'Jackwood'. He put the entire contents of the house up for sale, including the various Indian and Turkish rugs, Brussels carpets, tables, settees, farm carts, potted camellias, azaleas and ferns, garden seats and a donkey. The Crown Commissioners in turn decided to divest themselves of the estate and put the freehold up for sale.

The house was purchased by Lady Magdalene Harvey (nee Magdalene Breadalbane Pringle) widow of the Conservative MP Sir Robert Harvey who died in 1887. Once again, however, the occupancy was short-lived. Although Lady Harvey was still in residence in 1893, the house appears to have been abandoned again soon after that, and was certainly still for sale in

1899.[86] It was, however, about to be occupied by two of the most famous – and glamourous – residents to reside on the hill.

---

[86] Newsapaper reports in *The Scotsman* 1st May 1893, and the *Reading Mercury* on 6 May 1893, confirm that Lady Harvey was still in residence at that date.

Chapter 9 – Nat and Max

By the 1890's American theatrical touring companies had become a regular feature of London's theatre season and one of
the most successful of these was the Nat Goodwin Company.
Goodwin, himself had first appeared on the stage in Boston in
1874, but his talent for playing burlesque or comic characters
was only really acknowledged after 1888. By the mid-1890s
he had formed his own company and was constantly on the
road touring in the United States, with regular forays across
the Atlantic to play in London. In 1896, the company arrived in
San Francisco on its way to a season in Australia. When they
arrived in the city a rival company owned by T Daniel Frawley
was already in residence with a hugely successful staging of
The Two Escutcheons, a farce by Sydney Rosenfeld. One of the
main reason for the success of the Frawley company was its
leading lady, Maxine Elliott, widely claimed to be one of the
most beautiful women on the stage.

Maxine's real name was Jessie Dermott. She was born in Boston in 1868, the daughter of a sea captain. At the age of 15, the
dark-eyed brunette attracted the attention of a dubious character by the name of George MacDermott, a lawyer and New York

city Marshall at least ten years her senior. While she was still a pupil at Notre Dame Academy in Roxbury, he seduced her and the ensuing pregnancy - or suspicion of pregnancy – led to their marriage in the following year. The couple moved to New York where George had a reputation as a socialite. His occupation as a lawyer and his appointment as a city Marshall, enabled him to mix easily with theatre people and the city's wealthier residents. Unfortunately, his social activities included a large element of drinking and gambling, and he soon became unreliable as both a lawyer and Marshall. Within a few years his legal practice declined and he lost his job as Marshall.

Maxine Elliott, around 1890.

At the same time his relationship with Jessie became increasingly violent. In 1888, unable to stand it any longer she fled to San Francisco where her father had recently moved. A year or so later, believing that she had escaped MacDermott, she returned to New York and managed to talk her way into the drama school at the Madison Square theatre, adopting the stage name Maxine Elliott.

The school didn't last long, but Maxine, as she was now called, managed to persuade the English actor Edward Willard to give her a bit-part in his new play. According to some sources, her acting ability was negligible, but she had a visually striking stage presence which quickly attracted attention. For three years she worked with various companies, being joined in 1894 by her younger sister Gertude, who was also an actor. Maxine learned quickly and, as her acting ability grew, so did her reputation. By 1895 she had transferred to the prestigious Augustin Daly company. Unfortunately Daly had a policy of not employing relatives, so Gertrude had to remain behind with the Rose Coghlan Theatre Company while her sister's star rose. The Daly company staged *Two Gentlemen of Verona* and *A Midsummer Night's Dream*, with Maxine in leading roles, and toured the plays to huge acclaim in the United States. Things went less well when Daly brought the plays to England, where they were heavily criticised by, among others, George Bernard Shaw for being abridged. American interpretation also raised eyebrows among London's critical circle who complained that Daly's production had reduced Shakespeare to the level of vaudeville! In spite of this, Maxine herself was a huge hit, rapidly eclipsing the company's usual existing leading lady, Ada Rehan.

The company returned to New York for a run, performing *Twelfth Night* and then *The Two Escutcheons*. When Daly abruptly cancelled this program to stage a play with Ada Rehan in the lading role, Maxine resigned in company with the actor Frank Worthing, who appears to have been besotted with her. The two quickly signed up with T Daniel's Frawley's company in San Francisco – which is where this story began.

Maxine and Frank Worthing were starring in a very successful staging of *The Two Escutcheons* when Nat Goodwin and his company arrived in the city on their way to Australia. According to some sources, Maxine sent Goodwin a complementary ticket to see the play. When he didn't turn up to take his seat, she went to his hotel the following day to confront him. (This does rather sound like her! She had a formidable temper.) How that confrontation went we don't know. But it ended with Maxine agreeing to join Goodwin's Theatre company for the Australia tour, in company with her sister Gertude. The tour did not go well. Maxine's introduction to the company caused friction and resentment, resulting in the departure of the existing leading lady, Blanche Walsh, and rapidly escalating rumours about Maxine and Goodwin's relationship.

Max Goodwin around 1900.

Both of the latter were, at this time, still married to other people. As scandal erupted in both Australia and America, the two protagonists attempted to mitigate the criticisms by almost simultaneously seeking a divorce from their partners and announcing their own engagement. Following their return to the United States and the completion of their divorce settlements, the two were actually married on tour.

The company's next tour involved a long haul around the American West where cowboys, learning of Maxine's imminent appearance in the local theatre, rode eagerly into town to see her. And if there was any delay in her putting in an appearance on stage, they expressed their enthusiastic impatience by firing their pistols into the ceiling of the theatre. If some elements of the tour were alarming, there were compensations. The company toured in their own private train and, as a wedding present, Goodwin had bought Maxine her own personal railway carriage.

In June 1898 the company arrived in London for the summer season and Maxine and Nat decided to look for a house which they could keep on a long-term basis for their use whenever they were in England. Apparently, the day after their arrival Nat learned about Jackwood House on Shooters Hill and bought the leasehold immediately for $50,000 (about £1.5M at 2019 value). While they may been in accord about the purchase of the house, there is some suggestion that their reasoning was slightly different. As Nat rather sourly pointed out later, Maxine was somewhat enamoured with the English aristocracy. The fact that the house had been built by Lord Penzance may well have been part of its attraction. That said, Nat himself had no inhibitions about aping the part of an English country landowner and loved to ride round the local area dressed in the customary tweeds and going out with the local hunt. Maxine loved the gardens at Jackwood and frequently entertained guests on the lawn below the existing terrace.

After two months, the company returned to America and the house was shut up. Upon their return in the following year, their imminent arrival at Jackwood warranted a notice in *The Stage* – where the house was described as 'pretty'. Maxine herself was already attracting interest from beyond theatre land. In July 1899, an article singing her praises in the Illustrated

Sporting and Dramatic News reported:

'...her love of animals is so great, that she is almost capable of turning her new dwelling place at Shooters Hill into a sort of Battersea Home for all manner of domestic pets. When possession was taken the kennel department was one of the first attended to, and it is understood that the actress's favourite motto is Love me, Love my dogs.'

With its ample accommodation and beautiful grounds, the Goodwin's were quick to fill it with guests – and the Saturday to Monday weekend party quickly became the norm during the summer.

Maxine (left) and her sister on the terrace at Jackwood.

Given their profession, it was quite expected that guests from the theatrical and dramatic world would form the core of invitees. Frequent guests included the actor Sir Henry Irving, actor and theatre manager Herbert Beerbohm Tree, the caricaturist Max Beerbohm, the dramatist and theatre owner WS Gilbert (who had long-since fallen out with his former partner Sir Arthur Sullivan),the actress Ethel Barrymore and a host of other writers, actors, painters and musicians. The list also included the Australian soprano Nellie Melba who, invited to dinner one evening, unreasonably refused to sing for her supper!

Guests were free to wander at will round the rose terrace, or if they were feeling adventurous, through the woodland walks below the house. This was part of the garden which Nat was particularly fond of, nicknaming it 'Little Karlsbad' – though whether in honour of the town in San Diego or the Czech Republic is unclear.

Several years after their arrival at Jackwood, Nat and Maxine were visited by the American writer and journalist Margherita Arlina Hamm. Hamm was a paradoxical character. She was a suffragette; supported American Imperialism and reported from the front line during the Spanish-American War in 1898. In fact several of her books were based on her experiences during that war. She was also hugely enamoured of the American social elite and came up with the highly profitable idea of writing books about them. One of her books had the rather self-explanatory title, *Eminent Actors in their Homes*. To compile this Hamm managed to get herself invited into the homes of – yes, eminent actors, to give an intimate insight into their private lives. And who better to conclude the book with than two of the leading stage personalities of the day, Nat Goodwin and Maxine Elliott.

Hamm's account of life at Jackwood is interesting on two counts. Firstly it gives us a personal insight into the house and its grounds, and the social side of life there. Secondly, it reveals that while Hamm was capable of some thoughtful observation, she was extremely gullible. For it is clear that Nat, who was very fond of pranks, managed to pull the wool over her eyes during the visit. So it's worth quoting extracts from Hamm's account at some length.

The visit appears to have begun with Nat escorting the visitor around the house and grounds, explaining how he acquired the property:

'The strains of Gilbert and Sullivan's opera must have been lingering in his memory, because he selected a property belonging to the Lords of Penzance. The place was known as Jackwood, and, according to Mr. Goodwin, had some historical connection with the ancient English poem respecting "The House that Jack Built... The homestead dates from the fourteenth century. It is a low, irregular edifice with thick walls, roomy stairways, queer passages, and mysterious closets. It has been built piecemeal at various times, and while the softening hand of the years has united the various parts into a harmonious whole, yet both walls and roofs indicate the constructive efforts of different minds. Each part has a roof of a different design, so that an interesting chapter in domestic architecture could be drawn from the roofs alone.'

It is worth pausing here to note that as WS Gilbert was a regular visitor to the house, his name must have come up during the conversation – triggering some sort of vague connection in Margherita's mind between Jackwood and the Pirates of Penzance! My suspicion is that the mischievous Nat Goodwin then expanded on this misconception by claiming that the house was Mediaeval and of piecemeal construction; a 'fact' which the effusive journalist swallowed whole. The house was, of course, little more than thirty years old and had been built in one single endeavour. The guided tour *continued:*

'There is a stable near the house, surmounted by a cupola containing a clock which chimes the hours and quarters. From the road a circular driveway leads up to the main entrance of the house. Beyond the buildings are meadows into which the horses and cows of the establishment are turned every day. Beyond the meadows are wooded hills in which are little caves, sluggish streams, and cultivated farmland. Jackwood is an estate as well as a home. The lords who formerly owned it used it as a shooting preserve, and Mr. Goodwin has kept up the old custom. The woods and thickets are full of birds, and the place seems alive with rabbits. The immunity they enjoy from the outside world makes them bold. As the visitor strolls along the paths, they spring up from beneath the feet and hurry away to the nearest quickset or thicket. When the actor secured the place, it was comparatively wild. He went to considerable trouble and expense in improving and beautifying the grounds. The old paths were cleaned and widened; new ones cut to romantic spots; kiosks erected upon picturesque sites; benches placed beneath shady trees, or on the sides of hills from which there were fine views of the landscape; and the gardens, which had been neglected, were restored to their former high state of cultivation.'

One suspects here that Nat allowed his visitor to assume that the farmland on the lower slopes below the woodland were actually part of his estate, when of course they were not. Still, it added to the illusion of Nat Goodwin as an English country landowner – an image which he certainly coveted.

'One part known as Miss Elliott's rose garden is the fairest spot of all. In it are the plants presented to her by members of the nobility and royal family, and around these are specimens of nearly

every rose known to horticulture.... Arbors and trellises afford shade to the visitor and support to vines, the peach and other wall trees... It is near the rose garden that Miss Elliott holds tea-parties and levees in the afternoon, which are attended by the many friends — American, English, and French — of the host and hostess.

The interior of Jackwood Hall is as imposing in its way as the Tower of London. It was built at a time when the modern eco-nomical spirit had not come into vogue. The walls would stand a siege, while the beams seem large and strong enough to last a thousand years. The wainscoting is massive, and the floors have been worn by human feet, as well as by the hands of the cleaner, until they seem a work of art in themselves. The balmy climate of southern England permits the doors and windows to be kept open nearly all the year, and at many casements the vines and roses appear to have a mad desire to usurp the place of the cur-tains.'

Margherita was also privileged to be shown into the personal apartments of both Nat and Maxine. Nat's study, she noted, with delight was crammed with items of Americana, especially native American artefacts, weapons, costumes, pipes, cooking utensils, and even the trophies of war. Perhaps more reveal-ingly to us today was the collection of opium pipes and equip-ment which he also kept in his study. Items which, he ex-plained rather glibly, he kept to remind him of San Francisco!

Maxine's personal room, by contrast appeared to be full of a varied collection of knick-knacks with a vaguely Italian theme, which the hostess explained she had collected to help her pre-pare for playing the role of Portia in The Merchant of Venice.

Hamm seems to have been particularly impressed by the billiard room, around which much of the (male) social life seemed to revolve.

Nat felt no need to offer any apology for the rather self-indulgent life he and his guests enjoyed. As Margherita observed *'In their domestic life Mr. and Mrs. Goodwin make the most of the lighter and brighter phases of existence. "Some part of a man's daily life," said the host, "should be devoted to social enjoyment. All work and no play makes Jack at Jackwood a dull boy...".'*

But the observations with which she concluded her account of the visit, were remarkably percipient if actually wrong in their conclusion.

'In their domestic, as in their professional, life, Mr. and Mrs. Goodwin move along the same lines. They are enthusiasts in respect to dramatic art and its literature. Sociable and hospitable in nature, they attract and enjoy the society of the intellectual and cultured. They seem to be complementary to each other. Below the fun (and perhaps a part of it) which marks the husband is an underlying vein of melancholy; and beneath her poetic and pathetic qualities is a strong substratum of sunshine and optimism. The two qualities match in every respect.'

After the visit, I imagine that Nat drove their guest to a railway station in his American buggy – a ride which was reputed to be hair-raising, as Nat was notably reckless behind the reins. I also imagine – though I have no evidence for this whatsoever, merely a suspicion – that he drove her along the Shooters Hill Road to Blackheath, thereby avoiding any sight of the huge building development of Corbett's estate, which would have spoiled the whole illusion he had created. I can also imagine Nat chortling as he drove back, delighted with the little charade he had managed.

Margherita Hamm's account of life at Jackwood was not only rose-tinted, it was a deception. Things were far from rosy in Nat and Maxine's personal and professional relationships and, by the time of Margherita's visit, the cracks were widening.

According to Nat Goodwin, who later wrote a bitter account of his relationship with Maxine, the fracture in their relationship began before the purchase of Jackwood. According to Nat, Maxine was both scheming and ambitious, with a hankering to be accepted into the ranks of the English social elite. At first, Jackwood was thrown open to famous characters from the world of the arts, which Nat welcomed as an astute professional move – what we would recognise today as 'networking'. Alongside them were Nat's more personal chums, many of them American, with whom he liked to spend time, gambling, drinking and playing billiards. Both Nat and Maxine had a hand in the invitations, but Nat was increasingly conscious how much the weekend parties were costing him in board and lodging. By 1902 it was becoming clear that many of Nat's friends were no longer really welcome and, under Maxine's direction, the nature of the guests began to change. Invitations were extended to, and happily accepted by members (mainly men) of the English political and landed classes. Many of whom were very happy to accept an invitation to come and spend the weekend with the 'most beautiful woman on the stage'. Meanwhile, unable to relate to the army officers, politicians and members of the nobility who became the new weekend residents, Nat found himself increasingly isolated and uncomfortable.

Nat's own account suggests that he was deliberately humiliated during the dinner parties. On one occasion while strolling on the rose terrace after dinner, he overheard through the open library windows, a conversation between Maxine and one of the guests – an unnamed Lord. The latter was clearly flirting unashamedly with Maxine, and questioning why she was married to such a 'vulgar little person' who was so unamusing.

'I discovered the fair Maxine was being bored save when the house was filled with English guests. Americans bored her even more than I did! My repertoire palled and the anecdotes she screamed at when we first were wed met with but little response and that only when the dinner table was filled with English guests who found it quite as difficult to fathom my wit as Maxine.

Life at Jackwood was beginning to pall on me. Many Sundays found me a lonely host. Max was constantly accepting invitations to meet people at country houses, spending the usual Saturday to Monday outing away from her own fireside.

These...gatherings as a rule were the rendezvous for unblushing husbands and wives whose mates were enjoying the hospitality of opposite houses of intrigue. Generally no husband is ever invited to these meetings accompanied by his own wife, the husband always accepting invitations to the house party of his friend's wife...' [87]

At first Nat tried to stop Maxine attending these parties, but it was too late. By now Maxine was associating with the likes of Herbert Asquith (then Earl of Oxford and soon to become

---

[87] *Nat Goodwin's Book.* Nat Goodwin. 1914. Ch LVIII.

Prime Minister), Lord Curzon (Viceroy of India) and a certain Winston Churchill, among others.

Professionally too there was a split. Maxine had been urging Nat to take on more serious roles for some time. When he resisted she quite literally went her own way, eventually forming her own theatre company with financial advice and assistance from her friend J. P. Morgan.

In 1905, Nat decided to draw a line under their relationship and he put the leasehold of Jackwood up for sale. Initially it seems to have been sub-let to their friend Herbert Beerbohm Tree, but Nat eventually agreed to an outright sale, reluctantly accepting Tree's offer of just $25,000 – half of what he had paid for it. Beerbohm Tree did not occupy the house for long. In 1906 he leased the house to Lady Amelia Donaldson whose son, Sir Frederick Donaldson, held the rank of Brigadier-General and was Chief Superintendant at the nearby Royal Ordnance factories at Woolwich. Donaldson himself lived nearby at Wood Lodge at the top of Oxleas Meadow.

Jackwood must have been a daunting experience for the 74-year old widow. It was not only large (Nat Goodwin had employed sixteen servants in various roles) but it was expensive to maintain. In 1910 Lady Donaldson died and the house was put up for auction in the following year. It seems that no-one wanted it. The local area had changed, as Godson only half a mile away at Castle Wood House had noted, and large houses were of increasingly limited appeal.

In 1912 the house was let to a former Ceylon tea planter by the name of W. Saunders. According to Col. Arthur Bagnold, fellow hill resident, Saunders made considerable alterations to the house. Unfortunately we don't have any details. He left the house in 1918 and once again the house stood empty. This time, there was no-one to rescue it from semi-dereliction.

The leasehold was acquired by a Mr. Young who had grand plans to develop a 'garden city' on the site. But whatever plans he had fell through. The London County Council had already acquired the rest of Jack Wood and the Crown Commissioners weighed up their options. A report to the Commissioners from H E Davies in November 1926, advised: *'The character of our property in the Eltham neighbourhood is changing. There is no demand for large houses and grounds which formerly let well there. But we have a very considerable amount of local land which will sell well for smaller residential properties if we stand in with the LCC schemes for local town planning and the preservation of a certain amount of open spaces in the form of public parks and golf links.*

I think therefore that on all accounts we shall do wisely to sell Jackwood House and grounds to the LCC forthwith for £3,100, subject to the conditions of sale as now negotiated with them...' [88]

The LCC agreed to the terms of the purchase. The house was demolished but the brick rose terrace with its fountain, balustrade and formal beds were retained and maintained by the LCC's gardeners. The lodge at the end of the drive was retained for the use of park keepers, as was the coach house. Though the wash-house with its bachelor accommodation was demolished, and the greenhouses in the adjacent kitchen gar-

---

[88] One of the conditions stated the Commissioners right to insist on the woods being enclosed by a secure iron fence! Perhaps sadly, they never insisted on this.

den were allowed to gradually decay.

The woodland garden that Lord Penzance and Nat Goodwin had loved, was abandoned. On the hillside below the house, trees slowly grew up to fill the view of Kent; the carefully tended paths and little water course became choked with holly and bramble and were gradually lost. Today, apart from a hint of some landscaping beneath the undergrowth and a damp area where the spring still lurks below the lawn, all evidence of it has gone. But the presence of the mellow brickwork with its scalloped top, the steps and arbours, remain there still as a ghostly reminder of Jackwood.

As I said earlier in the account of Jack Wood, this part of the woodland more than any other, hints at the presence of the past, of history being a living connection. It is one of the loveliest parts of the woodland to stroll in on a warm summer evening. There is a tranquility and balmy atmosphere which even Nat Goodwin remarked upon. As the sky begins to shade with the falling orange light of dusk, and bats skitter across between the trees, a stillness sometimes seems to fall here. The sound of traffic diminishes.

One night as I stood here watching the stars slowly appear behind the twilight, I was conscious of music playing quietly somewhere nearby. It was the sound of a piano, a sad melody being picked out gently and with great sensitivity. Curious, I walked along the terrace, wondering where the sound was coming from. My initial thought was that it was emanating from an open window in one of the modern houses behind what was Jackwood's kitchen garden. But as I walked slowly forwards, I realised the sound was coming from the far end of the terrace – where Jackwood's library had been, where in

Summer the doors were kept open and where Maxine kept her piano.

Strangely, but perhaps predictably, when I reached the eastern end of the rose terrace, the sound faded, leaving me puzzled and feeling slightly bereft.

But I have to confess, this is not the only odd occurrence I have experienced. One afternoon, while carrying out woodland conservation work with the Friends of Oxleas Woodlands, I found myself alone, cutting back the banks of bramble and holly that choked the area formerly occupied by Jackwood's little woodland walks. The sky had been blanketed with cloud, but it was warm and close, and as mid-day passed the breeze which had been stirring the tree tops fell silent. The air became very still and even the birds stopped singing. I suddenly became aware of my own presence, as though I had somehow intruded into something. And then suddenly I was conscious of a perfume. A strong, definite perfume, old fashioned, heavy almost. It reminded me of the sort of rose-fragrance that one of my grandmothers used to favour when I was a child. It grew stronger, surrounded me, and then seemed to pass me by, as though carried away on a non-existent breeze or by a ghostly passer by. Maxine? I have often wondered.

Chapter 10 - Oxleas Meadow

Directly over my head a great tit is sitting exposed on a bare branch. Its tee-tee-tee call is ringing clearly in the woodland of Jack Wood. The sound is bright and crisp, and I can hear it being answered by other great tits in the surrounding wood. Crows are calling too, their voices sounding like echoes bouncing back randomly from all directions. In fact, this morning the woods are full of birdsong. It is more noticeable because a low mist hangs over us like a blanket, muffling the distant noise of the road traffic. Every now and again a little puff of vaporous cloud seems to drift down among the trees where the new hazel leaves seem to add their own green haze to the depth of the woods. But there is another noise too. From all directions come the echoing ring of children's' voices. High in the trees, three blue tits streak above me, dancing after one another in a line from twig to twig and branch to branch and tree to tree. I turn and carry on towards Oxleas Meadow.

It is mid-April, after one of the wettest winters that I can remember. Spring is definitely here, but it barely feels like it. Over the past few months, sunny days have been rare and short-lived and the temperature has been stubbornly below-average for just as long.

For the past four days South East London has been smothered by a blanket of low, grey cloud. A monotonous watercolour-wash that is drab and depressing. Beneath the cloud the air has thickened to a fog which has grown thicker with each day that passes. It has deterred me from walking in the woods and I feel increasingly ashamed to be put off so easily. So, in the end, I pull on the wellies (as opposed to the usual walking boots); and the ex-army Gore-Tex waterproof jacket – (cheap, tough, and suitably neutral-coloured jacket for walking in the woods or bird watching) and head into the woods.

The wellies are essential. Since last autumn the paths through the woods have been churned up on a daily basis, by feet, bicycle tyres and, occasionally, horses and (illegally) motorbikes. The soil has swollen with water, expanding into a mushy soup, and then turning into a yellow slush as the sandy soil beneath, exposed by the constant erosion, has washed out of the terraced gravel bed beneath the surface. Slowly, on the hillside, the paths are slipping away to expose the roots of the trees.

The wild shrieking of excited children echoes from all around, competing with the birdsong, reminding me that it is the third week of the school Easter holidays. Desperate parents and grandparents have now passed the limit of distraction and kids have been togged up and brought to the woods to let off steam and expend some of that tightly-coiled energy. And releasing that energy requires much shouting. For a moment I stand in a still, secluded place in the woods and the disembodied shrieks come from all directions. Suddenly I feel as a fox must, hearing the voice of the hounds, not sure which way they are coming, nor which way to run. It is almost as though a faint echo of some primeval fear has drifted through the trees in my direction from some past memory, drifting in the atmosphere like the mist itself. But the moment passes. The children are far enough away to not bother the birds around me, so why should it disturb me.

I am making my way to the café at the top of Oxleas Meadow. It's where most people start their visit to the woodlands. In fact, many people get no further. There is a car park a hundred yards uphill behind the café, and for many, sadly, the walk between the two is sufficient.

On my way to the café I pass two middle-aged women suitably back-packed and booted, with seven children of various ages. Two of the children are wearing eye-achingly vivid orange waterproofs. While the women follow the youngsters at a distance, deeply engrossed in their own conversation, the children are charging through the undergrowth, screaming. And I mean screaming. In most cases this is due to excitement, but inevitably, one of the smaller ones gets bumped, or tripped or just frightened, and the screams take on a different, harsher tone that expresses outrage and upset. As the budding bluebells are trampled underfoot – the daffodils were already beginning to collapse – the oblivious adults carry on their conversation. Still, at least they are outdoors.

The mist seems to have closed in noticeably. It sits low over the bare, top-branches of the trees below the hill in Shepherdleas Wood. If you didn't know better, it would be possible to think of the wood extending away to the south, much further than it actually does, to an undisclosed murky distance. As though it was still part of the ancient forest or its successor the great

West Wood.

When I reach the café, it and the tables outside are packed with women and yet more gangs of children – all well wrapped against the unseasonal cold and damp. Small ones are stumping around joyfully in tiny wellies, and I am reminded how much, as children, we could live in the moment, finding joy in simple things – singing together, running round in circles, playing chase, jumping in puddles. That ability to find engrossment in the here-and-now is something that we lose as we grow older though it is possible to find a way of reconnecting with it later.

The café sits on a terrace at the top of the long grassy slope which rises from the Rochester Way at its southern end towards the top of the hill. The café itself is a low, red-bricked structure with a steeply-pitched roof supported at the front on four brick columns. People often point out that from a distance, at the bottom of the hill, it looks vaguely like a Swiss chalet. The critical qualifier here is the word 'distance'. The character does rather diminish close-to but this does not detract from the excellence of the café itself, nor of its location. The tables and benches outside are often crowded, because the view from the terrace is one of London's best. From this position, overlooking the meadow, you can see across the falling hillside towards Shepherdleas Wood, which provides a woodland barricade running across the bottom of the meadow from side to side.

To the east of the meadow lies Oxleas Wood itself. A clear woodland edge running down the left-hand side of the meadow, with an isolated handful of mature oaks venturing out into the meadow like some forlorn hope. To the right-hand side of the meadow is Jack Wood, not as deep at Oxleas because half way down the hill the woodland crashes against the housing that was built right up against it in the late 1930s. However, from the café the houses are hidden behind a small outlying copse, dominated by a number of dead trees with ragged white branches still reaching skywards. The ground under these trees is sodden and marshy and may have become more so in recent years, which might explain the gradual decline in the trees here.

The lower part of the meadow is bisected by the remnant of an ancient hawthorn hedgerow which runs north-south and which can be seen on the mid-19th century Stanford's map of the area.

Between the meadow and Shepherdleas Wood lies the busy Rochester Way, now inevitably lined by cars parked by the commuters who use the nearby railway station at Falconwood. Fortunately, the road itself is largely hidden from view by a dip in the ground.

The reason to come here though is not just for the café, it's the view. On a fine day, the treetops of Shepherdleas Wood mask much of the suburban sprawl and the eye is drawn southwards beyond it, to the green belt beyond the edge of London. Out there in the distance are woods and fields, and in the far distance the North Downs form an impressive background, stretching all the way from east, where in the distance, the A20 can be glimpsed heading out for the M25; to south-west, where the tower blocks of Croydon can be seen to the south west, some fourteen miles away.

On a beautiful sunny day, it is easy to see why the wealthy

wanted to build their homes on the Shooters Hill slopes. The tranquility of the woodland, the clear, sun-washed air, the verdant landscape undulating towards the rim of the hills. On a clear day now, you can still make out the hedgerows and copses of the North Downs around Biggin Hill, where, in the late summer, the drying cornfields glow gold in the sunlight.

The existing café building was erected in 1937 on the site of a much older structure, Wood Lodge, built in the late 1780s by one of the Sir John Shaws who leased the estate from the Crown. There is a late-19th century photograph of the south front of Wood Lodge, taken from the lawn just below the house. It is a strangely lop-sided building. The left-hand side is dominated by two bays, while the right-hand side is a plainer more Georgian structure. From the south front, steps lead down into the grounds from tall French windows. The almost obligatory plant-filled conservatory stands against the eastern side of the house. Ivy and what looks like Russian vine grow up the walls on both the south and western elevation, softening the appearance and helping it to blend with the woodland behind.

William Skinner, who was the tenant here at the beginning of the 19th century, named it Nightingale Hall apparently in honour of the birds who sang so sweetly from the adjacent woodland. Sadly no longer! He extended the house, adding the double bay on the southern side which gave it its superb views. In 1806, he put the lease of the house up for sale and the ever-observant *Morning Chronicle* noted that the house, which was 'extremely commodious' contained 'a complete suite of three principal rooms, handsomely fitted up, and finished in the immediate taste..' [89]

I am not certain what immediate taste was – but guess this was the buzz phrase for 'the latest fashion'. The building had all the usual facilities of stables, servants quarters (of course), coach houses and out-buildings (presumably for the gardeners) etc. More importantly from our point of view, we are told something of the 34 acres of grounds in which it lay. There were *'pleasure grounds, lawn, shrubbery walks and gardens laid out in a pleasing manner, planted with the choicest fruit trees'*. The 'adjoining paddocks' were maintained in a high state of manurage (presumably from the stables). Furthermore the premises were well supplied with 'good water' – actually from a well behind the house – and it was immediately available, complete with elegant and 'well-adapted' furniture, if so desired.

July would have been an excellent time for a potential buyer to view. It may have been slightly different in September a few years later, when more of an emphasis was placed on the fact that it was *'delightfully situated...commanding extensive views of very rich scenery.'* It was also considered to be a house well-adapted *'for a family of the first respectability'* - and who wouldn't have wanted to buy into that? The house also seemed to have been extended this time, with the addition of drawing room, library, billiard room and brew house. The grounds, which were still laid out with lawns shrubberies etc., had also been extended to take in 60 acres of meadow and woodland.

In 1819 the leasehold was taken by Thomas H Longden, a Justice of the peace and Deputy Lieutenant for Kent. It was he who renamed the house 'Wood Lodge' and when, in 1838, he in

---

[89] *Morning Chronicle* 5 July 1806

turn put the lease up for sale it was taken by Samuel Francis Hooper, a broker in tea and other colonial produce in the City. He was understandably attracted to it because of its location. Hooper certainly thought it a 'beautiful' spot and particularly appreciated the fir trees (which stood both to the north-west and between the house and the Dover Road), as they gave *'free circulation to the atmosphere so special during the heat of summer and to prevent the damps in winter.'* [90] He was probably somewhat unimpressed when, in 1843 Charles Frensham who leased the fir wood cut the tops off the trees. [91] An act which cost him a fine of £10.

By the time Hooper acquired the leasehold, the house and its ancillary buildings had fallen into some disrepair. He spent £550 rebuilding the stables, coach house and brew-house. Then, finding the roof and gable end of the house itself had to be replaced, he wrote to the Commissioners asking for a contribution towards the cost of also installing a bathroom and conservatory. The Commissioners balked at this proposal but did allow him £850 towards general repairs and a new fence for the kitchen garden.

In 1848 Hooper assigned the lease to a Mr. Sergeant Adams who, with a colleague, had established the Shropshire Mineral Railway Company three years earlier. The company didn't last long. It was in trouble by 1849 and wound up in 1850. Adams' tenure was not altogether without controversy. Within a year of moving in he cut down 110 of the fir trees in Jack Wood [92],

---

[90] Letter to the Commissioners. November 1840. Crown Estate records at the National Archive. CRES2/356

[91] The technical term for this was 'shrouding'.
[92] The wood was called Jacks Hill Wood at the time.

claiming that he considered it necessary to improve the health of the place! A C Driver, the Commissioners' agent, was furious, protesting that he could not understand how Adams thought the commissioners would find this 'satisfactory'. To make matters worse, Adams soon got into a dispute with one of his neighbours, and the Commissioners had to intervene. But of this more later.

Adams' successor was a Mrs. Catherine Davis who appears not to have been totally at ease in the countryside, since she made a great deal of fuss about a nearby landowner keeping a flock of geese in a field near the house. Geese are such noisy birds, after all. In 1858 she moved on, assigning the lease to John Joseph Silva, a partner in a Portuguese trading company. Silva enlarged the stables.

Wood Lodge around 1870.

By 1868 Wood Lodge had been leased to the 36-year-old Sir Stevenson Arthur Blackwood, who sub-let it temporarily. He was soon back in residence with his family. Blackwood held a senior position at the General Post Office - which was more prestigious than it sounds today – the culmination of an astutely managed and very successful career. Following an education at Eton he was awarded a place at Trinity College, Cambridge, where his attention seems to have been more focused on riding to hounds, than reading for his degree. Perhaps sensing this drift, his mother intervened dramatically, calling in a favour of Lord John Russell, the Prime Minister, to find her son a position in the civil service. Russell acceded, and found Blackwood a position as a clerk in the Treasury – much to the latter's relief, he being doubtful about his exam prospects. Blackwood was still very much a socialite, and now took full advantage of the entertainment that the capital had to offer.

Stephenson Arthur Blackwood, around 1875.

Just two years later, however, in 1854, conflict erupted in the Crimea, and Britain began to mobilise for war. As preparations began for assembling and dispatching an expeditionary force, it quickly became apparent that the military administration was in a chaotic state, particularly when it came to the army commissariat (the forerunner of the Army Service Corps). Since the commissariat was a branch of the Treasury, volunteers were called for from the existing civilian staff, with the promise of both military rank and good salary. Although not quite sure what he was letting himself in for, Blackwood volunteered and found himself attached to the expeditionary force with the rank of Captain. He was quickly sent out to the Crimea and attached to the Guards regiment, where his main responsibilities involved the supply and provision food – especially fresh meat. He was present at the Battle of Alma, and was on hand during the famous Charge of the Light Brigade which, although he did not see it, he was able to report with information gleaned at first hand from fellow officers. Blackwood's account of the war is full of interesting detail and it is clear that he experienced much of it at close quarters, reporting critically on such matters as Lord Raglan's performance, conditions endured by soldiers during the siege of Sebastopol and treatment of the sick and wounded at Scutari. Perhaps predictably, as a ranking officer, he found some enjoyment from the experience, evidenced by letters from his father admonishing him for quite serious gambling debts. By the time he returned to England, however, he had become an irredeemable convert to Evangelicalism. His correspondence, which during his time in the Crimea, had been so full of lively and interesting detail, now became turgid and dull, full of endless – almost obsessive – repetition of the stock Evangelical phrases of the period. Happily, for him, he was able to resume his role in The Treasury, though now endowed with credit resulting from lofty recognition of his military service and contribution towards the war effort. In 1858, Stevenson very astutely married Sydney, the widowed Duchess of

Manchester. For several years the couple lived in Streatham,[93] where Stevenson dedicated himself (when he wasn't working at the Treasury) to preaching and proselytizing the Evangelicals' version of the Bible.

In 1868, the family took up the lease of Wood Lodge on Shooters Hill and moved in. The problem was that Stevenson soon found it a difficult location to reach late in the evening after his many Evangelical meetings. For a time the family moved to Crayford a few miles to the south-east, where Blackwood held open-air prayer meetings at both Crayford bridge and nearby Bexley Heath. At Dartford he encouraged local tradesmen to establish both a Temperance Hall and a 'lads' Institute. But he was also hugely active nationally, undertaking 'missionary' work in the East End as well as northern industrial towns. Predictably, he was hugely immersed in the Temperance Movement as well as being a trustee of Dr Barnardo's homes,;and he also became a prolific tractarian and parliamentary lobbyist.

In 1874 Stevenson became Financial Secretary to the Post Office, and then Secretary in 1880. His civil service work and Evangelical interest sent him almost constantly travelling around Britain and Europe for the next ten years, and then, in 1892, the family moved back to Shooters Hill. Here, Stevenson's missionary work intensified. Now he had the unemployed of Woolwich and Plumstead to minister to. With the help of fellow Evangelicals, he tried to help solve the endemic poverty and unemployment of the area by encouraging the victims to emigrate – (after they had received a suitable homily in

---

[93] By coincidence, the house they lived in there was also called 'Wood Lodge'.

the servant's hall at Wood Lodge). Even dinner guests were not immune from this attention. There are anecdotes of Stevenson inviting people to dinner so that he could interrogate them on the intimacy of their relationship with Jesus Christ!

Reading the official memoir [94] of Stevenson's life after his military career is a dull and almost mind-numbing experience. The memoir was compiled by a friend and edited by Stevenson's widow Harriet and contains page after page of extracts from correspondence consisting largely of Evangelical expressions of piety and Biblical homilies. The memoir itself was clearly intended as an assertion of Evangelicalism in its own right - almost a missionary hagiography. Were we to take it at face value, the memoir and Stevenson Blackwood himself, would rapidly be condemned to the bookshop-bottom shelf normally reserved for unsaleable old copies of bibles, prayer-books and Christian treatises. However, there was another side to Stevenson and one which we might suspect was excised from the official account. For if the impression we get is of Stevenson, in later life, ensconced in the overwhelmingly drab and claustrophobic aura of gospel halls, bible reading classes or tractarian meetings, it is not completely accurate. There was another side to him. He was also a man who loved the outdoors and enjoyed walking holidays in Scotland and Cornwall. He welcomed the arrival of spring with an almost pantheistic pleasure. Unfortunately, amongst the six hundred-plus pages of the memoir there are just a few fleeting glimpses of this side of his personality. In one of those rare moments we find him wandering alone in the woods on Shooters Hill, collecting wild flowers, *'delighting in the early singing of the birds, and all the sweet*

---

[94] Some Records of the life of Stevenson Arthur Blackwood. KCB. 1896.

loneliness of the Wood paths'. [95] In his final year someone introduced him to the poetry of William Cowper, which appears to have been something of a revelation to him – almost as though he had never been exposed to poetry before. Certainly he interrupted his almost incessant flow of biblical references in his correspondence to quote lines from Cowper's *The Winter Walk at Noon* which he confessed *'I am so enjoying ...Never read it fully before, certainly never in such absolute quietude.'* [96]

Towards the end of 1893 Blackwood was sent to the continent on speaking tour. Unfortunately, he had not sufficiently recovered from a bout of influenza and appears to have been struck down with pneumonia. He was hurriedly rushed back to England but died shortly after landing at Harwich on 2nd October, 1893. All of his family were at his deathbed except one. His wayward twenty-four year old son Algernon.

Algernon, who is best known as a writer – though his career was startlingly varied - was the third of the Blackwood's children, and was born at Wood Lodge in 1869. Algernon's first years were spent in the house at Shooters Hill before the family moved temporarily to Crayford a few miles away. The children were raised in a strict Christian environment and, perhaps because he was beginning to push against the restrictions, Algernon was sent to a school in Germany run by an even stricter religious order. When this didn't seem to curb his wilder nature, he was sent to Canada to try and make his own way in the world. There he worked at a number of occupations, including that of lumberjack, and developed a strong taste for the outdoor world. His adventures there were recorded in his very

---

[95] Ibid. P 523
[96] Ibid. p537

entertaining partial autobiography, *Adventures Before Thirty*.[97] A great walker and climber, Algernon continued these activities virtually all his life. But it really was as a writer that he is best known.

Algernon Blackwood.

During the course of his career (he died in 1951) Algernon wrote an enormous number of novels, plays and short stories. Although he is often categorized as a writer of ghost stories, this is not strictly accurate. Blackwood was one of a number of early 20th century writers who produced what has become known as 'weird' fiction. [98]   The nature of the stories this refers to hovers somewhere between the horror/ghost story and science fiction. It was a genre of fiction that was tremendously popular in the late 19th and early 20th centuries, and has continued with a cult following ever since.

Some of Blackwood's most powerful stories feature, not ghosts,

---

[97] *Adventures Before Thirty*. 1923
[98] This included Arthur Machen, Arthur, Conan Doyle, H P Lovecraft, Lord Dunsany (who lived a few miles from Shooters Hill at Shoreham in Kent), H G Wells etc.

but something much more elemental, something which emanates from Nature itself. In some of his most successful stories, like *The Wendigo* (1910) [99] and *The Willows* (1907) [100] travellers isolated in wilderness areas are beset by some powerful and malevolent natural force. Jack Sullivan in his survey of English horror fiction[101] notes a distinction in Blackwood's approach to the genre. In his case, Sullivan remarks, the focus has shifted from the claustrophobic world of old houses, churches and mausoleums, to *'the cosmic world of outdoor ghost stories, a world where ghosts and demons are apparitions of primal forces in nature...Blackwood envisions a world in which everything is alive and anything can be a ghost: trees, bushes, earth, snow, even the wind.'*.

One of Algernon Blackwood's most intriguing stories is *The Man Whom the Trees Loved*, a novella which he wrote in 1911. The story is set in the New Forest, where an elderly couple, Mr. & Mrs. Bittacy, live in a small house situated in a clearing amidst the trees. Mr. Bittacy is intrigued about the suggestion that trees might have some form of sentience – an idea which alarms Mrs. Bittacy, who is best described as a rather simple soul who clings tenaciously to a literal interpretation of the Bible. Any ideas which seem to stray in any way from narrow orthodoxy seem to her to be at best unhealthy and at the worst,

---

[99] The story first appeared as a novella in *The Lost Valley and Other Stories* (Eveleigh Nash, 1910)
[100] Published in The Listener and Other Stories. (1907)
[101] Jack Sullivan. *Elegant nightmares: The English ghost story from Le Fanu to Blackwood*. 2018.

heretical. (One can understand where this might have come from).

Mr. Bittacy purchases a painting, a portrait of a tree by an artist named Sanderson, who has a considerable reputation for his skill in being able to 'capture' the soul of a tree in his work. Sanderson is invited to stay with the Bittacy's in the New Forest, and to Mrs. Bittacy's growing alarm, he encourages her husband's speculation about consciousness in trees.

Following Sanderson's departure, she is deeply upset to discover that her husband has taken to walking in the forest at night and slowly realizes that, as his relationship with her fades, his relationship with the trees and the forest in general grows stronger. Some strange force present in the woodland around the house seems to be growing in strength and calling to him. In the end Bittacy responds to the call and becomes at one with the forest around him.

It is a strange tale. The portrayal of the stiff and fearful Mrs. Bittacy is somewhat unforgiving in its condemnation of religious narrow-mindedness. But it is the other side of the tale that is so intriguing. From an early stage Blackwood totally rejected his father's strict and confining religious views and began, instead, to explore the occult and eastern religions. In *Adventures Before Thirty* he confessed:

"By far the strongest influence in my life ... was Nature; it betrayed itself early, growing in intensity with every year. Bringing comfort, companionship, inspiration, joy, the spell of Nature has remained dominant, a truly magical spell. Always immense and potent, the years have strengthened it. The early feeling that everything was alive, a dim sense that some kind of consciousness

struggled through every form, even that a sort of inarticulate communication with this "other life" was possible, could I but discover the way—these moods coloured its opening wonder. Nature, at any rate, produced effects in me that only something living could produce..."[102]

Blackwood attributed this consciousness of Nature to his early upbringing, to being brought up as child in an environment dominated by trees, in 'the Kentish gardens' of his childhood in the manor house at Crayford and the woodlands on Shooters Hill. In later life, when he was under stress or in need of inspiration, it was to the countryside that he would turn. It might be the forests or the mountains or even 'the *simple fields, the lanes, and little hills.*' When, whilst in Canada, a telegram arrived reporting the death of his father, Blackwood fled to the woods for solace. Later he began to realise why the woods were so important to him. As he lay in the woods, especially at night,

"... the world of hotels, insurance, even of Methodists, [seemed] very far away. The hum of the city could not reach me, though its glare was faintly visible in the sky. There were no signs of men; no sounds of human life; not even a dog's bark—nothing but a sighing wind and lapping water and a sort of earth-murmur under the trees, and I used to think that God, whatever He was, or the great spiritual forces that I believed lay behind all phenomena, and perhaps were the moving life of the elements themselves, must be nearer to one's consciousness in places like this than among the bustling of men in the towns and houses."

In what some consider to be Blackwood's greatest novel, *Julius*

---

[102] Algernon Blackwood. *Adventures Before Thirty.* 1923. p13

Le Vallon, the main character has a strange mystical experience whilst walking on a hillside near a larch wood.

"*Somewhere about me on that bare hillside Nature had become aggressively alive....it was clear to me that the sensation of being watched, of knowing another living presence close, as also of sharing this tender beauty, issued primarily from the grove of larches. My being and their own enjoyed some inter-relationship, exquisite yet natural. There was exchange between us. And the wind, blowing stiffly up the heather slopes, then lifted the lower branches of the trees, so that I saw deep within the little grove, yet at the same time behind and beyond them. Something that their veil of greenness draped went softly stirring. The same minute it came out towards me with a motion best described as rushing. The heart of the grove became instinct with life, life that I could appreciate and understand, each individual tree contributing its thread to form the composite whole... The air, the larches and ourselves were marvelously entangled with the sunshine and the landscape. I was aware of an intelligence different from my own, immensely powerful, but somehow not a human intelligence. Superb, unearthly beauty touched the very air.'* [103]

Like Bittacy in *The Man Whom The Trees Loved*, the narrator becomes aware of a consciousness in the woodland before him, and once he understands and appreciates its beauty, he merges and becomes at one with it. Blackwood believed that everything had an energy or life force which linked it closely to everything else in the Cosmos. He believed that when in the presence of trees, or Nature generally, one could have a mystical experience that made it possible to see beyond the ordinary world. In this state "*..the ordinary world, and my particular little*

---

[103] *Julius Le Vallon*, Chapter 10.

troubles with it, fell away like so much dust; the whole fabric of men and women, commerce and politics, even the destinies of nations, became a passing show of shadows, while the visible and tangible world showed itself as but a temporary and limited representation of a real world elsewhere whose threshold I had for a moment touched."

The idea was not new, and had been powerfully explored by the nature writer and mystic Richard Jefferies, in his strange mystical book *The Story of My Heart* published in 1883. Like Jefferies, (who lived in Eltham between 1884-1885) Blackwood rejected the idea that the Christian God was responsible for everything. Like Jefferies, he felt there was something more elemental, something that emanated from within Nature itself, and that woodland could provide a window into whatever it was; and that a tree was, in some way, a messenger or a link to whatever that 'other' was.

Blackwood went further, becoming associated with esoteric organisations like the Rosicrucians and the more controversial Order of the Golden Dawn. However, time and again, like Richard Jefferies, he found a mystical experience in the presence of trees.

It is certainly thought provoking, while sitting at one of the tables outside the café which was built on the site of Wood Lodge, to realise that Blackwood's inspiration grew out of the natural and ancient woodland standing in front of you.

Following the death of Stevenson Blackwood in 1893, his wife, Harriet, continued to live at Wood Lodge for a while. But by 1905 the house had passed into the hands of Sir Hay Donaldson a mechanical engineer who been the Chief Engineer for The East and West India Dock Company before becoming the Chief Superintendant of the Ordnance Factories nearby at Woolwich. Shooters Hill combined the perfect location for him, being close to his place of work and yet still out of sight of the industrialized riverside on the other side of the hill. It seems as though Stevenson's Blackwood's inclinations towards moral improvement might have rubbed off on the building, because it provided a venue for a meeting of the Twentieth Century League on at least one occasion, in 1905. The aim of the League was to make good citizens of those who were likely to lapse into 'hooliganism and disgrace'.[104] By which they probably meant the working poor of Woolwich and Plumstead!

One of Donaldson's house guests was the social reformer and researcher Charles Booth, who stayed there while surveying Woolwich and the local area by bicycle. He seems to have been in the habit of exploring the town's streets during the night and was not beyond calling in at the Woolwich Music Hall for entertainment before arriving back at Wood Lodge after midnight

Donaldson was appointed to the Ministry of Munitions in 1914 and was selected to accompany Lord Kitchener on a diplomatic mission to Russia in 1916. Tragically, the ship they were travelling on, the cruiser HMS Hampshire, hit a mine off of the Orkneys, and Donaldson, Kitchener and all but twelve of the crew perished.

A few months later, Wood Lodge was damaged by a bomb dropped from a German plane and it seems that Donaldson's widow abandoned the house, because it reverted to the Crown

---

[104] *Morning Post* 28 February 1905.

Estate. They gave permission for the use of the site by an anti-aircraft unit for the remainder of the war, but thereafter the building was left empty and became increasingly dilapidated. The house, together with its ancillary buildings was finally demolished in 1932, just a couple of years before the entire site was purchased by the London County Council. The café building was erected on the site just a few years later.

With its fantastic view, woodland environment and handy supply of refreshments, the café, like its predecessor Wood Lodge, occupies a lovely spot. It is obviously less tranquil here now than it was, but there are occasional moments when it is quiet sitting outside the café. And I am conscious of that now when the mist suppresses the noise of traffic on the roads to the south or the planes as they roar across on their descent towards Heathrow. For the wealthy like the Blackwood's who lived in the grand houses in the woods on the top of the hill, that tranquility could be protected for a while by fences and 'Private Property' signs, but not for long.

It can sometimes be hard to imagine the tranquility of the woodland as it must have been before the First World War. Hard to recreate it. Nevertheless, despite the shouting and the surreal conversations of the children, the birdsong still rings out from the woods on either side. I guess if Nature doesn't mind the noise, why should I?

Then, as the fifth child trips up the café steps and falls flat on its face, I decide perhaps it's time to leave.

Oxleas Meadow photographed by Alfred Moore in 1951. The bottom of the meadow is still lined with prefabs erected during the war.

As I walk down the woodland edge on the east side of the meadow, the signs of spring start to become more evident. A few yards from the café three trees stand together on the edge of the woodland, not far from a garish outdoor gym from which children hang like washing. One of the trees is a London Plane. On the tips of its branches, buds are bursting into leaf, unfolding fresh dark-green leaves that are crumpled and wet like the new wings of butterflies. On some of the higher branches the buds are less well advanced. The soft pink outer casings splitting to reveal tiny grape-like lime green clusters which will expand to form a flower like a short green catkin.

On a nearby young beech, the buds are smaller and tight like bullets, but, changing slowly from amber to pink.

The third tree is a mature horse chestnut, slowly unfolding

clusters of tiny, narrow leaves, packed together as they unfold from the bud like a delicate dark green flower. Though in fact there is no sign of the tree's real flower yet.

I decide to follow the narrow tarmac path down the length of the meadow as it slips between the edge of Oxleas wood and the old laid-hedgerow which lines the path. Perhaps it is because of the mist, or the fact that the undergrowth is so thin at this time of the year, I suddenly notice an ancient woodbank running a few yards inside the woodland edge. I must have seen it before, but I am now aware how long it is and how complete. There is a ditch on the outer side and the bank itself is covered in ivy with mature trees and hawthorns growing on it. In the ditch, young beech saplings are taking advantage of the light from the woodland edge, and there is a young cherry, its flowers still opening.

As I follow the path I notice quite how many butchers brooms are growing along it. They have spread to the other side of the path and are more common in Oxleas Wood than in any of the others. It forms a broad shrub, sometimes called the box holly. The butchers broom is an evergreen with sharp, pointy leaves. Several of the specimens growing along here look a mess because, when they are ready to shed a stem, their leaves fade to a faint green, the flesh falling away to leave a delicate filigree skeleton. The spiky structure of the shrub also captures the falling leaves of surrounding trees in the autumn, and become untidily choked with brown vegetable debris. Here and there some of the plants have retained some of their bright red berries which look more like an artificial Christmas decorations, still brightly coloured and shiny, even though it is now April.

I carry on past the pumping station of the reservoir which is hidden under the lower portion of the meadow. Originally the Metropolitan Water Board wanted to install it half way up the meadow, but in 1975, after a three year battle, they agreed to excavate their site at the bottom of the meadow where it would be less intrusive. Seen from the air, the reservoir appears like a huge circular green plate laid onto the grass. It is less evident when you walk over it though, and the pumping station is reminiscent of a cricket pavilion, even it if it does stand behind a strong iron fence.

Opposite the pumping station the woodland edge has receded to a pretty grass covered glade. If you ignore the path, and the pumping station behind you, it is possible to imagine that this glade sits in the middle of a dense forest. In the centre stands a strong, mature oak. I have passed this way on a bright sunny day, and the sun on the grass is surprisingly inviting. If this was the centre of a deep woodland, it would be the perfect place to lie on one's back and stare up through the leaves to the sky beyond. There is plenty of birdsong here. But the glade is not hidden in the woods, it is beside the path. And I would get some very disconcerted looks if I laid down here.

The buds on the oak are turning pinky-white, like little spots of light on the ragged twigs at the branch ends. In the other direction a crow is burying its beak in the sodden turf over the reservoir. It eyes me curiously as I stand in the glade but seems to decide I am harmless, and casually waddles on, digging for food amidst the wet grass. On the far side of the meadow as I look back towards Jack Wood, the mist is thickening and the trees are turning grey and losing definition in the afternoon light.

It's time to turn for home.

Chapter 11 – Oxleas Wood

The seasons change with huge subtlety in the woodland. Perhaps no-one expressed it with greater poetry than the naturalist and writer, Walter Murray:

"Before the leaves of autumn fell I gathered sweet chestnut. The woods beckoned and I was not disobedient to their gentle summons...There was a quiet magic about the hush before the fall. Seed was ripened, fruit was full, new life was born. Rest and sleep were coming to the woods; and pervading the rides and brambly clearings there was a serenity and peace that beggared all telling. Work was done, nothing that was done could be undone. Life had expressed itself unstintingly, in energy and growth and sound and colour, life had made manifest in a thousand forms, and now it was all over, work was done, rest and sleep were coming." [105]

This subtle change is particularly noticeable in the Oxleas Woodlands in the autumnal months. Amongst the trees in the woodlands, there is a gentle re-shading of the light. The bright

---

[105] Walter J C Murray. *Copsford.* (1948) p160.

greenlight of the spring that became the dusty sage of late summer slowly ebbs into a hazy yellow and gold. It is the colour palette of the woodland autumn, and knowing that it is coming I look for the signs. The yellowing edges of the leaves, the little brown curls as the tree starts to prepare itself, withdrawing its vital energy from the extremity of its green fingertips. What you realise after a while in woodland though, is that the trees themselves are anarchic. There is no single start to this slow race into winter. Autumn is triggered in a myriad different ways in as many different varieties of flora and fauna. A tree of one species may start its journey one day, whilst a near neighbour may hang on for a little longer, reaching out for the last dose of sunlight for as long as possible before initiating its organic shut-down. Almost before I have noticed it, the change is upon us.

In our woodlands, one of the most obvious signals comes from the oaks. It starts as an occasional rustle through the leaves from the high canopy. Then slowly its pace gathers as the days pass until it sounds like a heavy shower is falling somewhere high above – as though heavy drops are making their way down from leaf to leaf, to land somewhere in the undergrowth. In intensity it grows day by day.

A small but sharp blow to the crown of my head startles me, and I look quickly round to see an acorn bouncing away into the bramble. Standing still now, I watch and all around me the oaken harvest is raining down in random little bombs. The oaks casting their seed in natural hope.

October brings wind and rain. At night I can open a window and hear the background swish of upper branches as the wind roars through the trees on the slopes above the houses. Next morning the paths are littered with large spear-shaped leaves, their ragged edges deadly-looking against the softer wet woodland floor. Then, one bright autumn morning, as I walk through the woods, the sunlight bursts through at a lower angle, and the path is suddenly a golden river of chestnut and beech leaves. I stop suddenly transfixed by the dispersing wash of colour as the light flickers and flushes around me. From bronze in the shadows to bright gold in the full sunlight. The canopy is thinning. The sunlight is beginning to strengthen on the woodland floor even as it weakens in the southern sky.

In Jack Wood, the air is filled for long minutes by the communal shrieking of the parakeets – the bright green ring-necked plague of the forest. In the 1990s, when I first started walking in these woods, the birdsong would be dominated by native species – tits, robins, blackbirds, together with the frequent coarse heckling of magpie and jay. Nowadays, those birds are still there, but often they struggle to make themselves heard against the din of the green devils and the rumble of the traffic from the motorways. In spring and autumn the parakeets seem at their noisiest, and even the bright flash of their feathers seem of little compensation for the inharmonious racket of their outraged voices.

As the canopy thins, some of our smaller bids become more evident, often making their way from the woodland, across the road, to our back garden. Goldfinches appear in greater abundance, and to my really great delight, the little long-tailed tits. .

The bird which really seems to come into its own in autumn is that cheeky little companion, the robin. They are with us all year, of course, and are as evident in the woodland as they are in the back-garden. But their scratchy little song somehow seems to be there in the soundtrack of the season in greater intensity than before.

On a blustery autumn day I take the lower path through Jack Wood and out onto Oxleas Meadow. Overhead, dark grey clouds are racing across a lighter grey sky and leaves loop across the air like blue tits blown on a breeze, not quite in control of their movements. The wind is pressing my jacket against my back with chilled hands. It is late morning. The robins abandon me as I leave the wood, and my passing is marked now by a crow calling to its mate from the stag-headed trees, bleached white against the sky to the left. I am heading for Oxleas Wood, and it is about time we talked about it.

Originally, Oxleas was part of, or connected to, the much greater West Wood, which was three times the size of Oxleas[106]. Sadly, West Wood was grubbed up in 1862 to create more agricultural land, which was itself lost between the wars in the great convulsion of expanding London. Oxleas is an orphan. A remnant of what once was. And I think there is a sense of loneliness about it. In some ways, although the trees were obviously harvested and managed for centuries, it seems to have been less interfered with than the other woods. So perhaps there are areas within in it that literally do date back thousands of years.

It is Oxleas Wood, of course, which has seeded its name to the rest of the woodland. At over 45 hectares, it is the largest wood in the group, and perhaps the most varied both in species and terrain. Thirty two different variety of tree of have

---

[106] West Wood appears as Runnets Wood, in the Andrews map of 1769. East Wood may have been its neighbour, stretching south-east to Blendon.

been recorded here, over 30% more than in the nearby Shepherdleas Wood and a few more than in Jack Wood – though there the variety was influenced by Lord Penzance's introduction of trees like the odd Wellingtonia, Lawson's Cypress and Red Oak. (There is also a Dawn Redwood – though as this wasn't introduced to Britain until the early 1940s it may have been planted by the London County Council's Parks department). Where Oxleas is unique (or at least it was until relatively recently) is in its Willow trees (both Grey and Crack willow), Highclere Holly, Wild Plum and Aspen.

Like the other woods it is dominated by oak – in this case the pendunculate oak. But Oxleas also has birch, sweet chestnut, ash, together with some aspen and wild cherry. There is abundant hazel, hawthorn and blackthorn, and scatterings of guilder rose, wayfaring tree and dogwood. It seems to be this rich variety which gives Oxleas its more diverse character. The cherry, for example, seems most abundant on the top of the hill on the northern side of the wood – its blossom filling parts of the woodland in springtime like a scattering of icing sugar. Then there are the wild service trees, always a delight to find because of their significance for the woodland. The tree is a key indicator of ancient woodland, and its presence helped save the wood when the government threatened to drive a motorway through it in the 1980s. The tree is best identified by its pretty pale gold leaves, shaped rather like elongated maple leaves, which is why it was sometimes called the 'maple service tree'. The Edwardian tree lover Francis George Heath, considered the leaves of the service tree to one of the great beauties of the autumn woodland:

'In autumn the fresh green leafy surface changes to a light gold-

en brown, which is relieved here and there, by patches of brighter colour...the handsome form of the leaf under rich, mellow shades of gold, and light delicate brown upon green that has not yet faded, presents an appearance, in the earlier part of the season of change, which contributes not a little to the loveliness of autumn foliage.' [107]

But it is the wild service tree's slow-growing nature that holds its greatest significance for us. Its seeds do not propagate easily. In both Oxleas and Jack Woods, small clutches of mature specimens can be found together; a colony that has taken a very long time to establish itself. Incidentally, the name 'service tree' is thought to derive from the word 'cerevisiae', the Latin name for beer. The fruit of the tree was, in the past, used in brewing beer, and even used on its own for brewing a potent drink called 'chequers'. (Which may account for the name of some country pubs!).

But the wild service tree is not the only one to add to the attraction of the wood. The presence of silver birch also contributes to both the variety and beauty of the wood. It is a tall and graceful tree, so much so that the poet Coleridge referred to it as the *'most beautiful of forest trees, the Lady of the Woods'*. [108] It is fitting that the tree is in Oxleas, a wood with an Anglo-Saxon name, because the tree also takes its name from the Anglo-Saxon word 'beorht' , meaning bright or shining. With its silver and white bark and light leaves which flicker in the sunlight, the name is delightfully appropriate.

If the birch is the 'Lady' of the woods, the ash tree also has its

[107] F G Heath. *Our British Trees.* 1907.
[108] From 'The Picture or the Lover's Resolution', Samuel Taylor Coleridge

appreciators. It is fast growing but can live over 400 years if coppiced. The canopy of the ash is high and open; the structure of its foliage is 'airy' with feather-like or 'pinnate' leaves which allow sunlight to pierce through to the woodland floor below. It comes into leaf later than most other trees, which allows woodland flowers like bluebell and wood anemone to grown beneath them in springtime. Like the birch, where it grows the woodland is lighter. But the ash had its practical uses too, which probably helps explain its presence here. The timber of the ash wood was useful, for tool handles, farm equipment and furniture – and it made what was probably the best firewood. It was commonly grown in coppice woodland like Oxleas.

In some ways the variety of the woodland in Oxleas Wood adds to a sense of confusion. Visitors who aren't familiar with the topography of the wood often get bewildered by the winding paths and subtle shifts in terrain. The north-west corner of the wood sits on the top of Shooters Hill, where there are thick plantations of laurel and rhododendron. It spreads eastwards along the south side of the Dover Road, level for a perhaps a quarter of mile before sinking abruptly down below the level of the road. To the south the wood descends evenly down the hillside to level ground. A winding stream-bed meanders through this lower level, and in the wettest winters, water flows through a deep winding cut made over several centuries.

The observant walker will also become aware that parts of the woodland are bisected by ditches and banks, often overgrown or partially filled in. They seem to serve little purpose now, but it is possible that some may date back to the middle ages. As mentioned earlier, trees and underwood could be exploited for different commercial purposes, and was often sold off separately. The wood itself could be sub-divided so that parcels of underwood could be separately identified – and the common way of marking this was by creating banks and ditches around an area. The most noticeable of these are known as 'woodbanks' and they most usually consist of a bank and ditch running side by side. Over time, the top of the bank often developed a hedge – and then trees. In Oxleas, there are banks that seem to share this feature, but they seem a little small to be medieval.

There is another explanation for at least some of the ditches, and that is simply drainage. In 1848, the Crown Commissioners' agent, John Clutton, wrote a report to his employers, following a detailed inspection of the woodland in company with the Woodreeve. In addition to recommending that more ash and chestnut be planted – to provide hop poles for the Kentish hop fields – he noted the poor drainage in the lower part of Oxleas and recommended that more ditches should be dug and at a greater depth, presumably to improve the water-logging which was a frequent problem for newly growing trees. Trees to the south of the hill had been harvested in 1818 and replanted. But around 1832 a further 528 trees were felled. These were in turn replaced – and these seem to be the trees we have now.

Clutton also noted that cattle were entering the woodland from the Dover road and causing damage, and he recommended a paling fence be installed there to keep them out. He finished his report with a rather laconic observation:

'Hedgerows and Timber in cultivated land are fast disappearing consequently the only stock of timber which will be possessed by

the Country will be that growing in Woods and Coppices. Underwood in most districts in England is becoming of little value as the effect of the Railways has been to reduce the price of Coals to so large an extent in Districts in which the only fuel of the Poor was before the Underwood of the District as to render the growth of Underwood a matter of Secondary consideration.'

Clutton's words were an uncanny echo of Defoe's observation a century and a half earlier. It was, however, probably this realisation which led to the leasing out of parts of the estate for country houses. But, apart from leasing land, the Commissioners had another source of income from Oxleas.

Sir John Shaw's long-standing lease of the Eltham estate was considerably reduced when it came up for renewal in 1809. To his intense chagrin, both Oxleas and Shepherdleas woods were taken out of his hands. [109] This reduction of his hunting and shooting rights rankled and the relationship between Shaw and Crown Commissioners declined until 1838 when he, or his son, either relinquished or lost all of his leasehold. The shooting rights to all of the woodland passed to a man by the name of Warren. His rights excluded the agricultural land, where shooting rights were retained by the farmers themselves. For the annual sum of £40 he was given exclusive rights over the woodland, with the specific instruction that he was *"... not to suffer or permit any stock of Rabbits to be encouraged but to do all in his power to keep all killed off."* He was assisted in this by

[109] Crown Estate records. CRES2/356 Notes about Tenancies. The National Archive.

a keeper by the name of Henry Wykes who occupied a cottage beside the turnpike road near what later became the site of Warren Wood house.[110]

Warren relinquished the rights in April 1839 and they were granted instead to Charles Webb, a City wine merchant. To take full advantage of the rights, and for both convenience and comfort, Webb persuaded the Commissioners to additionally lease him a small parcel of land beside the turnpike road upon which to build a new 'cottage' - almost certainly a small hunting lodge.

A dispute almost immediately erupted between Webb and the farmer who held the tenancy of Pippinhall Farm, whose fields extended north to the woodland edge from the Eltham-Bexley Road. Although the farmer had held the right to shoot over his own fields, it appears this was intended as a means of controlling rabbits, which threatened to damage young plants and saplings etc. Webb, however, was concerned that in addition to the rabbits, pheasants and hares were also being 'enticed' from the woods – game to which he believed he held exclusive hunting rights. The farmer, whose status obviously fell below that of a City wine merchant, was instructed he could no longer shoot in the fields adjacent to the woodland.

In 1841, Webb was in dispute again. This time with Benjamin Curry, the occupant of Eltham Park, the mansion to the south of the valley. Shooting rights over the 44 acres of the Eltham Park estate belonged to Curry as part of his leasehold. However Webb had taken to shooting on land belonging to the estate

---

[110] Wykes appears to have died shortly after because in 1839, the cottage was occupied by his widow.

without permission, so technically he was poaching. Of course, there was no question of him being sent to the local assize and transported to New South Wales! Instead he was given a firm written warning and told to desist.

In the end, Webb's leasehold of the hunting rights was rather brutally curtailed. Around Christmas 1841, Webb invited friends (or a friend) to a shooting party in the woods. Perhaps they prepared for the day's shooting with the traditional libation. If they did so it was particularly unfortunate. Once in the woods, Webb was shot twice in the face by one of his companions, causing irreparable damage to his sight. One of the friends in the party – if not THE friend in question – was William Matthew Coulthurst, one of the Directors of Coutts Bank.[111]

Not surprisingly, within days, the shocked and maimed Charles Webb declared he would never go shooting again, and determined to surrender his shooting rights to Oxleas. He dispatched a letter to A C Driver, the Crown Commissioners agent, announcing his decision. But before Driver could write to the Commissioners reporting the news, William Coulthurst, with questionable speed, acted. He persuaded the probably still shocked Charles Webb to accept a reimbursement for the cost of building the cottage beside the turnpike road; and then wrote directly to the Commissioners explaining what he had done '...*in the hope of being permitted by your Honourable Board to succeed him, I have made my arrangements with him. I am very desirous of acquiring this opportunity for occasional relaxation from business, and permit me to add I shall feel much*

---

[111] Coutts Bank was one of the most respected banks – and is still highly exclusive. It is also known as the Queen's Bank!

gratified by your acceptance of me as Tenant of the Manor to succeed Mr. Webb.' [112]

Reading this, and the following letter from AC Driver, one is instinctively aware of something darkly Dickensian. It is not only the speed with which the rich banker acted to benefit from his friend's misfortune, it's the calculating steps which he took to achieve his aim. By coming to a financial arrangement with Webb before the Crown Commissioners were involved or, indeed, had any knowledge of what was going on, Coulthurst had relieved them of any financial worries or complication which might accompany the early termination of Webb's lease. It also put him in an extremely favourable light. This was reinforced by the assessment of Coulthurst contained in AC Driver's report, which must have arrived after Coulthurst's application: *'Mr. William Coulthurst of the firm of Messrs. Coutts & Co. ... is now desirous of being permitted by the Board to become their tenant in the place of Mr. Webb, to which we appreciate there cannot be any objection as he is a Gentleman of the highest respectability and one who will be particularly likely to exercise the right, of shooting over the lands with the greatest possible good feeling & satisfaction to all the occupiers.'*

One can't help wondering if Driver also derived some benefit from the arrangement. One thing is certain though. Nobody seems to have drawn attention to the coincidental presence of Coulthurst at the shooting. Needless to say the Crown Commissioners were all too happy to lease the shooting rights to

[112] W M Coulthurst to the Crown Commissioners. *15 Jan 1842.* CRES2/362. Shooting Rights.The National Archive.

such a wealthy and respectable City gent. Incidentally, Coulthurst also gleaned an additional benefit from the leasehold. His holding gave him the right to vote in the local parliamentary constituency in addition to the vote he was entitled to at his home in Streatham!

Within months Coulthurst wrote to the Crown Commissioners again. He now wanted to cut a ride through the woods so that he could get to his hunting lodge from the Bexley Road, to the south, thus avoiding the inconvenient detour over the hill itself. A track already existed through the wood, running north-east towards the Dover Road from near the Woodreeve's cottage, (which appears to have stood in the south-east corner of the farmland which now forms Oxleas Meadow). [113] The existing track seems to have been cut through the wood to enable the extraction of timber, and the heavy carts used for this ploughed deep furrows into the surface. As a consequence, during the winter months, it was impassable by carriage. Neither the Commissioners nor their agent saw any reason to decline Coulthurst's request, though they made it clear he should try to avoid unnecessarily felling any mature trees along the route wherever possible.

At the same time, and possibly at the prompting of their agent, Driver, the Commissioners remembered the previous difficulty with Webb and wrote to Coulthurst clarifying that his shooting rights did not include the Eltham Park estate occupied by Curry. In 1849 though, a dispute did erupt between Coulthurst and Mr. Sergeant Adams, the former Director of the failed

---

[113] This is probably the small building which appears on the 1809 Crown Commissioners map. It is probably the site of what is now the Thames Water reservoir control building.

Shropshire Mineral Railway Company, who was resident at Wood Lodge. The Commissioners had already cautioned Adams for cutting down the fir trees in Jack Wood (see Chapter 10); now Coulthurst complained that when his keepers had gone onto Adams' land (the Wood Lodge estate) the latter had intervened, ordering them to leave. Coulthurst complained to the Commissioners and they, in turn, warned Adams that he was not to interfere. Coulthurst had exclusive right to hunt and shoot the rabbits across both farmland and wood,[114] unless – the Commissioners explained – the rabbits grew to so great a number they were damaging Adams' property. In which case the latter was entitled to trap and kill, but not shoot them for sport. It was an important distinction and illustrates how jealously hunting rights were guarded.

In fact poaching appears to have been a frequent problem here. In 1867, a policeman was alerted to the sound of gunfire in the woods. On investigating – probably rather bravely – he discovered two men from Plumstead poaching pheasants. He followed them as they made their way home, and when they stopped at a 'beer shop' in nearby Wickham Lane, he arrested them. They were charged with unlawful possession of two pheasants.   [115]

Rather more amusingly, In October 1869, an 18-year old from Woolwich, by the name of Mathew Wylie was given the choice between a 10 shilling fine or seven days hard labour, for stealing a chicken from Shooters Hill Woods. The chicken had probably wandered from one of the big new houses on the top of the hill. In excuse, poor Mathew claimed that he thought the

---

[114] Excluding, of course, the Eltham Park estate.
[115] *Kentish Independent* 27 April 1867.

chicken was living wild in the woods – (though this would presumably have, made him guilty of poaching). Nevertheless, the magistrate condemned his reasoning as 'nonsensical.' [116]

But lighter moment aside, poaching was an ongoing problem, especially with the increasing poverty among the growing populations of Plumstead and Woolwich. Almost immediately after Wylie's conviction, a fight ensued between three poachers and gamekeepers in Crown Woods Lane (which ran from the Shooters Hill road, south east along the edge of Oxleas Wood). The poachers who were armed with an air gun, were poaching pheasants, with which the wood was 'well stocked'. Two of the poachers escaped, but the third, a 33 year old from Woolwich, was given 2 months hard labour. [117]

A more serious incident occurred in 1886, and one which demonstrates how willingly wealthy landowners rallied round to help one another against any trespass on either their land or their strictly guarded hunting rights. On an early January morning, Lt. Col Kirby with four of his sons and a farmer by the name of Robert Allen from the village of Footscray, were riding through Oxleas Wood when they discovered a gang of at least a dozen men who were clearly engaged in some form of poaching activity. Kirby and his party challenged the men, who fled into the woodland, which then being very thick, made it difficult to search. Kirby sent someone off to the residence of Colonel North[118] at Avery Hill, where gamekeepers and beaters in

---

[116] *Kentish Independent* 16 October 1869

[117] *Kentish Independent* 15th Jan, 1870
[118] North was about the build himself a luxury mansion on the site, which

the service of the Colonel were quickly dispatched to assist. Twelve of the poachers were eventually captured and arrested.[119]

Sadly, neither hare nor rabbit have been seen in or near the woods for decades, though there are occasional reports of a pheasant. On the other hand, we no longer have the sound of gunfire.

Today, Oxleas is best appreciated when it is consciously explored. It is all too easy to wander along the pathways – and Oxleas has some very good wide pathways – in a mellow frame of mind without really noticing how the wood changes around you. In the northern part of the wood, for example, although you are assailed almost constantly by traffic hammering up and down the Dover Road, the wooded landscape offers a range of different aspects. There is the sunny glade of what is now called Hotel Field – which we will explore in more detail shortly – with its half hidden ornamental terrace lined with evergreens. There is the noticeably excavated area beside the Dover Road, where the labourers extracted soil in the early 19th century to build up the road level. There are several little

---

was renowned for its extravagance. For more information on this see http://www.londongardensonline.org.uk/gardens-online-record.php?ID=GRN001 (Retrieved 7.3.2020)

[119] *Norfolk News.* 9 January 1886

ponds – though these tend to be seasonal – and in wet winters an intriguing little stream appears running off to the north towards the Woodlands Farm. The wood's largest pond sits in the south-east corner of the wood between the Rochester and Welling Way. Since it doesn't appear on any of the early maps, it's difficult to know when it was created or why. It may have been part of the various attempts to improve the drainage of the woods in the later-19th century. Today, despite the inevitable sound of traffic it is a relatively tranquil corner of the woods where a heron may often be seen sitting motionless waiting for frogs or newts to stray too close in the springtime.

But perhaps the most noticeable variation in the woodland is to be found in the far south-east corner. This area contains many well-spaced ash and willow trees and the woodland floor is largely clear of the rampant bramble and choking holly bushes. All through this side of the wood there is evidence of the past coppicing activity which kept the wood so healthy. There are some large hazel and chestnut coppice stools which hint at centuries of managed woodland; and more recently the work parties of the Friends of Oxleas Woodlands have resumed a limited coppice regime to try and encourage a greater diversity of woodland flowers and invertebrates.

The feature which most people will know best, however, is Coulthurst's ride, which runs arrow-straight through the centre of the wood flanked by a ditch on one side and the avenue of oak trees which he must have planted at the same time. The drive has become a little less distinct at its northern end. Perhaps because it was here that it encountered the site of the hunting lodge built by Webb. Unfortunately there are no plans or maps which show the layout of this building, but presumably it had some form of enclosure around it, and this may account for the deviation at the end of the ride. Half way along the ride though, there is a broad and well-defined cross path heading north-west. It is a broad attractive path which glides easily through open woodland and then slowly begins to climb. It is a feature which appears on maps of the woodland in the later 1880s, and it is associated with what was probably the most impressive house to be built in the woods.

Chapter 12 – Warren Wood and Falconwood

We can only really guess why Sir James Plaistead Wilde chose to build his lovely country residence, Jackwood, on the heights overlooking the Eltham valley. It would obviously have been a tranquil and attractive spot (for a time), convenient for the City where he worked. Whatever the reasons, it appears the site also attracted other members of his family. Two years after Jackwood was built, Sir James' younger brother Edward, also applied to lease land on the top of the hill, and in 1865 the Crown Commissioners granted him a lease of land adjacent to the Dover Road just to the east of the crest of the hill. Almost simultaneously their cousin, Charles applied for and was granted a lease on the adjoining plot of land to the east.

Edward commissioned the architect Robert Edis[120] to design

---

[120] Robert William Edis, (1839 – 1927).

and build his new house, which he named 'Warren Wood'. Edis was a rising star in the world of architecture, and was making a name for himself designing neo-gothic style houses for the moderately wealthy.[121] The house he built for Edward Wilde possessed the gothic features which were characteristic of the style then popular, including a tower with a steeply pitched roof (according to a later resident this was not well built and developed a 'lean'). The front door of the building opened into a hall which was dominated by Gothic arches and was floored with imitation mediaeval-style encaustic tiles. Compared with Jackwood, Warren Wood was a modest dwelling, though its rooms were described as 'spacious'.

Its

Warren Wood from the south, around 1880

The grounds too were comparatively modest, extending to just two-and-a-half acres. The house itself stood on a slightly raised platform, and steep steps led up to the front door which

---

[121] Edis changed his 'trademark style' to Queen Anne imitations shortly after and his career benefitted considerably.

was set in the base of the tower. To the rear, French windows gave access from the dining room onto a terrace and steps which led down onto a lawn. The upper floor windows at the rear of the house, of course, looked out over Oxleas Wood.

Edward Wilde and his wife Mary didn't make use of Warren Wood for long. By 1875 they had leased the property to the civil engineer Leveson Vernon-Harcourt. The 36-year old Vernon-Harcourt had been employed as the resident engineer for the East & West India Dock Company, on the other side of the river. Following the completion of improvements there he had been commissioned to supervise several projects in Ireland and Alderney before returning to London to establish his own practice as a consulting engineer. Setting up an office in Westminster, he made good use of his previous experience, specialising in engineering projects which involved either river, harbour or dock improvements. [122] He wrote prolifically on the subject and by 1882 had been appointed the chair of Civil Engineering at University College London. In this capacity, he received a number of highly prestigious commissions, one of which involved a voyage to India to survey and report on improvements to the port of Calcutta. He resigned his seat in 1905 and died a few years later at Swanage in Dorset, an area he probably knew quite well as he had been previously undertaken work on the nearby Poole Harbour. By this time, however, Warren Wood had a new tenant, Colonel Arthur Bagnold.

Like other hill residents, Bagnold had very practical reasons for wanting to live here. In 1902 he had been appointed Chief Su-

---

[122] An astute move, as the port facilities of London began to grow dramatically from 1850 onwards, reaching a peak in the 1880s, when over expansion virtually crippled the port.

perintendent at the Royal Arsenal in Woolwich, though his connection with the area went back much further.

At the age of 16, Arthur had been enrolled as a cadet at the Royal Military Academy in Woolwich, where one of his fellow students was the future Lord Kitchener. Commissioned as a Lieutenant in the Royal Engineers, he served in the Egyptian Campaign against Mahdist forces and in the attempt to save Gordon at Khartoum. While there he was involved in some capacity in the re-excavation of the colossal statue of Ramesses II, an event which possibly sparked a life-long interest in history and archaeology (or 'Antiquities' as it was then usually termed).

Col. Arthur Bagnold, around 1930.

By 1887 Bagnold had married Ethel Alger, the daughter of the mayor of Plymouth where he was briefly stationed before being appointed to the School of Military Engineering at Chatham. The following year their first child, Enid, was born there - and it is with Enid that our interest really lies. Shortly after her birth, Arthur Bagnold was promoted to the rank of Lt. Colonel, and posted to Jamaica to command the Royal Engineers based there. [123] By the time the family returned to England, Enid had

---

[123] While there, the Bagnold's second child, Ralph, was born. Ralph Bagnold followed his father into the Royal Engineers, and survived three years on the Western Front during the First World War. He later became a spe-

grown into a wild and challenging thirteen-year old, prone to outrageous pranks and what would once have been described as 'unladylike' behaviour. On one occasion in Jamaica, for example, she had landed herself in trouble for spitting fruit-pulp and pips onto the caps of soldiers as they passed below her window.

In an attempt to haul their unruly daughter into line, the Bagnolds dispatched her to the newly opened Priors Field boarding school near Guildford. The school had been founded by Julia Huxley, mother of Julian and Aldous Huxley, and niece of Matthew Arnold. With such connections – family friends included George Bernard Shaw and WB Yeats – it is hardly surprising that the curriculum was heavily biased towards the arts, especially literature and the theatre. At this time there were only half-a dozen pupils at the school, most of whom were day pupils. Despite the intimate size of the school, Enid's behaviour continued to manifest its wilder character. According to her biographer, Anne Sebba,[124] Enid kept grass snakes in her desk and hatched silkworms in her bedroom. In the spring, she would climb down a drainpipe at night so that she could go and sleep out in the nearby bluebell woods. Perhaps the last straw came when she jumped from a first floor window and persuaded a fellow pupil to do the same. The school mate jumped and received serious injuries.

In what must have been a desperate attempt, the Bagnolds sent Enid to a finishing school in Lausanne. A year later she was back at Warren Wood, a tall and physically awkward 18-year

---

cialist in desert exploration and is generally acknowledged as the founder of the Long Range Desert Group in North Africa during World War II.
[124] *Enid Bagnold: A Biography*. Anne Sebba. Faber. 1986.

old with a strong will and very clear ideas of her own. She persuaded her parents to let her attend the Blackheath Art School and she began to write – probably encouraged by Aldous Huxley, with whom she had a brief relationship. Within a year her poems were being accepted in publications like the *English Illustrated* and the free-thinking *New Age,* and her father surrendered the tower room at Warren Wood to her as a study. In addition to poetry, she ventured into journalism, and took to haunting nearby Well Hall in an attempt to interview Edith Nesbitt, though she seems to have had more success with

Edith's husband Hubert Bland, who had something of a reputation as a womaniser.

Enid Bagnold around 1916.

Enid's literary and artistic ambition drew her fairly rapidly into Bohemian circles. She met and began taking lessons with the painter Walter Sickert, and she was drawn into the campaign for women's suffrage. She became friends with the French artist Henri Gaudier-Brzeska[125], who sculpted a striking portrait head of her which is now part of the

---

[125] More might have come of this relationship if Gaudier-Brzeska hadn't been killed on the Western Front in 1915,

Courthauld Collection.

In her mid-twenties, Enid moved temporarily into a flat in London, where she was able to indulge her Bohemianism to the full. Her regular social circle soon included poets and writers like W H Davies and Edward Thomas, and by 1913 she had taken a job with the Irish publisher and writer Frank Harris, who was then editing the weekly magazine *Hearth and Home.* Enid found herself interviewing and writing features on people like Katherine Mansfield, Annie Besant, and inevitably, Edith Nesbit. However, Harris had a reputation as something of a rake, and not long after meeting her, he seduced her after lunch in a room at the famous Café Royal.[126] In 1914 Harris began publishing *Modern Society* in which he satirised the activities of well-known society figures and soon found himself in court facing charges for libel. When he ended up in prison, Enid took over the management of the magazine, pleading with a range of literary figures to help out with contributions for publication. It was not a situation which could last long, and when, on release from prison, Harris fled to South Africa, Enid abandoned her efforts and returned to Warren Wood.

The return to Shooters Hill did not signify an end to her artistic ambitions. She resumed her lessons with Walter Sickert, and was still willing to keep up a distant correspondence with Harris – though she declined his request for nude photographs!

When war was declared in August 1914, Enid volunteered for work in the munitions factory at Woolwich. Here, however, she was horrified by the conditions in which the women had to

---

[126] Harris later wrote an illustrated four-volume account of his sexual adventures, *My Life and Loves*. Published between 1922-1927, it contained such explicit content it was banned until the 1960s!

work, especially the twelve-hour shifts and the primitive sanitary arrangements provided for them. She made a formal complaint to the Home office and when no satisfactory response was received, she resigned. Still eager to make some sort of useful contribution, she volunteered through the Red Cross to join a Voluntary Aid Detachment. Rather conveniently she was appointed as a nursing assistant at the nearby Royal Herbert Hospital which had become an important centre for dealing with casualties from the Western Front.

In 1918, Enid published her first book, *A Diary without Dates*, which gave an account of her experiences whilst working at the hospital. Sometimes, this could be arresting:

'I was sent down with a detachment to meet the trains with the wounded at the nearby station called Well Hall.[127] *The great trains with the Red Cross gleaming in front of them edged slowly, softly, carefully in against the platform. There was awed silence as the doors opened, nobody alighted, and the stretchers were carried to the train. There could have been no base hospitals in France then: there hadn't been time. The wounded came just as they were, their bandages soaked in blood.'* [128]

It is an interesting book for a number of reasons. One of these is the fact that it caused some controversy by exposing the disparity in care provided for officers and ordinary soldiers. Enid was promptly sacked.

But the other interesting feature of the book is the noticeable presence of the hill and its woodlands in her account. It would have been easy enough to write a narrative which focused sole-

---

[127] This was the original Eltham Station, and nearly on the same site.
[128] *A Diary without Dates.* p112

ly on the hospital and its affairs, but Enid does more than this. The physical presence of the hill and woodland form an elemental and natural backdrop which contrasts with the strangely unreal, almost surreal, experience of the hospital. This is made clear right at the beginning of the account:

'It is always cool and wonderful after the monotone of the dim hospital, its half-lit corridors stretching as far as one can see, to come out into the dazzling starlight and climb the hill, up into the trees and shrubberies here. The wind was terrible tonight. I had to battle up, and the leaves were driven down the hill so fast that once I thought it was a motor-bicycle.' [129]

And not many days later, she recorded:

' I walked up from the hospital late tonight, half past eight, and hungry...in the cold, brilliant moonlight; a fine moon, very low, throwing long, pointed shadows across the road from the trees and hedges...As one climbs up there is a wood on the right, the remains of the old wooded hill; sparse trees, very tall; and tonight a star between every branch, and a fierce moon beating down on the mud and grass...I turned into the wood... and the moonlight and the night vapour rising from the marshy ground were all tangled together so that I could hardly see hedge from field or path." [130]

Enid's description of the woodland gives us a glimpse of how elemental and wild it must still have been at that time. Admittedly her awareness is heightened by the contrast with the interior of the hospital and enhanced by the darkness and the winter weather. But she was clearly very conscious of the

---

[129] *A Diary without Dates.* p1.
[130] Ibid. p12

presence of Nature around her. For example, the change of the seasons also registers deeply with her, as she notes a little later;

'The crown of the hill here holds the last snows, but for all that the spring smell is steaming among the trees and up and down the bracken slopes in the garden next door. There is no moon, there are no stars, no promise to the eye, but in the dense, vapouring darkness the bulbs are moving. I can smell what is not earth or rain or bark.' [131]

Like Blackwood who lived at nearby Wood Lodge, Enid was aware that the woodland somehow seemed to emit some impressive primordial quality. The sight, sound and smell of the woodland all register in her writing. Sadly, this recognition doesn't really recur in any of her later work. But there is no doubt that she loved both Warren Wood and the surrounding woodlands. She was very clear about this in her autobiography.

'There was...such beauty in the garden. It wasn't that my mother was so good with flowers...it was the garden itself, its extraordinary position as it hung, hidden (query existing? Was it real?) at the edge of the Old Dover Road, on the crown of Shooters Hill, traffic pouring from London not a sound reaching in...in May the bluebells were solid; in June the bracken...' [132]

She particularly loved watching the summer sunrise and in her autobiography she recalled:

'...as each day opened in the garden there was an incandescence more lovely than a fire coming through the trees...time telescop-

[131] Ibid p84.
[132] *Enid Bagnold's Autobiography.* P37

ing inside my head brings back the garden...the compressed violet light is on the charcoal branches, and on a sequined twig a pigeon casts a shadow longer than itself.' [133]

On another occasion, feeling lonely, she wanders into a friendly neighbour's garden one night:

'Madeleine's garden next door [134] is all deserted now: they have gone up to London. The green asphalt tennis court is shining with rain, the blue pond with slime; the little statues and bowls are lying on their sides to keep the wind from putting them forcibly there; and all over the house are white draperies and ghost chairs. When I walk in the garden I feel like a ghost left over from the summer too."

Quite why Enid feels this way is an important part of our story, but in order to continue it is necessary to pause and step backwards. Because we have to take a moment to look through the garden hedge at Warren Wood to see what was happening on the eastern side of Warren Wood.

As mentioned earlier, when Edward Wilde submitted his request to lease the land for Warren Wood, his cousin Charles also applied for a plot. The 49-year-old Charles was, like his cousins a highly successful barrister, though he seems to have split his time between his position as Registrar of Deeds for Middlesex, a post which he held from 1851 until his death in 1891, and various appointments as Lt. Colonel of several army volunteer regiments. In 1858 he had succeeded to the title of 2nd Baron Truro, a title which no doubt had some impression on the Crown Commissioners.

---

[133] Ibid. p 101
[134] This is possibly a reference to Summer Court. See Chapter 14.

Unlike his cousin's more modest plot, Lord Truro was granted the leasehold of 40 acres of Oxleas Wood – virtually the entire woodland. But then he had greater ambitions for a country house. In fact what he wanted was a grandiose neo-Palladian mansion, and this is what he built. It was named Falconwood and it was certainly to be the grandest house built on Shooters Hill. The architect was possibly a man by the name of Frederick Thomas (though I have not been able to find any corroborating evidence for this). [135]

The house was a magnificent structure built in gleaming Portland stone. It was approached by a curving driveway which slid obliquely off of the Dover Road, past an entrance lodge which guarded the approach. Privacy and exclusivity seems to have been a passion of Truro's. Even as the house was being built, the local *Kentish Independent* newspaper was warning its readers; *'It may be well to warn intending trespassers of the fact that the privacy of the grounds will be strictly maintained, extra keepers and police constables being employed to apprehend all intruders.'* [136]

Within the grounds there were, in addition to the house and lodge, stables, greenhouses, farm buildings, and a bailiff's cottage. Visitors arriving by carriage were driven through a short belt of woodland, to find themselves at the main entrance on the north side of the building. Falconwood was almost square in plan, and four storeys high, though this was not obvious from the exterior. The roof-line was hidden behind a stone

---

[135] The only possible candidate for this is the Frederick Thomas who was based at 5 Queen St, (Possibly Great Queen Street in Covent Garden) in 1868. If this was the same man, he would have only been 25 years of age when he designed Falconwood; and had emigrated to Canada by 1872.
[136] *Kentish Independent.* 19 August 1865

balustrade, which hid the windows of the servant's quarters, and matched an identical feature ground level balustrade which also hid the basement area where the service rooms, (e.g. kitchen, store rooms etc.) were located.

Falconwood from the south, in the 1940s after it had become a hotel.

The north elevation was symmetrical with a tall central door-way, and two tall sash windows to either side. At each end of the front elevation were a pair of full-height stone classical columns. To the left of the main façade and adjoining it was a five-arched neo-classical arcade which seems to have been the winter garden. Upon entering the building, visitors found themselves in a bright, circular atrium under a domed lantern, which allowed natural light to brighten the interior. On either side, elegant stone stairs curved up to a short landing on the first floor. On both sides of the central hallway were four lesser reception rooms, including the inevitable billiard room. More importantly, two wide doorways at the back of the Atrium led into the three principle reception rooms which stretched across the whole rear of the building. These three rooms could be opened up into a huge single room for balls or similar large functions; or they could be separated into three rooms by cleverly designed sliding partitions. The partitions were fitted with large mirrors, and the effect created when the screens were either partially or fully drawn across was stunning, if not a little disorienting. Floor-to-ceiling windows filled the walls on the south side of the rooms – the central of which was bay-fronted with French windows opening out onto the grounds. The walls at either end also featured bays with tall windows. The space was a spectacular architectural tour de force. On bright summer days, the rooms were flooded with sunlight and dappled with the dancing shadows of foliage from the garden and woodland beyond. In fact, large striped awnings were later installed over the windows to reduce the temperature and glare in summer. In 1941 the rooms were the subject of a painting by the artist Sir John Lavery which vividly depicts the interior with the slightly confusing perspective created when the mirrored partitions were in use. On the upper floor there were nine bedrooms for the use of the owners and their guests. The floor of the atrium seems to have been laid with stone or perhaps marble, but the main reception rooms were laid with oak parquet flooring.

The Palladian theme was continued in the interior with neo-classical columns and large stone fireplaces. From the French windows in the central bay, visitors stepped out onto a broad 160' long stone-ballustraded terrace which ran right across the back of the building and round the sides, connecting with the Winter Garden on the east side. The terrace mirrored the shape of the back of the building, having a large central bay with wide curving steps which swept down from either side onto a wide lawn, where comfortable wicker chairs and tables were laid out in the summer. Beyond that a banked flower bed separated a lower lawn with a large semi-circular stone bench of classical design. This lower lawn later contained one, possibly two tennis courts.

Falconwood cost Lord Truro around £20,000 to build, (or around £2.5 million pounds at 2020 prices), though it should be said that in 1907 a correspondent for the *London Evening Standard* thought this to be an underestimate as the Winter Garden alone cost the equivalent of '*a good suburban house*'. [137]

To make the site more attractive, the Crown Commissioners seem to have given their approval for a wide, straight ride to be cut through the woodland, in a south-easterly line from the back of the house, towards what is now Falconwood railway station. This feature gave the house a clear view over Oxleas Wood to the hills and woodland of rural Kent. A small discrete gate, the base of which still exists, probably gave access to the woodland from the ornate terraces and pond below the lawn, and visitors were able to wander along a range of paths through the trees. Where the ride levelled out at the bottom of the hill – and before it intersected with the ride cut through the woods by William Coulthard - there appears to have been a circular feature which may have been another pond with a fountain, or an ornamental stone flower bed. Either way, this feature has long since disappeared.

Truro filled the house with custom-made carpets to his own design, as well as statuary and paintings, including at least two Van Dyck portraits; and statues of 'Diana' by Holme Cardwell,

---

[137] *London Evening Standard.* 10 June 1907.

and 'The Bather' by Matthew Cotes Wyatt who had produced the infamous equestrian statue of the Duke of Wellington which was commissioned for the arch at Hyde Park Corner.

Despite all the wealth lavished upon Falconwood, Lord Truro's occupancy was not a particularly happy one, nor was it without controversy. It seems that his wealth and desire for privacy, attracted exactly the wrong attention. In March, 1866, he had fencing installed along the Dover Road; however, in doing so he appears to have enclosed an area of land which was not his. Objections were raised but as the parishes of neither Eltham nor Plumstead could agree whose side of the parish boundary had been infringed, his Lordship was acquitted. [138] Eight months later one of his Lordship's horses was stolen from the stables during the night, along with bridle and hunting saddle. Bizarrely, the horse was found in an adjoining meadow the next morning, minus the tack. Eventually a man by the name of George Ryan was arrested after trying unsuccessfully to sell the saddle and bridle at nearby Erith and Dartford. It was thought he had abandoned the horse after it had rejected his attempts to saddle it.

In 1877, Lord and Lady Truro's coach was being loaded for a trip to the Continent when it was discovered that a quantity of valuable jewellery was missing.[139] The items had apparently been packed by the housekeeper and included an enamelled gold locket and brooch, pearls, emerald clasps, an antique

---

[138] It may be recalled that disputes between the two parishes over the exact course of the boundary had been rumbling on for years. On this occasion, Truro was the beneficiary of their inability to come to a sensible agreement.
[139] It is possible that in fact their carriage was attacked and robbed on the Dover Road just after leaving Falconwood – according to a retrospective comment in the *Biggleswade Chronicle* in August 1898

cameo brooch depicting St George and the dragon, diamond studded locket, gold bracelets and gold and coral chains. The items do not appear to have been recovered and Truro responded by using his position in the House of Lords to launch a scathing attack on the police. Almost simultaneously a large black turkey was stolen from the grounds of the estate and at least one satirical journalist made use of the moment to lampoon his Lordship's response to his 'poultry' losses. [140]

Charles Robert Wilde, Lord Truro. A satirical portrait. 1887.

At this precise moment, Lord Truro's butler chose to resign. There are no details to explain the reasons for this, though it is tempting to want to link the reason to the thefts. A replacement was immediately sought for the position of 'butler and valet'. The successful candidate had to be aged around 31, married without family (so presumably accommodation and employment for the spouse would be provided) and he had to be 6' tall! In the event, as we shall see shortly, the lucky candidate proved to be a poor choice.

---

[140] See for example the *Edinburgh Evening News*. 14 August 1877.

Within months, Falconwood was beset by a bizarre and controversial event. In 1838 Charles Wilde had married a woman by the name of Lucy Ray, and in due course she received the Title of Baroness Truro. They had no children but she occupied Falconwood with her husband until the middle of October 1879, when she appears to have died suddenly. Under what might be interpreted as strangely sinister circumstances, Truro had her body placed in a lightly built plain wooden 'box' and buried during the night somewhere in the lawn in front of the house. His Lordship and the gardener were apparently the only witnesses to the interment. Lady Truro's family and some local residents raised objections, but the local authority had no power to intervene provided the grave was a minimum 4' deep and well-marked. Truro gave assurances that in due course a marble monument would be erected over the grave and there the matter rested. However, as far as is known, no grave marker was ever put in position and when, over fifteen years later Lady Truro's family attempted an exhumation, the grave could not be found. On the contrary, according to several sources, after repeated attempts to locate the grave, only one containing the bones of a dog were found.

Perhaps the circumstances of his wife's death and interment left some darker shadow on Lord Truro. Either way, his luck did not improve. Or perhaps it did. In December 1882, Truro had been obliged to employ yet another replacement butler. This time a 30 year–old man by the name of John Walter Cowley (or Corley). In September, of the following year, one of the Falconwood footmen, Gerald Keighly, had attended a fancy dress ball at the Kensington Town Hall on his day off. There, to his astonishment, he had seen the butler, Cowley, parading round the ballroom dressed in Lord Truro's state regalia, including hat and gown, ruffles, cuffs, a diamond chain about his neck and diamond buckles on his shoes.

The amazed footman returned to Falconwood, where he duly reported what he had seen. The Butler's personal quarters were searched and a quantity of valuable items were discovered, including yet more of his lordship's state costume and a number of waistcoats. The police were summoned and Cowley/Corley was arrested though he claimed that the stolen items actually belonged to his wife (who does not appear to have been there at the time). For his crime, Cowley/Corley was sentenced to a tough five years of penal servitude. Such was the penalty for robbing or attempting to rob a member of the peerage.

In 1885, Truro was appointed Volunteer Aide de Camp to Queen Victoria. Almost simultaneously, he decided to abandon Falconwood and put the house up for sale. But, before that could happen, he travelled to Rome where he died suddenly in March 1891. He left behind a summons for unpaid rates from the Plumstead Vestry committee (who presumably had finally ironed out their boundary dispute with their colleagues in Eltham!)

Once Truro's estate had cleared probate, the house and estate with all its contents and effects were put up for sale. The sales catalogue issued in the following October gave detailed information about Truro's art collection, which in addition to the aforesaid Van Dyke's, included a large collection of mainly early-18th century silver-ware and a large library collection of antique books and prints. Other paintings included a collection of Dutch landscapes, and watercolours; collections of porcelain and clocks, antique and modern furniture. In the grounds, his lordship's state carriage, a phaeton, four farm carts and a cart-mare were for sale, as were chaff and turnip cutters, and a large number of greenhouse and bedding plants.

The lease of the house had a further seventy-one years to run, and it was purchased by Sir Clarence Smith who was a City stockbroker who had just been elected the liberal MP for Kingston-upon-Hull. Smith's parliamentary career was relatively short; he was defeated in an election three years later and was never able to regain a seat in parliament. He appears to have been a keen Wesleyan. For many years he was Secretary of the Metropolitan Chapel Building Fund, and he used Falconwood to host a number of charitable functions, including in 1901, a garden party for 200 Wesleyan soldiers and wives from the nearby Woolwich Barracks. By 1905 he had become a Director of the Star Assurance Society, but he no longer had need of Falconwood. In 1907 the house was once again put up for sale. The *London Evening Standard*, in reporting this, described it in a rather interesting way:

'Falcon Wood , on the southern slope of Shooters Hill, is a very beautiful residential property ...When Shooters Hill was yet a distance from Town, it was a highly esteemed residential locality, and no wonder, the views of Kentish scenery from Shooters Hill being very fine. Moreover, it was never contemplated by the builder of this fine place that anything would ever come between the wind and its nobility. The 40 acres comprised in the estate contain some exquisite spots of rusticity and woodlands. There is an imposing stone terrace ...whence the view of the lovely country for miles around unfolding itself must be a keen enjoyment... Altogether Falcon Wood is a gem of a place, and is held from the Crown for a remaining term of 56 years of the lease at a ground

rent of £300 a year.' [141]

Unfortunately, although Smith made several attempts to sell the lease he was unsuccessful. According to Enid Bagnold, the house was too grand for the local army personnel and it was difficult to heat – therefore expensive to run. [142]

In the end Smith gave up and simply surrendered the house to the Crown Commissioners. Fortunately for them, they were more successful and in 1908 a new occupier was found. This was probably the most flamboyant personality the hill has known, the Baroness Catherine d'Erlanger and her husband Emile.

---

[141] *London Evening Standard.* 10 June 1907.

[142] *Enid Bagnold's Autobiography.* P 101

Chapter 13 Enid and the Baroness.

In 1908 Falconwood was bought by Baron Emile d'Erlanger and his wife Catherine. The couple were fabulously wealthy and had the behaviour to match. Catherine came from French aristocracy, being the daughter of the Marquis Rochegude who not only owned a chateau and land in Provence, but more pragmatically, had a ship-owning business based in Le Havre.

Emile was the second son of the banker Frederic d'Erlanger and followed his father into the banking business. In addition to owning a major continental bank, the d'Erlangers had railway and transport interests in England and Emile, who was a major City of London banker, was appointed president of several of the companies. In 1895, he had married the 21-year-old Catherine (her real name was Rose Marie Antoinette Katherine Robert d'Aqueria de Rochegude – though she doesn't appear to have used this) and the two had settled in London.

Emile had a passion for travel and was impressively multilingual. He was also regarded as a rather cultured man and a passionate collector of antiques and art. He had assembled a valuable collection, some of which was put on display at Falconwood, but the couple also had an impressive town house at 139 Piccadilly, which was affectionately known as 'Pic'.[143]

It is at this point that we pick up the thread of the story of Enid Bagnold. As mentioned earlier, with the commencement of the war in 1914, Enid moved back to her parents' home at Warren Wood. Now that she was back at Shooters Hill, away from the distractions of Frank Harris and his literary circle, she became interested in the new neighbours at Falconwood. One weekend afternoon, in a moment of boldness which was typical of her, she literally pushed her way through the hedge which separated the two properties, to go and introduce herself.

Her timing was immaculate. Apparently, the Baroness had just installed a tennis court on the lawn below the house and, together with some house guests, was trying to fathom out how to play. Enid was apparently quite a keen tennis player and was immediately seized upon to explain both the rules and playing techniques. By the end of the afternoon she had not only been welcomed by the Baroness, she had been warmly accepted into their social circle.

This is not altogether surprising. Catherine d'Erlanger was an astonishing socialite who loved to surround herself with unusual, sometimes eccentric, often young and always entertaining people. She was financial patron to Cecil Beaton and Sergei Diaghilev, and the Ballet Russe de Monte Carlo. Her more famous acquaintances included, at one time or another, the composers Ravel and Debussy, the dancer Nijinsky and the writer Proust.

By 1914 Falconwood had become the venue for regular weekend parties at which, apparently, no form of behaviour was ta-

---

[143] The house had once been the home of Lord Byron.

boo and anything could be taken to excess. At the centre of everything was the tall, striking figure of Catherine d'Erlanger with her vivid red hair, flamboyant dress and extravagant behaviour. Enid Bagnold left a brilliant portrait of her.

Catherine, Baroness d'Erlanger, around 1925.

'She was tall, red-haired, with nostrils that flared like an Arab horse, and a way of dressing that was not chic, but grand. She had no French art of dressing. She spoke rapidly a slight accent tingling in her words, and gave out an alarming sense that one's replies must be brief. She had a social cruelty, logical and French. She was haughty and shallow and swift in her judgements. Her health was unassailable. She went to a dentist and he couldn't pull out a tooth. Her delight in each day sprang alive as

she woke.' [144]

Enid was fascinated by the Baroness's attitude towards dress. In the morning she would carelessly throw on anything; clothes which Enid described as 'jumble sale-ish'. But in the evening it would be Parisian haute couture. Somehow the Baroness had little idea of the traditional convention regarding dress espoused by the English well-to-do, e.g. the difference between clothes for 'town' and clothes for 'country'. More excruciatingly for Enid, once the Baroness had taken her under her wing as her latest protégé, she had a habit of randomly selecting dresses from her own wardrobe for her to wear; clothing which Enid considered not to her taste at all. In fact, so close did Enid and the Baroness become, she was given her own room in the house at Piccadilly.

Already accustomed to a relaxed Bohemian lifestyle, Enid found herself drawn closer into the cosmopolitan Falconwood circle, attracted by its brilliance, lack of inhibition, affluence and, frankly, danger. She was confused and mesmerised by Catherine especially, who openly kept a transvestite lover by the name of Hugo 'Hugh' Rumbold. It was a relationship that Enid could never quite understand. Perhaps made more confusing by the fact that Rumbold was a captain in the Guards regiment who served with distinction in both the Boer and First World War. By profession he was also a stage designer and friend of Charlie Chaplin and Noel Coward.

On one occasion the Baroness confessed to Enid that she had really bought Falconwood as a 'joke' because she found it so amusing to make her guests drive through the poorer suburb

---

[144] *Enid Bagnold's Autobiography.* P103.

of Bermondsey to get to her weekend parties. And what parties there were. Enid was enthralled to find herself socialising freely with likeminded young people, writers and artists included. They were not quite, as she admitted, of the same artistic or literary gravity as some of her other acquaintances (e.g. Walter Sickert or Augustus John, or Edward Thomas), but they were gay and fashionable. At Falconwood she met the likes of Nancy Cunard (the shipping heiress who was also a writer, anti-racist and (later) anti-fascist activist); Phyllis Boyd ('lovely and kind' – married the Comte Henri de Janze in 1922 and close friend of the eccentric socialite Lady Diana Manners); the Marchesa Casati (a hugely eccentric Italian patron of the arts who often wore live snakes as jewellery); [145] Princess Marie Murat, and the Italian princess and actor Maria Carmi; the witty Lady Drogheda was also a regular. Then there were the men; the French writer Paul Morand (later Nazi sympathiser); Matila Ghyka (a Romanian prince, author and diplomat), there was the prominent Tory politician Duff Cooper (Viscount Norwich, who married Lady Diana Manners in 1919) and his political colleague Basil Blackwood (Earl of Ava but better known as a lawyer and the book illustrator 'BB'). There Enid also met the comedian George Grossmith, (co-author of *Diary of a Nobody*), and Prince Antoine Bibesco, a Roumanian diplomat, with whom she had an affair. Two other influential regulars at Falconwood were Ivor Guest (Viscount Wimborne) and his brother Freddie. Ivor was not only wealthy, he also had a reputation as a womaniser and there was certainly a brief connection between him and Enid, but she regarded it as unsatisfactory and it didn't last long.

---

[145] She was also famous for attending one of her own balls with two chained lions in hand.

The drawing room at Falconwood, 1917, by Sir John Lavery. The painting was commissioned by Catherine d'Erlanger.

The Falconwood parties usually lasted all weekend. On fine days there were often tennis 'tournaments', with guests required to spectate from the grassy bank above the lawn, while servants delivered drinks on silver trays. Sometimes the parties transferred to Piccadilly and then extended even later into the night. On these occasions the Baroness and her companions would sometimes lapse into the sort of behaviour for which the wealthy could often be notorious. For example, it was not unknown for the Baroness to lead the party to a favoured restaurant in Soho, after midnight and hours after it had closed, and bang on the doors demanding to be fed. On other occasions she would book a box at a West End theatre for the opening night of a play, and then arrive there with her party just in time for the final act – causing considerable fuss and disturbance in the process.

But there was a darker side to the Falconwood parties. As will have been noted, some of the younger men were drawn into the conflict of the First World War and as the war progressed their numbers diminished, leaving haunting gaps at the table. One of the Baroness's friends was the handsome young air-ace, Gilbert Mapplebeck, known as 'Gib' to his friends.

Mapplebeck had originally joined the army in 1910. But in 1912 he decided to pay for flying lessons which enabled him to transfer to the Royal Flying Corps in the following year. In August 1914, he was sent to France and there served with distinction despite being shot down several times behind enemy lines, wounded and temporarily captured, before making his escape back to England. Following his return, in 1915, he was appointed as the Officer Commanding No. 10 Reserve Squadron, based at the Joyce Green aerodrome at Dartford, some dozen miles to the north-east of Shooters Hill. This was convenient because Gib was also one of the invitees to the parties at Falconwood - if not one of the Baroness's protégés.

Not long after his appointment he invited the Baroness to bring a party down to Joyce Green to watch him give an aerial display. The Baroness wrote to him several days later expressing her delight in a letter which is characteristic:

'Bravo! It was lovely to see you. We all lay flat on the grass & were quite sick with fright & had to have cocktails! Do come

again soon for any meal you like.' [146]

The letter was signed by the Baroness and eight other people, including Hugo Rumbold and Paul Morand. Whilst Enid was not one of the party, she and Mapplebeck were certainly acquainted, if only recently. Not many days before they had been playing tennis at Falconwood when Enid had fallen and torn her dress. Rather gallantly, the young Captain Mapplebeck had given her his tie pin to carry out a temporary repair. She obviously made quite an impression on him

On 24th August, Mapplebeck arrived unexpectedly at Falconwood driving a new car which had been issued to him by the War Office. He had already been invited there for dinner that evening, but was proud of his new appointment and insisted on driving the Baroness and Enid, together with the Baroness's 13-year-old daughter and a Miss Peto, to visit the airfield. Unbeknown to his guests, he was actually scheduled to test a plane for potential Royal Flying Corps service, [147] and his plan was to put on a private display for them. Shortly after their arrival at the airfield, he excused himself and went off to climb into his plane leaving them to wander round the airfield in the company of a Sergeant Major. Minutes later they saw a plane take to the sky, and correctly identified its pilot at Gib Mapplebeck. Enthralled, they watched as he put the plane through its paces, flying out over the nearby Thames and then reappearing suddenly. As they watched, Mapplebeck put the plane into a climb and then brought it down in a series of spectacular banking spirals. Suddenly, their excitement turned to fear and

---

[146] *The Extraordinary Life and Times of Captain G.W. Mapplebeck DSO.* Peter Mapplebeck. 2015.
[147] The plane was a French Moreane Saulnier. Mapplebeck had already flown one of these and was not impressed by its airworthiness.

then horror. The plane's manoeuvres became sharper, steeper and 50' from the ground it tilted into a vertical dive and smashed into the ground. Officers and ground crew rushed to the crash site but the young pilot was seriously injured and unconscious. He was rushed to hospital in Dartford, but died on the way. [148] Desperately shocked, the Baroness and Enid made their way home. Not long after, the d'Erlangers shut-up Falconwood for the duration of the war. The fun had somehow evaporated.

Towards the end of the war Enid enrolled as a Voluntary Ambulance Driver. She was trained in automobile maintenance and repair, and sent to France as the war ended. The story of her experiences there were recalled in her next novel, *The Happy Foreigner* (published in 1920).

The departure of the d'Erlangers from Falconwood didn't completely sever the ties between Catherine and Enid but their relationship seems to have become more distant. The d'Erlangers had other interests which the end of the European war meant could now be resumed. These were to include a villa in Italy and a night club in Hollywood.

Enid also now had other contacts. One of these was the literary socialite Lady Ottoline Morrell, who was a supporter of D H Lawrence and the Bloomsbury Group, some of whom Enid had

---

[148] Sadly, the official RFC inquiry into the cause of the accident stated: *'The accident appears to have been due to the machine "spinning" on a heavily banked turn, the pilot not having sufficient speed and height to regain control before hitting the earth...Conclusion:- The accident was due to an unfortunate error of judgement on the pilot's part.' Ibid. p138.*

already met. But one of the most significant of her contacts was Irene Cooper Willis who lived (or had lived) close to Shooters Hill. Irene was one of the first women to be admitted to Girton College, and on graduation she had become a barrister – and a convinced socialist. Enid and Irene met (probably in 1916) and became close friends. Irene introduced Enid to another of her friends, the writer and aristocrat, Vita Sackville West. Vita and Enid also became friends, on one occasion meeting for lunch with Violet Trefusis (one of Vita's lovers). It was probably through Vita that Enid met John Galsworthy and HG Wells, with whom she stayed friends (on and off) for many years. Through Ottoline Morrell and Vita, Enid was also introduced to Virginia Woolf, but it seems that the two did not get on terribly well, and Virginia declined to write a review for the *The Happy Foreigner.*

Vita also introduced Enid to Sir Roderick Jones, the owner of Reuters, and before long he was making regular trips to Warren Wood to visit her. The two of them married in July 1920, though Enid's connection with Warren Wood continued and she stayed there during the pregnancy of her first two children. [149]

Enid's final break with the Baroness was rather spectacular and somewhat controversial. In 1924 Enid published her third novel *Serena Blandish.* The book was actually a sharp satire based on her experiences with the d'Erlangers. Her father, Colonel Bagnold, had been given the manuscript to read before publication and he was horrified. He condemned it as a 'loathsome production' and tried to persuade her not the publish it.

---

[149] The writer Rudyard Kipling was a friend of Roderick Jones, and godparent to their first child.

She ignored him but to avoid his embarrassment, published it anonymously.

The novel sold out in three months and received many enthusiastic reviews from publications like the *London Evening Standard* and the *Times Literary Supplement*. One review described it as *'a bitter comedy of manners, blithely capturing the wicked and gay spirit of post-war London society.'* However, the source which inspired the novel did not just relate to post-war society. The main character in the book is the Countess Flor fi Folio, and this is how Enid described her in the book:

"She had the mind of a child, the energy of a wild animal, and the health of an immortal. She was no snob, and though still beautiful and very rich she had a delightful flair for bad society. There had been a time when the most exclusive persons had accepted her invitations, but having everything in the world that she wanted she had tired of them, and her growing fondness for the disreputable, the curious and shady, for all quacks and purveyors of sham goods, sham art, bogus literature, her passion for imitation fur, imitation tortoiseshell, imitated antiquity, had led her at last to the pitch of appreciating an imitation aristocracy, and with the cunning of a child, which thinks it takes in all the world, it had delighted her to palm off bogus dukes upon genuine duchesses. She adored the abnormal and the extravagant."

It might have been something of a distortion, even of exaggeration. However, to anyone who knew her and the Falconwood set, it was obvious that this was based on Catherine d'Erlanger. Catherine knew it too and promptly tried to sue Enid for libel. The latter, however, had a very capable defence barrister. When the matter came to Court, he read the offending description aloud in Court and then, turning to the Baroness, asked her point blank if she recognised herself in the description. Unaware that a trap had been set, she answered 'no'. The barrister then pointed out that if the description was not about her, it could hardly be considered a libel against her. The Baroness's case collapsed. And so too, finally, did the relationship between Enid and the d'Erlangers.

Although the d'Erlangers virtually abandoned Falconwood after the war, they did not do so completely. In fact in 1924 they decided to convert it into a hotel, leaving a manager to run it on a day-to-day basis. Sadly, whether it was too uncomfortable (Enid had said it was hard to heat), or just in the wrong place, or too expensive, Falconwood did not prosper as a hotel. In 1932 the d'Erlangers decided they had had enough of the place and they surrendered the lease once again to the Crown Commissioners.

The hotel was taken over by a W. F. Mills, who promptly submitted an application for a licence to hold regular dances in the 'drawing-room' for 150 people. A licence was granted [150] and during the 1930s and 1940s a succession of would-be hotel owners tried to make a successful business from the building. Adverts in local papers publicised tea dances and balls in the elegant ball room, and the hotel became the location for wedding receptions. All of the bedrooms were ensuite; the convenience of the near-by golf-course was emphasised, as was the fact that the building would make an 'admirable home for military gentlemen and their families.' A postcard available to guests at the time featured a photograph of the south side of the building. It is clear from this that use was still being made

---

[150] The curtains in the 'ball-room' had to be changed as they did not meet the ten fire regulations.

of the tennis court, and that tables and chairs still stood on the lawn. But there are subtle signs of neglect too, of 'standards slipped'. Towels and table cloths have been left untidily on chairs on the lawn, and the presence of a tennis ball abandoned on the court is suggestive of a lack of enthusiasm.

The attempt did little good. Customer numbers fell, especially during World War Two when the building was perhaps too obvious a target for the bombers of the Luftwaffe who regularly flew over the hill on their way to or from blitzing London. By the end of the war, the last lessee had given up and the building was empty. The windows were boarded-up and the shrubs over ran the flower beds once so lovingly managed by the Baroness. Then the trees began to reclaim their inheritance

In the 1950s, the London County Council purchased the site to complete their acquisition of Oxleas Woodlands for the public. There were no plans in place for the old mansion on the hill. It continued to moulder and crack, and the ornamental features in the grounds slowly disappeared. In 1954 a draftsman was sent down to make some records of the building. The architectural line drawings he produced, together with the plan of the ground floor, are not only informative, they provide a sensitive and almost affectionate portrait of the building. The grass may have grown overlong around its foot, but it is still an attractive building. Unlike the stark greyness of the wartime photograph, the drawings make it look appealing. Then in 1958/59 the LCC gave up on the building. Vandals broke in repeatedly, lit fires in the ballroom, smashed windows and what remained of the chandeliers. The LCC decided to demolish the building, and almost without notice or public record, the once magnificent neo-Palladian mansion was destroyed.

Vandalised and boarded-up. Falconwood just before demolition in the late 1950s. (City of London Collection).

Slightly to the north-west though, Warren Wood survived. Edward Wilde's house might have been more modest than that of either his cousin or brother, but it was perhaps this which gave it slightly greater longevity. It was simply more affordable and adaptable to other uses. Colonel Bagnold was still in residence when the Second World War began. Very pragmatically, he had a solid looking bomb shelter built in the garden not very far from the house. But in 1944 he died and the house was sold. Its final few years were very unsettled. The lease from the Crown Commissioners was due to expire in 1963, so by the late 1950s it became increasingly unlettable. The last lessee, a Miss Moore, submitted a request that the final few years of the lease be reassigned to the Ockenden Venture so that the house could be used as a hostel for refugee children. The request appears to have been declined and Miss Moore remained in residence until the lease expired. She was then offered a quarterly tenancy, but finding this too uncertain, she decided to leave. For a while Warren Wood was used as a hostel by the Save the Children Fund, but then it was abandoned again and this time more or less permanently. It stayed vacant for years as the garden grew rampant and the lawns vanished under holly and hazel. Enid, who still loved the place, watched sadly from a distance as the building deteriorated.

During the 1970s, inevitably, it attracted the attention of vandals. And, in the early 1980s, after it had finally been handed over to the local authority, it was demolished. By this time Enid was no longer there to witness it. She died in 1981 with dementia and having suffered for years following a disastrous hip-operation. Her literary career had been a mixture of huge success and controversy. She had written several very successful plays and novels, including *National Velvet* which was made into an even more successful film; and *The Chalk Garden*, which ran at The Haymarket in the West End for twenty-three months. But she had had some very dark moments too. In 1938 she was sent by *The Times* to Germany, to write a feature on the Nazi regime. Her hosts very cleverly hoodwinked her, showing her exactly what they wanted her to see – and blinding her to the reality of Nazism. She returned to England full of enthusiasm for a country which – she had been led to believe –

was full of youth, enthusiasm and energy. Like so many other people, she saw a country that was the anti-thesis of the old regimes that had plunged Europe into the disaster of the First World War; and the opposite of the crusty old regime that still ruled Britain. She very publicly sang the praises of the Nazis, and most of her friends (including H G Wells) disowned her. [151] Although she had success with *The Chalk Garden* most of her other plays failed to achieve any success. As several critics noted of her later plays, her viewpoint was that of a wealthy and aged member of the minor aristocracy and her plays showed badly after the revelation of John Osborne's *Look Back in Anger* in 1956.

But all of that has taken us far away from Warren Wood and Shooters Hill. Today the site of Warren Wood is all but lost beneath the trees and foliage that have reclaimed what was rightfully theirs. The low platform that the house was built on can still be traced with careful scrutiny, and traces of the demolition debris exist embedded into the compact surface of the woodland. The blast shelter installed by Colonel Bagnold is the most obvious clue to the house's location – an ugly structure which echoes the ugly reason for its existence. It is not really a happy relic of the building or its occupants. Perhaps the only real memento of the house is the remnant of the hedge, through which Enid walked to go in search of the d'Erlangers.

Today though, the site of Falconwood is a pleasant spot. When the LCC demolished the building, they virtually eradicated it and its garden features completely from the landscape. What

---

[151] HG Wells's criticism stung her badly. They had been close friends, and in (probably insincere) retaliation to his admonition, she threatened to join Moseley's Blackshirts!

they left, though, was a pleasant grassy meadow where the house had stood. Surrounded by trees that almost screen the noise of traffic on the nearby Shooters Hill Road, it is a quiet, tranquil spot where butterflies dance in the summer and cowslips can be found in the spring. The meadow tilts down slightly, presenting itself fully to the sun and on the hillside below, a series of terraces which Enid once likened to the superstructure of an ocean liner. If you stand at the bottom edge of the meadow, with your back to the ornamental ride that drives down into the woodland itself, you can just make out a slight ridge half way up the meadow where the Baroness's guests sat sipping champagne to watch the tennis.

Chapter 14 – The Enigma of Summer Court

Historical research can be hugely rewarding – even exciting. It can also be wearyingly disappointing. Ask any historian. You'll know what it's like also if you have tried researching family history. There are gaps where there shouldn't be in the information you want; there are false trails that can mislead you for hours. And then there are puzzles, things which simply don't make sense because time has played its tricks with memory and records and the landscape.

Virtually all that you have read in this book so far is the result of hours and hours of research in archives, books and even – especially nowadays, and with caution - online. The historian is always looking for source material, comparing what s/he finds, seeking corroboration, evaluating material, and always, desperately, trying to fathom out where information might have gone, what it might be, and what might have happened to it. Sometimes it's like doing a jigsaw puzzle with half the pieces missing. Except that when putting our findings together we can't resort to checking under the table or looking accusingly at the dog!

Sometimes, the information just eludes us. And even worse, sometimes when we finally conclude the evidence has vanished, and we commit ourselves to print – that missing information comes to light. It is infuriating, even embarrassing at times. But it is all part of writing history.

So now I have to confess I have reached this impasse, and there is nothing to do but own up to it. For there is a building which should feature in this story of Oxleas Woodlands which has proved to be pretty elusive.

The series of 25-inch to the mile ordnance survey maps produced in the later-19th century were amongst the finest ever produced for showing detail. The sheets for Shooters Hill dated after 1866 are a vital and accurate source of information on the woodlands as they were recorded at that time, especially when it comes to considering the houses that were built on Crown land. They show Castle Wood House, Mayfield (Jackwood) and Wood Lodge, with the layout of the houses, outbuildings, grounds and pathways etc. The following edition, surveyed in 1894, shows the houses built later, e.g. Warren Wood and Falconwood. But when we look at the map detail for Warren Wood we see a significantly larger property on its western side. It was called Summer Court, and it stood in extensive grounds. From the map we can see that the house was approached by two drives. One approached the house from the Dover Road, passing a lodge. A second, longer driveway approached the house from the south, from Crown Woods Lane (just south of the lodge for Jackwood House). From the map we can see that the house itself was substantial, set in large grounds with winding pathways – with a few trees. Unlike its neighbour Warren Wood, which the map clearly shows to have been set in the woodland itself, Summer Court stood in much more open, formal grounds.

According to the 19th century local historian and journalist, W T Vincent, the house was built by the shipbuilder William Henry Courtenay in 1866. He also states that Courtenay sublet the property to the iron and steel merchant William Carter in 1870. There is some question about this as neither the house nor any occupants appear in the Census records for 1871. But the Register of Leases in the Crown Commissioners records at the National Archive do confirm that 4 acres and 1 rood were leased to Courtenay in December 1865.

The 1871 Census return also records the fact that by that year Courtenay was both 'out of business' (i.e. bankrupt) and living in nearby Lee. So it is possible that he built the house and then had to abandon it when his business failed. The Carter family were certainly in occupation in 1881 at the time of the next Census. So, if WT Vincent is correct, the house must have been built at some point between 1865-1871.

The Crown Commissioners' Register of Leases also records that a new lease for Summer Court was issued in 1887, and although the lessee is not specified, it must have been the 64-year-old William Carter. In 1881 he was in partnership with his 32-year old son Henry, who also lived at Summer Court along with William's unmarried sister, Jane.

The Carters sold Summer Court in 1899 and a careful scrutiny of the information provided by the estate agent provides us with interesting detail about the house and its grounds – actually more than was usually available in these occasions. There is the standard information regarding the house itself, which is important since no visual record seems to have survived. We are told, that the house was of two storeys only, though the individual rooms were apparently spacious with high ceilings. On the ground floor there was a 'fine' entrance hall leading to a large billiard room, a morning room which probably faced south as it was described as 'cheerful'. A drawing room 30' x 24' and a dining room with a large bay window. A lavatory appears to have been installed on the ground floor and there was the usual suite of service rooms including the housekeeper's room, butler's pantry, large kitchen, larder, dairy and offices for staff. On the first floor there were eleven bedrooms and dressing rooms, (more than any of the other buildings in the hill) - and two bathrooms! In the grounds stood stables for four horses, coach house and wood store, a conservatory, vinery, cucumber house etc. From the ordnance survey map, it would seem that a range of greenhouses stood against the western perimeter of the estate, near additional tool and potting sheds.

But the sales information also contains some unusual and revealing information. So, for example, we are told that the house was *'tastefully decorated and fitted with the comforts and conveniences that only a long occupying ownership can supply.'* [152] This suggests that the leasehold hadn't changed for some time and possibly confirms that William Carter may have been in residence there for over twenty years.

We are also told that the grounds were *'well wooded and shrubbed and laid out with great taste in wilderness and shrubbery walks, fernery, tennis and other lawns, and well stocked kitchen and vegetable gardens'.* [153] This is reminiscent of Jack-

---

[152] *Kentish Independent.* 15 July 1899.
[153] Ibid.

wood, and of course, it was probably expected that the owner of a fine house would also have tastefully laid-out grounds and a well-cared for garden. Most of the larger houses kept a full-time gardener in residence, though some owners, of course, were known to be very hands-on. Either way it is an indication of where the owner' interests lay.

The Carters' occupation of the building had not been without tragedy. William had at least three other children, though they were not at Summer Court when the census was recorded in 1881. One of these, possibly the youngest, was suffering from some form of mental illness. In November 1889, according to a story reported in the *South Wales Daily News,* she left the house to go and visit a friend. When she failed to return, the family became alarmed, and servants were sent out to help search for her. In the grounds of the house next door to Summer Court stood a small patch of woodland and in the centre of this was a large pool. It was here that the gardener found her body; her hat, jacket and gloves had been left neatly folded beside the water.

As we have already noted, in 1899 the leasehold of the house and its estate were put up for sale. The following September all of the contents of the house were removed and taken for sale at an auction house in Woolwich. It seems that every item of furniture and fitting was ruthlessly removed along with three pianos, a collection of about 40 'valuable' pictures and paintings, two iron safes and seven chickens! [154] The older William Carter would have been 82 by this time if he was still alive, however, it seems more likely that his son, William Carter Junior had become the head of the household. He was a

---

[154] *Kentish Mercury* 8 September. 1899

ship owner with a ship brokering business, with offices in both Leadenhall and Billiter Streets in the City. In April 1900 his company collapsed and he was declared bankrupt. It seems most likely that the house and its contents were seized by the official receivers. Hence the sale of the household contents.

The lease was purchased by a building contractor by the name of Joseph Randall, who moved in with his wife Martha who died there in 1906. Joseph and his eldest son were in partnership with premises at Warren Lane in Woolwich, from where they carried out a range of building services, specialising in steel and concrete construction. In 1912, they went into partnership with a Leonard Kirk (forming the company of Randall & Kirk) and attempted to negotiate some major contracts. In 1914 they were in the process of finalising proposals for a dock-building contract in Harwich when the declaration of war brought all such projects to a halt. The company certainly struggled for the next few years and by 1920 seem to have been in serious difficulty. It probably collapsed around 1924.

We don't know when the Randall's left Summer Court, but at some point during the 1930s it became the home of Sir Andrew Scott, who had been the secretary of Lloyd's Register – and was in that position at the time of the sinking of the *Titanic*. He died in 1939, still resident at Summer Court.

What happened for the next couple of decades is still a mystery. However, in 1962 the site was taken over by Greenwich Council who used the house as a homeless hostel for a number of years, installing extra bathrooms and a larger kitchen. They appear to have come under some pressure because the Greater London Council (who succeeded the London County Council) had to remind them that they had acquired the site under the

Open Spaces Act, which obliged them to make it part of a public amenity. [155] This seems to have finally prompted the demolition of the house, and the site became one of the depots for Greenwich Council's Parks & Open Department. Although the house had been demolished, what appears to have been the coach house certainly survived until 2012 when the site was taken over by Hadlow College as a Horticultural Skills Centre.

Summer Court is the only house on the hill which appears to have left so little trace of its original building – of course the site is not easily accessible, so it is less easy to check. However, if you wander through the adjacent woodland, it is possible to find – in addition to the rubbish and the rotting remains of an abandoned car – a few lumps of shaped Portland stone which just may have come from the demolition debris of the house. [156]

---

[155] GLC Records at the London Metropolitan Archive. DG/AR/6/44

[156] Without further evidence and/or photographs it is impossible to know what material was used in the construction of Summer Court. Of course, Falconwood was also built of Portland stone, but it seems hardly possible that building debris could have travelled that distance.

Chapter 15 Shepherdleas – in which the author takes a ramble and wanders off the track a bit!

I haven't been able to find out when exactly, Shepherdleas Wood got its own identity. The Andrews map of 1769 show that all of what we now call the 'Oxleas Woodlands' stretched as a single entity from Eltham Common in the north-west, about five miles to the hamlet of Blendon in the south-east. However, on that map the whole woodland is named 'Runnets Wood' – but this a common type of error: in this case the cartographer appears to have carelessly taken the name of one of the lesser woods to the south (i.e. Upper or Lower Rennets Wood) and simply misapplied it to the whole woodland. By the time the much more accurate Crown estate map of 1807 was drawn up, Shepherdleas was clearly identified as 'Shepherds Leys' (sic), so it must have been well known by that name by that time.

Today Shepherdleas is sandwiched between the Rochester Way to the north, and the Bexleyheath Railway line and the motorway status A2 to the south. The southern part of the wood was shaved off by the railway line in the early 1890s. The eastern section of the current Rochester Way, between what is now Falconwood Station and Welling Way, was originally known as Sanders Lane. This appears to have been a narrow country lane which ran through the northern edge of Shepherdleas until it connected with Crown Woods Lane between that wood and Oxleas. When the 'Shooters Hill Bypass' was built in the late 1920s, the new road ran eastwards following the route of Sanders Lane and shaving off the top of Shepherdleas wood.

The Rochester Way in the late 1930s, looking east. Jack Wood lies behind the houses to the left. Behind the vehicles lies Oxleas Meadow, some of which will shortly be built upon.

Shepherdleas lies below the slopes of Shooters Hill and leads from it in a curve around the top of the Eltham valley, so that from a distance the whole resembles a wooded crescent. Along its south-western perimeter the woodland ends abruptly with some pleasant meadowland. In 1807, these meadows were part of the farmland on the Eltham Park estate leased by Lord Rancliffe but by the end of the 19th century they had become the manicured expanse of a Victorian parkland – Eltham Park North. The area still features a semi-ornamental pond which continues to attract ducks and moorhens and the occasional heron. But the broad sweeps of grassland have more recently been allowed to grow wild, promising a haven for insects and butterflies and, one hopes, swallows etc., in the summer months. Unlike its still-manicured partner south of the rail and motorway, it seems appropriate that this area should be allowed to keep its more natural character. The meadowland, which sweeps over a gently falling slope, provides a pleasant and appropriate transition between the natural ancient woodland and the more formal parkland donated by Cameron Corbett, the Victorian property developer.

In many ways Shepherdleas is similar to Oxleas with pedunculated oak the dominant tree. But there is perhaps more birch and sweet chestnut, and happily, another colony of wild service-tree on its western side. As in the other woodlands, the oak was harvested by the Crown Commissioners for the navy up until the early 19th century. In fact it was possibly more ruthlessly harvested because in 1811 A C Driver, the Crown Commissioners Agent, reported that there were very few trees in the wood and virtually none of those were more than five years old.

Some of the woodland was also destroyed by fire in September 1906. It was thought that a match carelessly discarded by a Sunday rambler had ignited some of the dry undergrowth and in a very short time, the woodland was enveloped in flame. As the *London Evening Standard* reported the following day. *'In a few hours a black and smouldering mass was all that was left of what had been a charming expanse of trees and undergrowth.'* [157]

Perhaps it is these clearances, planned or otherwise, which gives the wood a less crowded, more open feeling. Certainly it has much less holly than the other woods, and the fact that no houses were built here meant that there were no artificial introductions (e.g. rhododendron or laurel). As a result the wood looks and feels lighter, less dense. And, if you can ignore the threatening rumble of the traffic in its motorway cutting, the wood feels a quieter place. In spite of the longer distance footpaths (e.g. the Green Chain Walk) which run through it, you are less likely to encounter other walkers here than in either Oxleas or Jack Wood. Perhaps this is because there is no convenient car park to attract visitors from further afield; (though at weekends, there is ample parking space along the roadside to the north of the wood).

Walking in Shepherdleas, though, can be a slightly disorienting experience. Except towards the west, where the ground tilts down towards the Eltham valley, the wood largely lies on flat ground. There are numerous small ditches, probably dug in the mid-19th century at the recommendation of John Clutton, the Commissioners agent (see Chapter 11). But apart from the busy roads and railway on the perimeters and the large expanse of grassland to the south-west, there are no landmarks to help you locate your position in the wood. There are many pathways – as indeed there are in the other woods – but in Shepherdleas they seem to meander in an unhurried fashion,

---

[157] *London Evening Standard.* 3rd September. 1906. i

as though having no particular wish to get you anywhere else. In the centre of the wood the sound of the traffic seems to come at you from all directions – and the curiously shaped outline of the wood means that its edges are misleading. When you think you have worked out where you are going to emerge, you find yourself in a different place entirely. It can be very confusing, even a little frustrating. Perhaps that's why it is less walked than the other woods.

However, Shepherdleas has its own natural glory. On its western side, where the ground begins to fall down into the Eltham valley, the slopes of the woodland fill in springtime with an exquisite carpet of bluebells. During the early months of 2020, during the Covid-19 lockdown, the display was particularly spectacular. High rainfall over previous months probably helped, but then ironically, as the lockdown was implemented, the weather improved and a long period of warm weather followed. It transformed this part of the wood; and the sunlight, shafting down through the fresh new canopy, turned into a stunning lilac wash on the woodland floor. Gazing at it for more than a few minutes gave you the illusion that a blue mist was rising from the thousands of little flowers, rising and drifting hazily in front of you. With a warm breeze sifting between the trees, the fragrance was heady, yet subtle and powerful at the same time. And it was noticeable how people walking through the wood slowed down to fully appreciate the spectacle, as though literally entranced by the scene. Only Shepherdleas now offers this spectacle, though conservation work parties in Oxleas Woods hope that their work there will in time encourage more displays elsewhere.

Probably no-one could really have anticipated the effect that the Corona virus lockdown would have on the woodlands in general. It was evident that the longer we were all locked-in to our homes, the more the national media began to focus on what we were missing – not just the obvious losses of friends and family, pubs and restaurants, and football – but the access to Nature which so many had taken for granted for so long. For some of us it was a little reminiscent of the Foot and Mouth outbreak in 2001, when 'the Countryside' was closed to us city dwellers. Day after day, morning radio programs featured articles about the springtime we were all missing and how evident it was becoming that access to Nature was vital for our physical and mental wellbeing.

Told that we were only supposed to leave our homes to exercise for a short time – and somewhere locally - the woodlands became suddenly much busier. Those of us living within walking distance of the woods found them to be the obvious place to go. The Friends of Oxleas Woodlands' Facebook page suddenly started receiving posts from new contributors expressing their love and appreciation of the woods, the trees and the spring wildflowers. Many were suddenly seeing birds and flowers they had never noticed there before. In some cases, it seemed as though many people were seeing the woodlands for the first time.

The trees and woodland had, of course, been there all along. But something seemed to have changed in people's consciousness. A new sense of appreciation seemed to be arising as some deep need was being fulfilled - as though people had suddenly realised that they needed the woodlands. And for some, another connection was made: that being the realisation that what is good for us mentally is also good for us physically. We need the woodlands – and the planet needs the wood too.

This strain of thought may seem to take us away far away from Shepherdleas Wood. But, as will be seen shortly, our woodlands have not always been and may still not be regarded as a valuable, even critically vital asset.

The value of woodland for the environment hardly needs to be stressed here. We all know that trees are a vital element in the resistance to climate change. But the danger is that the 'vital element' thus recognised is thought to be 'somewhere else' – somewhere more 'obviously' important, like the Amazon basin. The assumption is that as long as – or even IF - the rain forest is preserved, there is still hope. But what then gets overlooked is our little local woodland, whether it be by the corner of a farmer's field or the junction of a busy road, a tree at the bottom of the garden or even trees in our streets. By focusing on the distant object we fail to see the important one under our very noses – and we fail to notice when it is damaged or lost. For the truth is that **every** tree counts, especially the ones close to us. And this is not just for us but for the entire eco-system and bio-diversity.

A friend of mine once observed that 'there was plenty of countryside for everyone.' To which I pointed out they had used the word 'everyone' not 'everything'; and that is our problem. We tend to think only of ourselves. The tree in the street or garden may be an inconvenience to us, but it is vital to the insects, birds and myriads of other life forms that depend upon it. Neither the environment nor the planet belong to us alone – and the same is true of the woodland. It is something we share with other creatures who have as much of a right to a successful life as we do.

But even if we do recognise the value of woodland to biodiversity and the environment, do we really understand why it is so valuable to us individually?

Over the last couple of decades there has been a renaissance in new 'nature writing'. Nature writing itself is not a new phenomenon. There have always been writers who appreciated 'Nature', whether it be the natural world, the countryside or the landscape, or any combination of those. The popularity of this genre in the 19th century largely reflected a sense of loss. The social changes ignited by the enclosure of agricultural land and the industrial revolution resulted in both an unplanned and uncontrolled expansion of towns and cities, and a simultaneous depopulation of the countryside. As mentioned earlier in this work, it wasn't that many decades ago that the majority of people living in the British Isles lived outside of the cities. Up until the Second World War there were still large, if declining numbers of people who lived and worked close to the land (for which read 'close to Nature' whether they were conscious of it or not.) My own paternal grandfather still worked on the land in the mid-1930s following a family tradition that stretched back centuries.

And as we moved into the cities, a hunger slowly grew for some form of literary reconnection. If the urban Victorian couldn't get to the countryside, he or she could at least still read about. In the 19th century there evolved a stream of writers whose work focused on Nature and the British countryside. The most famous were men (usually) like Richard Jefferies and William Henry Hudson, whose books eventually sold in great numbers. But by the mid-20th century, the tradition of nature writing had gone into something of a decline - as did our interest in Nature. It was as though we took our eyes off the ball because we were distracted by the 'modern world'. In the new post-war regeneration of the cities, the possibilities of science and 'Space' (of final frontier variety), offered a more tempting distraction. When the personal computer came along, followed closely by the internet and the Apple Corporation, it seemed as though all we really needed was the digital world. And as television channels proliferated, we flocked to watch film of the natural world at the same times as that very world was being destroyed. We failed to notice the consequences of the intensification of agriculture, the loss of millions of miles of hedgerow, the extinction of birds, insects and butterflies. We didn't notice as the towns and cities spread, as woodland and meadows disappeared.

It was only towards the end of the 20th century that we began to wake up. The losses were being noticed. Writers and journalists and television presenters began to bring it all to our notice. A new stream of Nature Writing appeared; but this new emergence has been different from what came before. On the whole, earlier writers were largely content to write about what they saw and appreciated in Nature. They only rarely suggested how Nature might impact on them personally, or might be essential for our individual or collective wellbeing. [158] They were conscious of the greater attraction of the countryside and although some of them hated the cities, they thought of this as a very personal response.

---

[158] The importance difference here is, of course, Richard Jefferies, who desperately sought to explain the psychological, even mystical importance of Nature in *The Story of My Heart*. (1883) Though even W H Hudson had his mystical moments.

However, now, an increasing number of scientific/academic studies are revealing just how damaging urban living can be to mental and physical health. (This is the not the place to review all of the arguments and studies, though I would strongly recommend further reading on this).[159] Overcrowding, air and light pollution, noise, an unsympathetic concrete and steel environment, financial deprivation, all have long term and serious effects on our well-being. On top of this, the way that we live our lives creates unnatural stress which we find harder and harder to alleviate in the city environment. Seeking relief in drugs, alcohol or even the internet may provide temporary respite, but it rapidly makes the problem worse.

It is against this background that the genre of 'New' nature writing has emerged. Authors of New Nature writing often begin with an acknowledgement of the social and psychological trauma they have personally experienced; and drugs, alcoholism, or a dysfunctional relationship, may form the starting point from which they depart. In fact the new genre has evolved a trope in which it is implied that some form of mental illness, personal trauma or crisis has to be experienced in order that someone can reconnect with Nature. It is certainly a valid claim, as I confess I can myself testify. But it also contains a danger. For in many of these books the writer retreats to some extremely isolated spot or wilderness-area to find the Nature 'cure' which they need.[160] As readers we might identify with the trauma that the writer shares with us, but most of us

---

[159] Two really excellent books on this are *Nature Fix:Why Nature Makes Us Happier, Healthier, and More Creative* by Florence Williams (2017) and *Losing Eden: Why our Minds Need the Wild* by Lucy Jones. (2020)
[160] My apologies to Richard Mabey here, whose work does not follow this pattern and whose book *'Nature Cure'* is not guilty of this.

cannot escape to the same wilderness. It is the same with writers who regale us with tales of how they escaped from the city to find peace in a cottage deep in the country, where they began to rediscover Nature and a different more meaningful way of life. We cannot all escape to an isolated cottage in the country.

The books may be really entertaining, but they are a misplaced form of escapism. We may recognise the trauma but, because we cannot reach the location or environment of the cure they identify for us, it remains beyond our reach in the pages of a book. Yet the truth is that the cure is much nearer to hand. We just have to learn to recognise it in the green spaces around us. The Nature that we need to reconnect to may be on our doorstep or at the end of our street. But it is not just a case of learning to recognise it: we need to protect it before it is destroyed, lost both to us and the wide diversity of species that also depend upon it.

Like woodland everywhere in Britain, the Oxleas Woodlands are critically important, and they face threats from many directions. What is different here is that those threats are exacerbated by the fact that the woodland is imprisoned by a heavily populated urban environment. Not only does it have to contend with environmental damage, disease and changing climactic conditions, it has to cope with the pressure of heavy use by the local population – some of which is unsympathetic, and some simply damaging.

Our woodlands are a precious resource, not just for us, but for a wide range of species who are clinging on desperately, just like us, trying to survive in an increasingly hostile environment. As communities we need to act together, to defend Nature as a resource which is vital to us as both individuals and community. We need to defend our local woodland, just as much as we need to stop the destruction of the hedgerows in the countryside and the ancient woodland along the route of HS2.

Our trauma is our alienation from Nature, and for many of us our cure lies not in flight to a distant 'wilderness' but in the wild nature that surrounds us, in our gardens, parks and urban woodlands, for these are all part of the same Nature.

When it comes down to it, the experience that the New Nature Writers discover in their wilderness areas, the thing which brings them relief or a cure or restoration, can also be found much nearer to home. In this case, in our beleaguered suburban woodland. And the 'thing' that those writers find is really two 'things' – 'reconnection' and meaning.

It is possible to reconnect with Nature in your own garden, if you give it time. The difficulty is that two key elements in the process of reconnecting with Nature - solitude and tranquility – are two of the things that are hardest to find in the urban environment. Nevertheless it is possible, and it is even more possible in a suburban woodland. It may be just a question of finding the right time – when the woods become quieter – and of finding the right place – away from the main footpaths.

There are techniques to reconnecting with Nature – and the increasingly popular Forest Bathing (or Shinrin Yoku), for example, is all about learning and practicing those techniques. Essentially, the practice teaches the user to see, smell, hear, feel and even taste Nature. The process enhances consciousness and, when it is fully and finely honed, has a dramatic effect on the human psyche. It can be a form of 'awakening' – the recognition that meaning lies in something greater than ourselves, the very Nature of which we are part. It was something that the poet Robert Bloomfield recognised (see the Introduction) and which Wordsworth identified so powerfully in *Lines Composed a Few Miles above Tintern Abbey (1798)*. It was also recognised by many, many writers thereafter. One of these was the psychiatrist and psychoanalyst Carl Jung, who acknowledged woods to be the place where he connected with nature the most and which enabled him to find meaning to life. In 1947 he wrote, *'You must go in quest of yourself, and you will find yourself again in the simple and forgotten things. Why not go into the forest for a time, literally? Sometimes a tree can tell you more than can be read in books.'* [161]

And what comes out of the experience is a sense of awe, the reaction that comes with being in the presence of something greater than ourselves. As Wordsworth described it

'How oft, in spirit, have I returned to thee,

O sylvan Wye! Thou wanderer thro' the woods,

How often has my spirit returned to thee!

... And I have felt

A presence that disturbs me with the joy

Of elevated thoughts; a sense sublime

Of something far more deeply interfused,

---

[161] Quoted in Jones. Losing Eden. P161-162.

Whose dwelling is the light of setting suns,

And the round ocean and the living air,

And the blue sky, and in the mind of man:

A motion and a spirit, that impels

All thinking things, all objects of all thought,

And rolls through all things. Therefore am I still

A lover of the meadows and the woods

And mountains; and of all that we behold

From this green earth;' [162]

And that thing which is greater than ourselves, is Nature. Nature, vast and astonishing, recognisable and yet mysterious. Beautiful and comforting because we are part of it. Poets and philosophers have been telling us that for a long time, because they knew the recognition gives us a sense of perspective about our own lives and existence. We are part of something that is greater than ourselves, something that is rich and long-lasting.

But there is the problem. The very thing which we are a vital part of and which gives our existence meaning, is the thing we are destroying. And that is why we have to protect it. Just like our suburban woodland. We need it for a whole range of reasons. But it needs to be protected.

---

[162] Wordsworth. *Lines Composed a Few Miles above Tintern Abbey*. 1798.

Chapter 16 – Saving Oxleas Wood – A lesson from the past and a warning for the future.

I have strong memories of driving along the A21 in the evening at dusk. I'm sure many drivers of a certain age will have the same memory. The A21 is the road that connects the south-east corner of London and the M25 with the south coast at Hastings. It is a busy road, but in many ways a pleasant one as it winds its way south through Kent and East Sussex, passing fields and woodland, rolling over the undulating landscape and through villages and hamlets. It's quite an old road and stretches of it were managed by various turnpike trusts in the eighteenth century.

However, the A21 was also a pain. Just south of Tunbridge Wells, at Pembury, there was always a long, long traffic jam. It was a pain, but there were compensations. Because depending on the speed of the traffic – you glimpsed the terracotta tiled roofs of ancient farm buildings nestled among the trees high on either side. At dusk sometimes tawny owls and nightjars hurtled headlong overhead, just glimpsed in the beam of the car headlights.

However, the road lobby are a powerful bunch and they wanted something done about the delays. The old road was replaced by a new multiple-lane roadway which opened in 2017. Drivers could now speed through the Kent countryside, saving minutes on their journey. But for several years, road users had been passing a landscape of terrible destruction. A half mile-wide swathe of Wealden woodland had been torn out. The farm buildings largely demolished or moved to the Downland Open Air Museum. Even once the road opened, the most noticeable thing was the wide, largely barren expanse on either side of the road. Admittedly, thousands of saplings had been inserted into the new grass-sown banks beside the broad tarmac highway. But there was no escaping the huge scar that now ripped across this part of the Weald. And what had happened to the wildlife? It had gone.

This little trip down the A21 might seem a literal diversion – but it might so easily have been Oxleas and Shepherdleas Woods. It seems incredible now, when walking through the relative tranquility of Oxleas, that we came so near to losing so much of it. But the story of how this ecological tragedy was averted needs to be recorded and remembered, not just because of the heroic commitment of those who saved it – but because the threat could so easily be resurrected.

I have already mentioned the proximity of the A2 Rochester Way relief road, which was cut into the bottom of Shepherdleas Wood. The road, which was built in the 1980s, was really part of the legacy of the wider post-war road improvement scheme for the capital. This had first been thought of in the mid-1930s as a new 'ringway system' for London. It was dropped when its proposer, Sir Charles Bressey, realised – somewhat ahead of his time – that new roads simply generated more traffic and therefore defeated their object. Nevertheless, the post-war period saw a gradual shift in transport policy in favour of the car. By the 1960s motorways and road schemes proliferated, at the expense of public transport – especially, of course, of the railways. By the mid-1970s the focus in London shifted back to public transport, but this policy conflicted with the ideology of the new Conservative Government led by Margaret Thatcher, elected in 1979.

One of the key aims of the new Thatcher Government involved the regeneration of the depressed dockland area of east London and key to this was a plan for a new Thames river crossing in that area - the East London River Crossing (ELRC). The scheme which was totally opposed by the Greater London Council, proposed a new bridge across the Thames downstream from Woolwich. The bridge and its ancillary roads would provide additional access to docklands from both sides of the Thames. From the south, traffic would find its way to the new river crossing from the A2. To achieve this a major new interchange would have to be constructed at Falconwood. This would lead to a motorway-grade link road running through Shepherdleas and Oxleas Woods, across the Woodlands Farm and through Plumstead to cross the Thames at Gallions Reach.

People living near the proposed route of the new motorway quickly realised that the construction work would devastate the both the ancient woodland and other green space along the route, and the increased traffic would have an appalling impact on the local environment. Those most concerned quickly gathered together to organise opposition to the scheme. A number of local groups were formed, including Welling Against the Road, Plumstead Against the Road, the Slade Action Group, Shooters Hill Defence Committee – and these eventually merged into PARC, Plumstead Against the River Crossing. (Or People Against the River Crossing as it was later known. [163]

In September 1985 a formal public inquiry began. At the time it was to prove the longest in road transport history, running until December 1986. The scheme was supported by some powerful lobbying organisations, including the London Docklands Development Corporation, the Confederation of British Industry, the Transport & General Workers Union, the London Borough of Newham and the British Road Federation. In opposition stood PARC and a large number of ordinary members of the public, together with the Labour controlled Greater London Council (which the government conveniently abolished during the course of the inquiry) and Greenwich Council. Also opposing the scheme were an array of conservation groups including Greenwich and Lewisham Friends of the Earth groups, the Nature Conservation Council, Campaign for the Protection of Rural England, Royal Society for the Protection of Birds, London Wildlife Trust, the Ramblers etc.

For those fighting to save the woodland, the Inquiry was a frustrating and cynical event. When for example, the Inquiry seemed inclined to agree that the overall cost of the project exceeded the value of the time which motorists would save by using the new route, the Department of Transport claimed that the **type** of motorists who would be using the route would be engaged in more important work and so their time was of

---

[163] I am hugely indebted to Maggie Jones, one of the original campaigners, for some of the detail in this chapter.

greater value than that of ordinary motorists; recalculated on this basis, they argued, the scheme would have a positive economic value.

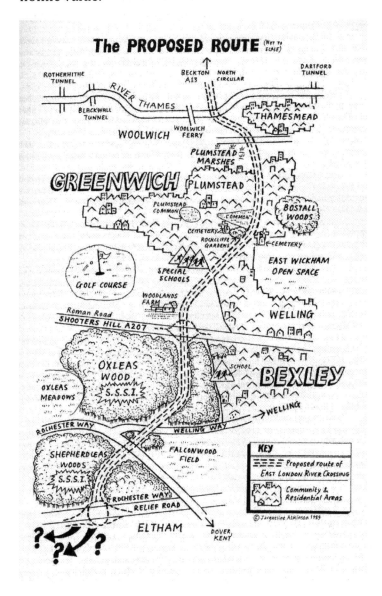

Jacqueline Atkinson's illustration of the route of the new road, produced for PARC in 1989.

Similarly, when the inspector presiding over the Inquiry, Maj. Gen. M E Tickell, agreed with objectors that a tunnel bored under the woods would be a solution if the scheme was approved, the Department of Transport countered that this would cost an additional £400M and make the scheme financially unviable. Furthermore, Nicholas Ridley and Paul Channon, Secretaries of State for Transport and the Environment, both issued statements arguing that concerns about an adverse effect on the woodland justified neither the need for a tunnel of any sort - even a 'cut and cover' model, - or a rejection of the project in its entirety.

On 28th July 1988, formal approval was given for work on the ELRC to begin. However, the woods were temporarily reprieved because of an interjection from an unlikely direction. In the early 1980s the London Docklands Development Corporation had backed another scheme for the building of an inner city airport on a site in the middle of the old Royal Docks in Newham. Objections to the environmental impact on local residents were partly overcome by promises that the airport would only be used by relatively quiet turboprop aircraft. Whether this was a sleight of hand or genuine claim is open to interpretation, but by 1988 the airport was already submitting plans to extend the runway so that jets could be used, increasing the profitability of the facility. The problem was that jets required a longer approach route, and the height of the new suspension bridge across the river at Gallions Reach, obstructed that. The government hastily backtracked, temporarily halting work while a new bridge design was developed.

When the design for the new bridge was made public, the Dept. of Transport received over 3,000 objections from the public, and a new inquiry had to be convened. The bridge plans were quickly withdrawn and new designs appeared a month later. There were suspicions that the Government had hoped that, since objections would have to be resubmitted, the level of opposition would be less. In fact, it grew. Over 7,200 objections to the scheme were received and the Dept. of Transport was forced to convene a second inquiry.

To the frustration and fury of local residents and conservation groups, the terms of reference of the inquiry were changed by the Dept. of Transport, so that only the changes themselves could be taken into account, not the entire scheme. As far as the government was concerned the fate of Oxleas Wood and the housing in Plumstead had already been 'settled'. To make matters even more difficult for the protesters, the venue of the inquiry was moved from Woolwich Town Hall, to the more sympathetic (to the government) environment of Newham, where the Council supported the scheme. The time of the sessions was also changed making it almost impossible for objectors to attend.

The Government had other worries. A hundred miles to the south-west, in Hampshire, a major battle was going on over the extension to the M3 near Winchester. The original route chosen for this was thwarted because Winchester College refused to sell its long-held water meadows.[164] The alternative route involved a tunnel under the chalk down at Twyford, but the Dept. of Transport balked at the cost of approximately £75M. Instead, they proposed carving a huge gash through the centre

---

[164] One might be entitled to wonder why the Government didn't simply impose a Compulsory Purchase Order on Winchester College, as they did on the people of South-East London? (see p5)

of the ancient chalk landscape of Twyford Down. Public opinion was quickly roused against the destruction of such a well-loved beauty spot. Opposition was beginning to result in violence which was being screened on the television, and the Government were becoming anxious not to see a repetition in the suburbs of south-east London. There was another problem. Things were not going well with the Docklands redevelopment, where a wider financial recession was seriously threatening regeneration. Business interests had been lobbying the Government for improved transport links to Docklands since the early 1980s, and the new river crossing was becoming increasingly central to the financial success of the project. To add to the Government's woes, a number of prominent architects and developers publicly criticised the poor design for the new Thames bridge – now a box-girder structure rather than the elegant suspension bridge formerly proposed.

Then it was discovered that in calculating traffic speed projections for the new scheme, the Dept. of Transport had failed to include the impact of traffic concentrating at the Falconwood and Dover Road interchanges. Furthermore, their predictions only covered the initial five years of road use. Consultants employed by Greenwich Council predicted huge increases in traffic in the adjacent area with an 83% increase on the Shooters Hill Road and 123% at Westhorne Avenue where traffic would join the South Circular Road. To the fury of objectors, the Dept. of Transport responded to this by proposing that the four-lane carriageway would be widened to six lanes, resulting in the potential loss of an even greater area of Oxleas and Shepherdleas Woods.

To the astonishment of campaigners the environmental assessment (such as it was) undertaken by the Dept. of Transport, concluded that the impact of the road increase would be negligible. And this despite the fact that evidence about increased levels of carbon pollution, and its impact on children's health, was submitted by Dr Barry Gray (Chair of PARC) and Dr Malcolm Owen – both chest Consultants. (Their evidence was contemptuously dismissed as 'mistaken' by the Dept. of Transport).

The second inquiry closed in January 1991, and things were looking extremely bleak for the woodlands on the east side of Shooters Hill. However, the Dept. of Transport's own failings were soon to have a major impact on the progress of the scheme. Under European Commission Directive 85/337, governments were required to carry out a full Environmental Impact Assessment on projects like motorway construction, where there might be a damaging effect on human health and the quality of life and especially where they passed within 100m of a Site of Special Scientific Interest. The Assessment also had to 'ensure *the maintenance of diversity of species and maintain reproductive capacities of ecosystems as a basic resource for life.*' It was expected that the full data of this assessment would be made available as part of the meaningful public consultation. European governments were entitled to apply for exemptions for projects which were already underway when the Directive came into force, but the British Government had failed to make such applications for ELRC, Twyford Down and other similar road schemes.

When it was realised that the Dept. of Transport had failed to carry out a full Environmental Impact Assessment in June 1989, PARC had written to the European Commission, pointing out that the British Government were technically in breach of the Directive. The government responded to the European Commission by arguing that 'development consent' for the East London River Crossing project had been given on 28th July 1984, before the Directive came into legal force in Britain. The European Commissioners then closed the files on the case without notifying PARC.

However, the 28th July 1984 was not the date on which development consent had been granted. It was the date on which the planning application had been submitted. Final decision to build the East London River Crossing was actually dated exactly four years later on 28th July, 1988, seven days after the Directive came into effect (under an amendment to the Highways Act of 1980). Furthermore, since full development consent could not be enacted until after the new bridge design was agreed after the Second Inquiry, the effective date for consent was actually 27th September 1991. A delegation from PARC cycled (several times) to Brussels to lobby for support and succeeded in getting the case reopened. A month later the European Commission announced that it was issuing a Section 169 Notice of Impending Action against the British Government for non-compliance with the terms of the Directive on a number of projects (including both ELRC and Twyford Down), and requested that the Secretary of State for Transport, (then the Rt. Hon. Malcolm Rifkind) put a halt to all work on the projects.

The announcement was a hammer blow for the Government. The Conservative Party was still in power, but Margaret Thatcher had been toppled by her own parliamentary party in November 1990 and was replaced by John Major. Public opinion had slowly been turning against the brittle policies of the

Thatcher period which had been characterised by a harshness that some party members saw as an electoral liability. At the same time, the Conservative party had become increasingly divided over the country's greater involvement in the European Union – an issue which had certainly contributed to Thatcher's downfall.

At the same time, public concern about the state of the environment was growing, with new and more active conservation organisations attracting wider public support and attention. In March 1991 the former Secretary of State for the Environment, Michael Heseltine had called for a new emphasis on environmentally-sympathetic politics, and spoke at a conference with Carlo Ripa de Meana (the EC Environment Commissioner) who promised that under the proposed European Union, there would be tighter environmental regulation. Ironically, it was Heseltine along with Rifkind, who had announced on 27 September 1991 that the ELRC project would proceed.

When the news of the impending Infringement Proceedings were announced, John Major was at a Commonwealth Conference. He left abruptly to give a furious statement to the press denouncing what he (and the dominant right wing of the Conservative Party) saw as an outrageous 'violation of national sovereignty'. He complained to the President of the European Commission, Jacques Delors, and threated to withdraw co-operation from the forthcoming summit meeting in Maastricht, which was to negotiate the terms of what would become the Maastricht Treaty, setting up the single market.

Initially it seemed as though the government were simply going to ignore the Directive. Instructions were issued for the compulsory purchase of houses and land along the route to the river crossing. Details of the Compulsory Purchase Orders appeared in the local newspaper, *The Mercury,* on 28th November 1991. A few weeks later PARC convened an extraordinary meeting to decide how to respond. Strategically, it was realised that if they could successfully challenge the Compulsory Purchase Order on Oxleas Wood, this would block the route and should save all of the houses and green spaces further down the planned course of the motorway. As an organisation, PARC itself could not take the matter to the High Court, but nine of its leading members put themselves forward to lead the challenge and subsequently became known as the 'Oxleas Nine'. All were prepared to mortgage their homes to fund the case if necessary. PARC also launched an Oxleas Challenge Fund appeal to raise money for the legal costs of the nine, who would be personally liable if the case went against them. However, the appeal to supporters to fund the case met with astounding success. As Maggie Jones, remembers, when a stall was set up in the local Eltham High Street, members of the public queued up to donate to the fund. At the same time Greenwich Council lodged a similar motion with the High Court.

The basis of the challenge focused on the validity of the 'Certificates of Land Exchange', which the government had issued. Essentially, if public amenity land was going to be taken, a suitable and comparable area of land had to be provided in its place. Certificates had to be produced testifying that the exchange was a fair and equitable one. In this case, the Government were required to offer comparable land in exchange both the woodland and parts of Woodlands Farm. The Oxleas Nine submitted their motion before the High Court on 7th January 1992. The case wasn't actually heard until 18th January 1993.

There was however a set-back. In Brussels Delors signalled that there might be a 'relaxation' of the European Commission's environmental standards in return for Britain's cooperation with the Maastricht Treaty. Ripa de Meana, the European Environment Commissioner, resigned in protest. His successor, under pressure from Delors, withdrew most of the Section 169 Notices including that relating to Twyford Down, but ironically, not the one for the ELRC project.

In the High Court, things did not go well. The Oxleas Challenge Group's motion had contended that the land being offered by the Government in exchange for both the woodlands and woodlands farm, was not of equal quality. They pointed out that the ancient woodland was unique as being the only Site of Special Scientific Interest which was fully open and accessible to an urban population. Woodlands Farm was also farmland of high landscape value in its own right. Both the Oxleas Challenge Group and Greenwich Council pointed out that what was currently a publicly accessible asset would inevitably be lost when fences and a six lane highway were installed.

By this time some high profiled people had rallied to the cause of Oxleas Wood, including the late (Sir) David Bellamy and Jonathan Porritt (former Director of Friends of the Earth). The woodland expert Oliver Rackham was also recruited to offer expert academic advice on the value and ecological irreplaceability of the woodlands. The Counsel for the Dept. of Transport responded by arguing that the value of the wood and farmland should be assessed in terms of its 'recreational' not ecological value! (The Secretary of State also commented that the exchanged land would become of equal value 'in time').

As television images continued to show ordinary people desperately combatting the destruction of the beautiful and ancient chalk downland at Twyford, thousands of members of the public threw their support behind the campaign to save Oxleas Wood. Local people organised, becoming closely involved in everything from mass letter-writing campaigns, adopting trees or rallying 10,000 people to pledge to physically obstruct the bulldozers.

Horrifyingly, on February 19th, the High Court ruled against both the Oxleas Challenge Group and Greenwich Council, (though only half of the Dept. of Transport's costs were allowed against them). The decision was based on the assessment that the Secretary of State had not acted unreasonably in issuing the Certificates of Exchange. The judgement did however include a wry note mocking his claim that public access to Oxleas Woods was already restricted because of the brambles and other undergrowth.

Neither the Oxleas Challenge Group nor Greenwich Council were ready to surrender and referred the case to the Court of Appeal on 19th March 1993...

With work due to start on the destruction of the woodland in 1994, things began to look desperate. Especially as the Government were making it clear that they weren't prepared to await the outcome of a Court of Appeal hearing. A delegation from PARC returned to Brussels in April 1993, and were informed that in January the British Government had been given two months to respond to the Section 169 Notice over the ELRC scheme, and that having failed to do so, formal legal proceedings would be initiated in the European Court of Justice. To add to the Dept. of Transport's worries one of its main allies, the British Road Federation, announced that it no longer considered it necessary to take the new road through Oxleas Wood. It proposed instead that the new crossing could link to an existing road, the A2016, which ran close to the Thames several miles to the north.

Then suddenly on 7th July, 1993, the Transport Secretary, John MacGregor, made the astonishing announcement that the plans to build a motorway through Oxleas Wood were dead. As the news was broadcast in the media over the next two days, senior Conservative ministers scrambled to dissociate themselves from the ELRC project. In what has now to be regarded with a degree of cynicism, The *London Evening Standard* claimed for itself a leading role in the campaign to save Oxleas Wood and stated: *'After over a decade of arrogant Thatcherite rule that would brook no dissent, we have a Government which actually takes into account the will of the people. At last: we have a Government that is prepared to listen to us...Our politicians are learning that the arrogance of the Thatcher years is behind us and the will of Londoners, sensibly and responsibly expressed, and with the full-blooded backing of London's newspaper, has to be attended to.'* [165] The veracity of this claim can be measured against the fact that just months later, another London environmental protest exploded onto the television screens. This time over plans to build a new motorway grade link road between the Blackwall Tunnel, just a few miles away, and the M11. Within months the campaign gathered in both ferocity and publicity. Physical obstruction became more determined and better organised, and met what many saw as a brutal response from the police. On television, the film footage recorded the destruction of ancient trees and the violent arrest of pro-

---

[165] *London Evening Standard.* 8 July 1993.

testers. The road went ahead.

The campaign to save Oxleas and Shepherdleas Woods, and Woodlands farm has always been known as the campaign to save Oxleas Wood, though in fact Oxleas Wood itself was only the focal point. In saving Oxleas, the people who worked on the campaign or who supported it in whatever way they could, not only saved the precious ancient woodlands of Oxleas and Shepherdleas, they saved a swathe of green space and homes stretching from the woods to the river; and they saved the local environment too. It was an astounding achievement by a local community, a victory won in the face of powerful and seemingly overwhelming odds.

The campaign seems a long time ago now, but the pressure that lay behind the threat to destroy our ancient woodland is still there, rumbling like a volcano waiting to erupt and growing more powerful as the years pass. The road lobby is powerful once again and demands for an additional river crossing in the area have been resurrected. Now though, the (now) Royal Borough of Greenwich and Greater London Authority have given their support for a new river crossing at Blackwall. It will be fed by the same A2 Rochester Way Relief Road which would have fed the motorway through Oxleas Wood. Questions remain, however, about whether that road is wide enough to cope with the additional traffic which the new crossing will attract. And what happens if, once the capital has been expended on the new crossing, the approach road is deemed insufficient? Will it need to be widened? Do past pledges that Oxleas Wood is now safe mask the fact that Shepherdleas is not? The lessons from the past and the experience of the more recent HS2 project clearly indicate that when it comes to valuing and protecting our ancient woodland, there is a limit when weighed against the desire for 'growth'.

Chapter 17   A walk in the dark

As I have been asserting in this book, Nature is vitally important to us in many ways and for many reasons, and one of the ways that people access Nature is through what we could call 'the wilderness experience'. It is, as I have said, the subject of much Nature writing, and it lays stress on the need to get 'out there' and 'away from it all'.

The great advocate of the wilderness experience was the Scottish-American John Muir. His writing and campaign work in America in the 19th century, led to the preservation of the great National Parks and set the foundation for the popularity of the 'Great Outdoors' experience. Muir always saw nature as the natural home of humankind, to be shared with all other life forms. To be admitted into that home one had to travel alone and lightly. But the reward of this was that you would be bathed in the spirit of the beauty of Nature and *'Presently...lose consciousness of your own separate existence; you blend with the landscape and become part and parcel of nature.'* [166] The desire

---

[166] John Muir. *Twenty Hill Hollow*. 1872.

for and appreciation of this experience helped establish the value of Wilderness. So in America the great National Parks were eventually preserved and millions of Americans make use of them every year. But what about us here in the UK?

If we value the experience of connecting with Nature (at whatever level) then we also imply a value in the place where we have that experience. And that is true whether it's Yosemite National Park or our own Lake District. But what Muir recognised as the precondition for connecting with Nature was solitude and 'space ' – that is, space in our minds to slow down, lose distraction and lose the self-consciousness which dominates our everyday lives. It's fine if you can get to the mountains or the Outer Hebrides, where there are far fewer people to distract you and the grandeur of the landscape can exert its own power over you. But what if you can't get there?

What I want to suggest is that the essence of what is identified as the 'wilderness experience' can be found much closer to home. What is needed for this is, as Muir asserted, the ability to be alone and without distraction, and time to be still, to 'stand and stare'; and with this, a sense of being detached from the normal baggage of the everyday and to become transferred to another place – Nature. It is what some philosophers have described as a state of 'transcendence'. But call it what you will.

The point is that this can be done much closer to home, if you find the right place. In the urban environment it is doubly difficult. There are more people, there is the incessant sound of traffic and of planes roaring overhead. It is hard to break away from the distraction. It is more difficult but not impossible.

In Oxleas Woodlands, in my experience, the most effective time to do this is as night. I have always loved night walks in the country. Once one's eyes have adjusted to the lack of light, it is sometimes astonishing just how visible everything is. But the heart of the experience is the sense of the elemental.

I started walking in our local woods at night several years ago as part of a national survey initiated by the British Trust for Ornithology. It was, as I expected, a totally different experience from walking the woods during the daytime. And now, in the summer months, I do it often. Background noise is usually diminished, (though this can vary depending on the wind direction) and there is rarely anybody else around. Sometimes, in the early evening, a small group of young people might be observed 'smoking' or drinking furtively away from home. Very rarely there might be the occasional late dog-walker. But usually, the woods are devoid of people.

Walking from the amber aura of the lit streets into the woodland is to pass through a liminal space, like stepping off of a cliff into the unknown. There is a moment of hesitation, of uncertainty, until you feel the atmosphere of the night-time woodland envelop you. I usually stop at this point, waiting. As the minutes pass my eyes adjust, the stars become brighter despite the over-glow of London's light pollution (which fortunately is largely hidden by the shadow of Shooters Hill itself). The outline silhouette of the trees becomes sharper and the darkness of the foliage changes from black to greyscale. I listen. Hearing is vital when walking in the woods at night. It is not only that some deep-seated instinct makes us want to hear better when our vision is reduced, but sound contains clues to what is going in in the wood. So I start by listening intently, as though training my hearing to the ambient soundtrack of the woodland. If there is a light night-breeze, there will be the soft susurration as it stirs the top-most branches of the trees, brushing the leaves gently. You can almost hear as the zephyrs roll along the hillside, almost like waves rippling onto a shingle shore.

Then I turn from the meadowland at the entrance into the woodland itself. In the summer, the woods are warmer than outside, you feel it very quickly once you enter. If there is a bright moon, the light beneath the trees has a dappled quality. Sometimes, where there are unseen gaps in the canopy, a soft silver light seems to fall on the foliage and the pathways seem to mirror the moonlight in a strange, almost eerie way. At times the footpaths almost seem to be lit by this light, as though there were some strange luminescent quality in the soil itself. The ground though, is hard. Through the soles of my trainers I can feel the hard ripples where the winter mud has dried, and the tough tubular rolls of tree roots that snake across the footpath. Occasionally a stick will snap under foot, but I always try to tread softly, to be as quiet as possible, for I am an intruder into another world and do not want to disturb it.

Deep in the woods, the sound becomes close, almost tangible. Once the ears adjust to the background ambience, one can hear the silence pressing in. And then gradually one becomes more alert to the sounds of the night creatures. A fox pads across the path ahead, its feet treading quickly with a soft and regular step which is unmistakeable. If it senses me, it will break into a sudden gallop, forefoot and back-foot working together to pro-pel it noisily and with speed through the undergrowth.

A short, sharp scurry in the dried leaves, as a mouse or rat nudges something in its passage. There are voles, though I have never seen one, and there are hedgehogs. They are easy to identify, as they trundle like tanks through the leaves and undergrowth. There is nothing furtive about their movements. They forge around intently seeking food, their spines scraping and snagging so that sometimes it sounds disconcertingly as though something is being dragged through the woods. Emerging to cross the footpaths – which they themselves have no use for - they amble unconcernedly across open space with a comic rolling gait, sometimes myopically pausing to sniff the air.

It is good to know that they are there, though sadly their numbers may have been falling over recent years. In prolonged dry spells, food is hard to get and they may take to exploration of the local gardens, though many of these are barred to them. It is unforgivable. There surely cannot be a gardener anywhere who would not donate a few slugs and snails to keep our hedgehogs alive – and yet they still turn their gardens into an impregnable fortress, when all it would take is a hole six inches square at the bottom of a fence. Hedgehogs will travel miles foraging for food, so virtually all of the gardens adjacent to the wood could have one of these delightful night-time visitors.

Not all sounds in the wood are so identifiable. Perhaps because I am listening so intently, I hear odd sounds, a click here and there, almost a soft whir. I admit there has been the rare occasion when curiosity overcomes me and I have turned a torch to these sounds. Several times, almost unbelievably, what I see in the light of the torch is a moth of some variety.

In the woodland dark, time seems to stretch in different ways. Footpaths seem longer, the familiar landmarks changed or diminished. Turns in the path or junctions look different. Some are lit by moonlight, beckoning and inviting exploration. Others become strange, tunnels, alien caves of darkness that can almost deter – but not quite. The wilderness 'experience' sometimes requires us to step outside our comfort zone

With no agenda or external pressure, I can relax and surrender to the impulse to just wander. Just to allow my feet to take me somewhere. I don't necessarily need to know where I am going, I am concentrating only on the sense of immersion. The woodland is living and breathing around me without being concerned about my presence. Its wild population may notice my passing but as I am doing nothing harmful, they can ignore me.

Startlingly, a robin will sometimes break into song, especially near the woodland edges. Its voice, a scratchy trilling in the darkness, is mysteriously without aim. It seems to be singing to itself. But it is welcome nonetheless.

Depending on the humidity or the recent weather, or the times of year, the woodland is full of fragrance. In autumn, coffee and spice dominates but in summer the scents are warmer, sweeter and more soothing. Wild honeysuckle and jasmine grow in the woods. Away from the commonly trod footpaths, they hang like vines from the trees and in warmer weather the night air drifts their fragrance through the woods. In Oxleas Meadow there are several sweet chestnut, and when in flower they emit a powerful fragrance that is not altogether pleasant. But the most noticeable fragrance comes from the pines. There is a small, almost hidden clump right in the centre of Jack Wood. Once upon a time they probably stood out noticeably on the hillside – possibly planted by Lord Penzance as a deliberate landscape feature in his 'natural' garden below Jackwood

House. Now, the clump has itself become immersed in the largely oak woodland. But in warm weather, the scent of pine is unmistakable, and lovely. I know when I am approaching the pines, not just because of the smell, but because the ground under my feet becomes softer and quieter. I can feel it quite clearly, the ground becomes spongy, almost springy. It is the result of the laying down of countless pine needles over the years. People forget that although coniferous trees are 'evergreen', they still lose their leaves. It's just that they don't do it at the same time and in the same way as deciduous trees. With them it is more of a continuous process a much smaller scale, which is why the ground beneath them gradually changes in texture as the needles fall and very gradually decay.

The middle of the wood is the place to stop, to close my eyes and keep as still as possible. The idea that trees are sentient seems to have gathered in credence over recent years. They can sense things around them. They probably 'hear' movement in the form of vibration, and they can feel damage – especially when attacked by insects. But they do not see (or at least I haven't come across anyone who suggests that). So, amusing though it might seem, one of the best ways of connecting with the night-time woodland is to find a place where you feel completely safe, close your eyes and stay completely still. If you stand completely still in the woodland in daytime, a magical thing happens. It almost feels as though nature has been holding its breath while you pass by. But if you keep still for long enough, it relaxes and comes back to life. As long as you stay completely still you feel this happen. The life of the woods regains its confidence and carries on. Birds appear where you hadn't noticed them before and come close. Butterflies and other insects proliferate. The trees themselves recommence their slow dance if there is a breeze.

At night, the experience is similar. But what you experience is closer to what must be the tree's experience. Keep still. There is a soft breeze stroking your cheek, a moth may whir close by, its wings may even brush your face. If you listen intently you will hear the conducted dance of the tree tops and the rustle of small things around your feet. But wait long enough and there is something else as well, something harder to define. A sense of difference, of something deep-rooted and of great age, of permanence. It is as though you yourself have become invisible to the present and slipped into a past.

In my semi-consciousness, imagination flows and images and sounds flash as though on a cinema screen. The people I have spoken of in this book pass by, their voices echoing down through time: the houses in the woods rise and fall: the trees grow are felled and rise again; the echo of history lingers. It feels as though I could just stay there forever, gradually become part of the woodland, part of the landscape, letting time pass.

Of course I don't. Eventually I notice the physical sensation of my own breathing, part of me moves and the spell is broken. I open my eyes and the woodland springs back into dark focus. But there is still magic to be found in the woodland and it is the reason I started walking there. I can never tell where it will be found or when – and sometimes this particular magic never appears. But if I am not there I will never experience it.

I walk on, listening intently, treading lightly. And there it is. The magic that I have been seeking. It comes fluting through the woodland. A soft liquid warble. A sound which drifts echoing between the trees, somehow as ineffable as the breeze itself. It is the contact call of a male tawny owl. Often it will be accompanied by a response from a female – a sharp, high-pitched 'ke-wick'. Sometimes two females will duet from different parts of the wood, each taking their turn to call, as though they are holding a conversation.

If any creature evokes the mysterious and magical spirit of the night-time woodland it is the tawny owl. It is rarely seen, so its presence is often missed. But the owls have been in our woodlands for many thousands of years. The soft call that lingers amidst the trees reminds us of the long heritage of the ancient woodland. It is, in a sense, the voice of the ancient woodland, a voice from its past.

To me, the experience of standing in the woodland at night, listening to the music of the tawny owl, brings the deepest connection with Nature at its most secretive and inspiring. It is a humbling yet fulfilling. It brings both awe and joy. And that is the same reward, the same experience that lies at the centre of the Wilderness experience.

For those of us who, for whatever reason, cannot flee to the geographical wilderness, or live in a cottage deep in the isolated countryside, there is still a way of connecting with Nature. And that is why woodlands are so valuable to us and so important. And this is especially so in the overcrowded and unforgiving suburbs of our cities.

Nature is here.

ABOUT THE AUTHOR

Tom Wareham lives in south-east London, within a few yards of the Oxleas Woodlands. Since his retirement, in 2014, as the Curator of Community and Maritime History at the Museum of London , he has devoted much of his time to the woodlands, and is a founder member of the Friends of Oxleas Woodlands.
He also spends rather a lot of time learning to play traditional Scandi music on the fiddle. In 1999 he was awarded an M.A. by University College London and, in 2000, a PhD from the University of Exeter.

He can be contacted at tomwareham54@gmail.com

The Friends of Oxleas Woodlands was formed in 2018, to work with the Royal Borough of Greenwich on the conservation and protection of the woodlands. The organisation organises a range of activities ranging from practical conservation work, rose garden restoration, guided walks and a wide range of woodland activities.
You can find out more at their website:
 www.oxleaswoodlands.uk
or at their Facebook Page.
https://www.facebook.com/OxleasFriends/

Printed by Amazon Italia Logistica S.r.l.
Torrazza Piemonte (TO), Italy

16853436R00181